Hopscotch,

Hangman,

Hot Potato,

and Ha, Ha, Ha

Hopscotch,
Hangman,
Hot Potato,
and Ha, Ha, Ha

A RULEBOOK OF CHILDREN'S GAMES

Jack Maguire

Foreword by Bob "Captain Kangaroo" Keeshan

Produced by The Philip Lief Group, Inc.

A FIRESIDE BOOK
Published by Simon &
New York London Toronto

FIRESIDE

Rockefeller Center
1230 Avenue of the Americas
New York, New York 10020

FIRESIDE and colophon are registered
trademarks of Simon & Schuster Inc.

Manufactured in the United States of
America

20

First Fireside Edition 1992

Library of Congress Cataloging-in-
Publication Data

Maguire, Jack.
Hopscotch, Hangman, Hot Potato, and Ha,
Ha, Ha/Jack Maguire.
1. Games—Rules   2. Sports—Rules.
I. Title.
GV1201.42.M34   1990
793'.01922—dc20   89-27200
                                                CIP

ISBN 0-671-76332-6

Designed by Barbara Cohen Aronica

Illustrated by Gary Zamchick

Acknowledgment

Thanks to Patricia Leasure at The Philip Lief Group, and to John Thornton and Chung Han at Prentice Hall Press for their enthusiasm and editorial guidance. Special thanks to Pamela Ivinski, whose research, creative input, and "field-testing," were invaluable contributions.

Contents

ONE   INDOOR GAMES FOR SUNNY DAYS AND RAINY DAYS

TWO   GAMES TO PLAY ON GRASS AND PLAYGROUNDS

THREE   GAMES TO PLAY ON PAVEMENT, STEPS, AND STOOPS

FOUR   GAMES TO PLAY IN WATER

FIVE   PARTY GAMES FOR ANY OCCASION

SIX   TRAVEL GAMES FOR FUN ON THE ROAD

Foreword by Bob "Captain Kangaroo" Keeshan

On the playground of life, game playing equips each of us with the "rules of the game." As youngsters, games taught us how to work together, to accommodate, and to help one another. Through playful moments, children can act out real-life situations. In imagined contexts, they can learn how to solve problems, look for options, and resolve conflicts.

By winning or losing at games, children experience the real world but in less harsh fashion. Children learn about their environment and how to relate to other children, as well as grown-ups. They learn about healthy competition and about trying to do their best. And, because most games have winners and losers, children learn to accept positive and negative outcomes. Game playing offers opportunities for children to build self-confidence and enhance self-esteem.

By following the rules of a game children learn to work within defined guidelines. However, rules should not be inflexible, but instead should provide a springboard for a child's imagination. The rules presented in the following pages are just that: Wonderful starting points for play and fantasy. By encouraging children to develop their own versions of these popular pastimes, we help to unleash the powerful forces of their creativity.

What a dull and serious world this would be if we didn't have games to enliven the spirit and refresh the soul. Games provide a launching pad to fun and fantasy for children of all ages!

Hopscotch, Hangman, **Hot Potato,** and Ha, Ha, Ha

Introduction

Children's play is children's work, even though children wouldn't express it this way. Only gradually, as they are conditioned by adult culture, do they put games, fun, and free time into one category called "play," and tasks, tests, and lessons into another category called "work." Anyone who regularly spends time around kids, however, soon realizes that they play to learn more about themselves and the world around them.

Ironically, child's play can all too often become work for an adult. While kids may be born to play, they don't play interactive games by instinct. More experienced minds are needed to teach them the methods and means of organized cooperation and competition. Most grown-ups have fond memories of childhood games but scratch their heads in forgetfulness when the opportunity arises to share these games with children in their care.

Hopscotch, Hangman, Hot Potato, and Ha, Ha, Ha solves this problem for parents, grandparents, teachers, day-care personnel, camp counselors, baby-sitters, and other people who facilitate games for children of every age. It contains complete, easy-to-read instructions, recommendations, and scoring procedures for more than 250 popular games: games to play on grass; on the pavement, steps, and stoops; in water; inside houses for rainy days and parties; and games to play while traveling. (These games are listed under the setting in which they would most likely be played. And because many games can be played in a variety of environments, I've offered other recommendations for "Where to Play.") You'll find not only your own favorite games but scores of others that can be as entertaining for players today as they have been for generations past.

When it comes to orchestrating children's games, having all the details at your fingertips is an indispensable aid; but there is another, vitally important, resource. In addition to knowing *how* to play a wide variety of children's games, it is imperative for a facilitator to appreciate the essential nature of children's games. Understanding some of the reasons *why* children like games, *why* certain games have retained their appeal for centuries, and *why* particular types of games appeal to particular types of children can help us bridge the gap between the adult's world and the child's world. In doing so, we help individual games come alive for children and individual children come alive through games. This appreciation begins, then, with a look back to the childhood of our civilization.

How Did Children's Games Originate?

Once upon a time there were no children's games. There were plenty of games, but they belonged to people of all ages. For most of human history, the young and the old enjoyed the same pastimes, just as they shared the same labors. Experienced players certainly jumped rope, hurled balls, or ran bases with better effect than inexperienced players; and, therefore, players in general tended to group together according to age. Nevertheless, the basic structures of play remained the same throughout one's life. Work situations followed a somewhat different pattern. Physically immature or weak workers took over simpler tasks, leaving more challenging ones to their elders; but everyone strove for a common cause: the family's and the community's livelihood.

Like the distinction between childhood and adulthood, the distinction between work and play for all ages was less clear in the past than it is today. Many games had a definite practical purpose: they trained young people, or kept older people in shape, for key responsibilities. Various games of **Tag*** and **Hide-and-Seek** paralleled the occupations of stalking wild animals and herding livestock. Games of **Marbles** (more frequently played then with peas, beans, nuts, stones, or clay pellets than glass or marble spheres) exercised critical skills of judgment and dexterity needed for killing prey. Relay races mimicked the crucial communication service performed by message runners.

As one territorial group made contact with another, games were avidly traded; and over the centuries they became a

---

*Note: Whenever a game that has an entry in the book is mentioned in the text, it will be in **boldface** type.

kind of international language. Given this mode of distribution, it is not surprising that games played on roadways acquired special prominence. The game known in English-speaking countries as **Hopscotch,** for example, developed from a favorite leisure activity of Roman soldiers occupying the Great North Road in ancient Britain. These original hopscotch courts, some of them more than 100 feet long, simulated the 400-mile journey from London to Scotland and back. Often players would hop through them carrying heavy loads to test their strength and agility. Other soldiers practiced this sport on other highways and byways of the Empire, establishing the roots of present-day children's games like *Marelles* in France, *Templehüpfen* in West Germany, and *Hinkelbaan* in The Netherlands. Similar games have grown up along the roads of India (*Ekaria Dukaria*), Vietnam (*Pico*), and Argentina (*Rayuela*).

Soldiers, of course, don't spend all of their time training. They battle for food, wealth, treasure, territory, and—sometimes—for principle. Inevitably, games evolved to imitate such warfare. **Prisoner's Base,** for instance, which Shakespeare mentions in *Cymbeline,* has been played across Europe throughout recorded history. The earliest documented game of **Tug-of-War** occurred in ninth-century England, where players were either on the side of the Saxon or the side of the Dragon (i.e., the Viking).

Frequently, quarreling factions played **Tug-of-War** to settle differences before those differences could lead to bloodier fights. *Crik Crak,* an African version of **Tug-of-War** from Gambia was, and still is, played among hunting teams who disagree about who should get the trophy portions of captured animals. In Japan neighboring villages used to play a tug-of-war game called *Tsunahiki* at planting time, as a symbolic means of determining which village would have the best harvest. Today, in England, Gambia, Japan, and around the world, tug-of-war games are standard money-raising competitions at fairs, celebrations, and civic gatherings.

Aside from imitating work or combat, some games were meant to reenact or ritualize specific historical events. In both cases, the games themselves often functioned as a way of mitigating hardships, of gaining symbolic control over stressful situations. The game we know as **Musical Chairs** (which people in France, Germany, Poland, Bulgaria, Czechoslovakia, and Turkey know by other names) can be traced back to the First Crusade, when long-distance travelers play-fully spoofed their desperate scurry for coach seats. **London Bridge** dates back to the eleventh-century destruction of the major bridge in that city—along with the Britons standing on it—by Norway's King Olaf and his troops.

One of the grimmest stories of the origin of a game involves the apparently sweet, innocent game now called **Ring-Around-the-Rosy.** The first line of this verse, originally "Ring-a-ring o' roses," refers to the circular body rash that was an early symptom of the Great Plague of London, which killed more than 70,000 people between 1664 and 1665. The healthy attempted to thwart the disease by carrying herbs ("A pocket full of posies"). In the final stages of the disease, the victim would start sneezing violently ("A-tishoo! A-tishoo!," later corrupted to "Ashes! Ashes!"). Death followed quickly ("We all fall down").

Through the ages, in virtually every civilization, certain games have also functioned as spiritual rites. Contemporary **Tag** games featuring a tree as home base evolved in part from ceremonial dramas in which the faithful, by touching a special tree, were rendered safe from the malign forces that pursued them. Egyptians in the biblical era considered the sycamore sacred in this manner. North American Indians, Homeric Greeks, and Druids revered the oak, a frequent target of "divine" lightning. Today, the tree magic of yesterday survives not only as a game-playing fantasy but also as a common superstition: the habit of "knocking on wood" to ensure protection and/or to avoid being "caught" boasting.

Codified in many of the other games kids now play—notably games involving chanting or rhythmic activities—are ancient incantations and movements originally designed to impose some order on the mysteries of the universe. Pre-Christian natives of northern Europe jumped rope and tossed balls to invoke favorable weather. Their Christianized Mediterranean counterparts engaged in question-and-answer drills that reinforced acceptable behaviors: the forerunners of such games as **Simon Says** and **Mother, May I?**

In the aftermath of the Roman Empire, game playing became such a bonding element in every facet of group life that great halls were built so that large-scale games could be played indoors as well as outdoors. These halls were commonly called ball houses, because so many games involved balls; but they were also the scenes of running, chasing, singing, and dancing games. The generic name *ball house* accounts for the origin of the current terms *ballad* for a narrative-style song, *ball* for a celebratory dance, and *ballet* for a dance performance.

Game playing as a transcendent social activity was not destined to last much beyond the Middle Ages. Shortly after the Great Plague of London inspired **Ring-Around-the-Rosy,** Western culture began making the distinction between childhood and adulthood that we take for granted today. The catalyst was the Industrial Revolution. On the one hand, it ushered in new, highly sophisticated technologies that required extensive formal education to master. No longer could the old and the young so easily involve themselves in the same basic enterprises; and games lost their universal efficacy as a means of job training and social commentary. On the other hand, increasing prosperity spawned a large, relatively wealthy middle class that could afford to indulge children—to give them for a time a world of their own where they could be free from many of the harsher real-world responsibilities and where they could take time to prepare themselves for a variety of possible adult careers.

The old games persisted, but now they were designated "children's games." Adults created more intricate and intellectually demanding games of their own: versions of the old games but with a twist. Complicated card and board games, for example, seemed especially suited to large numbers of adults whose daily lives were now more sedentary and clerical. At the same time, complex team sports like **Baseball, Football,** and **Basketball** (all derivatives of "children's" games) replaced simpler group games. Far fewer people actually played—or *could* play—these sports on a regular basis; but they were able to enjoy them well enough on a vicarious level simply by watching them. Nevertheless, being a spectator is a far cry from being a player.

Fortunately, all adults must still start out as children; and children continue to cherish, preserve, and revitalize the games with which humankind grew up. As the folklorist William Wells Newell wrote in his 1883 classic, *Games and Songs of American Children,* "the old games, which have prevailed and become familiar by a process of natural selection, are usually better adapted to children's taste than any new inventions can be; they are recommended by the quaintness of formulas which have come from the remote past, and strike the young imagination as a sort of sacred law."

How Can Today's Children Benefit from Games?

To an adult, a child's life seems enviably carefree. In the process of growing up, we tend to forget that being a child entails constantly braving unknown natural and social dangers. Children must obey older people who are more powerful than they are without always understanding why and often without any alternative. They must always strive to master mental and physical challenges that keep changing as their minds and bodies grow. Every day carries a high risk of uncertainty, discomfort, and failure.

Games help children not only cope with this situation but also flourish in it. Through games, children can create a delightful, controlled environment in which to exercise their minds and their bodies. They can also safely experiment with interpersonal relationships, exploring how it feels to be the leader or the follower, the champion or the challenger, the attacker or the defender, the pursuer or the pursued, the acceptor or the accepted, the rejector or the rejected, the winner or the loser. By living through each of these situations in mind and body, children accumulate experiences that will prove to be invaluable during their adult years, when they must deal with real-world goals and conflicts.

Aside from the overall fun of playing a game simply for the sake of the game itself, the benefits children derive from games can be divided into two general kinds: *comprehension-building benefits* and *skill-building benefits.* Here are some of the specific benefits in each of these groups:

Comprehension-Building Benefits
- Gaining respect for rules and procedures
- Learning the value of goals—and of the patience, determination, and balanced self-assessment required to meet goals
- Realizing one's capabilities and the capabilities of others

- Cultivating patience and acceptance regarding one's limitations and the limitations of others
- Appreciating that one can compete against someone and still be his or her friend and that one can be close to someone without losing one's independence
- Understanding what it means to be fair and honorable

Skill-Building Benefits
- Improving one's physical coordination, strength, flexibility, and energy management
- Increasing one's powers of concentration, memory, and creativity
- Learning how to follow directions, interpret signals, make decisions, solve problems, and resolve conflicts
- Enhancing the way one uses language and communicates
- Developing a better ability to estimate and utilize time, space, and resources

Naturally, different games emphasize different combinations of skills. To benefit the most from game playing, therefore, children need to master a wide repertoire of games. One of the main objectives of this book is to help children do this.

Which Games Are Appropriate for Which Ages?

This book contains more than 250 of the best-loved and most-played children's games. The total number of children's games is no doubt incalculable, but surprisingly, all games for children—regardless of age—are concocted from the same six basic formulas (with room for overlap). These formulas can be described as follows:

Circle Games—Players perform the same activity, taking turns or, in some cases, in unison (includes **Ring-Around-the-Rosy** and **Pin the Tail on the Donkey** for younger players; **Jump Rope** and **Hopscotch** for older players).

Acting-out Games—Players engage in imitation, impersonation, or dramatization according to cues (includes **Simon Says** for younger players;

Cops and Robbers and **Charades** for older players).

Race Games—Players compete to reach a goal first (includes basic foot racing for younger players; Wheelbarrow Race and **Relay Races** for older players).

Capture Games—Players alternate between being searchers or chasers and being the objects of searches or chases (includes **Hide-and-Seek** for younger players; **Ring-a-Levio** and **Sardines** for older players).

Combat Games—Players wage mock battles or stage "attack-defense" situations (includes **Tug-of-War** for younger players; **Dodge Ball** for older players).

Strategy Games—Players use physical and/or mental skills in a series of maneuvers to outscore opponents (includes **Marbles** for young players; **Baseball** or card and board games for older players).

■ ■ ■

As this breakdown indicates, children experience a continuity in game playing through the course of their childhood, with older children proceeding smoothly into more evolved variations of the games they played as toddlers. To assist facilitators in determining which types of games may be best suited to particular developmental stages in a child's life, here is a synopsis of what experts in the field (among whom Brian and Shirley Sutton-Smith, authors of *How to Play with Your Children,* and Arnold Arnold, author of *The World Book of Children's Games,* are especially instructive) have to say:

EARLY CHILDHOOD: AGES 2 TO 5

Children under the age of five are very self-absorbed. They have difficulty collaborating and cooperating with other children in games that require concentration, and they don't easily accept the idea of losing. When a child is two or three years old, one-to-one imitation exercises or chases are the games most likely to please, although children in this stage of life may be able to participate with small groups of older children in simple circle games like **Ring-Around-the-Rosy** or **Mulberry Bush.** Above all, children in their early years crave rhythm, repetition, and order: not just in their play, but in all aspects of their life.

For three- to five-year-olds, any circle game is appropriate, with the possible exception of games having strong "acceptance-rejection" themes. **Farmer in the Dell,** for example, can be upsetting to a child of three or four because the game hinges on choosing or being chosen from among other players. **Musical Chairs** and **Kitty Wants a Corner,** on the other hand, are usually well received. Because children from three to five are rapidly accumulating language skills, they tend to relish games with chants, verses, and nonsense words.

Three- to five-year-olds are also just beginning to experiment with ways of getting along together. To bridge the gap between this dawning era of social play and the relative solitude of their earlier play years, they often invent imaginary playmates and put them through "learning drills." In a similar spirit, they respond favorably to group acting-out games that are easy to follow, like **Simon Says** or **Hot and Cold.** At parties, they can appreciate mildly competitive games like **Bobbing for Apples** or **Pin the Tail on the Donkey.** Basic foot races and tug-of-war games are best reserved for the older, more physically coordinated children in this age range.

MIDDLE CHILDHOOD: AGES 5 TO 9

Children at this stage are swiftly acquiring interpersonal skills as they rise through the primary grades of school. They can tolerate losing, being "It," and trading the pretend roles of "friend" and "enemy" with their peers. More advanced circle games like **Farmer in the Dell, Blindman's Buff,** or **Run for Your Supper** are now appropriate.

For younger children in this age bracket, this is the golden era of beginning-level capture games like **Cat and Mouse** or **Hide-and-Seek;** role-playing, acting-out games like **Cowboys and Indians;** and that grandparent of all strategy games, **Marbles.** Physically, most of them are also ready to be more boisterous with one another, enjoying outdoor games like **Leapfrog, Potato Relay, Obstacle People,** or **Log Roll;** and water games like **Chicken Fights** or **Water Keep Away.**

Older children in this bracket, logically enough, prefer more complicated circle games like **Jump Rope** or **Hopscotch;** more intricate capture games like **Ring-a-Levio,**

Kick the Can, Freeze Tag, Prisoner's Base, or **Octopus;** more demanding strategy games like **Jacks, Treasure Hunt, Gossip,** or **Free Association;** and more sophisticated races like **Relay Races.**

LATE CHILDHOOD: AGES 9 TO 14

Children in this age range are keenly interested in expanding their repertoire of task-related skills and techniques. They are generally enthusiastic about card games like **Crazy Eights** or **Concentration;** board games like Backgammon or Chinese Checkers; and table games like Ping-Pong or Pool. They also take to games that give them a chance to display their intelligence and perceptiveness, like **Twenty Questions, Lemonade, Assassin,** or the **Memory Game.**

Most nine- to eleven-year-olds enjoy capture games that have advanced to the level where two teams oppose each other, like **Red Rover** or **Sardines.** They have also matured sufficiently to play more aggressive attack-and-defense games like **Army, Dodge Ball,** or **King of the Hill.**

Eleven- to fourteen-year-olds still play these games, but they are increasingly attracted to team sports that combine physical action and strategy—notably ones that have adult counterparts like **Stickball, Baseball, Touch Football,** or **Basketball.** Team water sports, too, are popular, such as **Underwater Football** or **Water Volleyball.**

■ ■ ■

Though the above schedule may seem quite logical, assigning specific games to specific age groups is a problematic issue. Individual children of the same age can differ greatly in their mental and physical capabilities, interests, and experiences and in the range of their personal game preferences, depending on the group that is playing. One thing children of all ages *do* have in common is a keen sensitivity to age prejudice. If eight-year-olds, for example, are invited to play a game that is too narrowly defined as a game for five-year-olds, they almost always will balk.

For these reasons, the games in *Hopscotch, Hangman, Hot Potato, and Ha, Ha, Ha* are not rigidly classified according to age group (although some games are noted as most appropriate for younger children). Instead of depending on any chart, it is much better to leave matters open-ended. Invite multiple suggestions from children about what games or kinds of games they would like to play, and then rely on your own common sense—both as an adult and as a former child—to make suggestions regarding games that you believe are suited to the group and situation at hand. Any final decision about what particular game to play should be a collective one.

How Can I Help Children Play Games?

One of the beauties of any game is that its rules enable it to run by itself. A good game facilitator, however, can make the experience all the more lively and pleasurable. If you are a parent, relative, friend, or teacher who regularly spends time with the same children, the best way to help these children derive happiness from games is to set an inspirational example. Let them see you reveling in your own games, and share their enthusiasm over the games they play. These are important first steps toward enjoying yourselves together.

As for assisting children to play specific games, a facilitator can assume one or more of the following three roles, according to what seems most appropriate at the time.

INITIATOR-COACH

In this role (by far the most common for a facilitator), you arbitrate the decision-making process concerning what game to play, and then you help to get it started. Allow the players to take the lead in making game suggestions; however, if you are also the supplier of game equipment, or if the game is taking place on your property, you have a special interest in this process and a right to press your interest. Once a decision has been made, lead a discussion about how the game is to be played so that everyone understands and accepts the rules.

In preparation for team games, particularly with younger children or a group of mixed ages, it may be advisable for you to supervise the picking of teams and team captains. To be as fair as possible in both situations, try drawing straws or counting off. During your discussion of how the game is to be played, you may want to anticipate potential dominance conflicts by steering the players to accept a rotation of leadership. (See "Helpful Hints to Get the Ball Rolling" on page 18.)

REFEREE-SCOREKEEPER

In this role, you observe the entire game closely, keep score, and—in response to appeals from the players—help settle disputed points. The trick is not to be too intrusive and not to embarrass individual players in public by correcting their mistakes or accusing them too bluntly of improprieties. In a dispute, whenever possible refer to the rules, not you or your role, as the authority.

Before automatically assuming this role, consider whether a child who is present—a player or nonplayer—may want the role or even need it: for example, as a means of feeling important or of avoiding direct participation in a game that he or she doesn't really want to play. If neither you nor anyone else is officially designated "referee-scorekeeper" in a game, then the pregame discussion should cover how to manage conflicts.

PLAYER

In this role, you actually participate in the game, which can be a joy for everyone, as long as you are careful to tailor your participation to fit the overall skill level and physical capabilities of the other players (without, of course, ruining your own fun!). In many situations, you may be compelled to participate in a children's game in order to even the number of players or to fill in for a player who quits. That is when being familiar with game-playing rules really pays off!

Remember that playing a particular game may involve being a partner, a competitor, or both to any or all of the other players; so think ahead about whether individual relationships of these types might pose problems. Above all, bear in mind that once you are a player you cannot suddenly step out of that role and be an authority figure, unless you are also the designated referee-scorekeeper or something serious comes up that forces you to quit. As a player, it is expected that you will have the same degree of commitment to playing the game as any other player.

■ ■ ■

Not all game situations need a facilitator, but most can profit from one. If nothing else, having a game facilitator makes the game itself appear more earnest. In the paradoxical world of child's play, the more seriously one takes a game, the more entertaining it is likely to be. A party game for young children almost always works best with a facilitator. On the other hand, a pavement, step, or stoop game—like street life in general—gets much of its energy from the independence of the players.

Any specific role you assume as a facilitator, no matter how vigorously you enact that role, requires knowing the rules of the game. Keeping this book handy will ensure that you can fulfill this responsibility; it will also give you a "higher authority" to cite. In order to be prepared for the overall role of a game facilitator, however, it is a good idea to familiarize yourself with a wide variety of games. Browsing through this book from time to time will introduce you to new games (which may, in fact, be tried-and-true games with a different angle). It will also jog your memory and feed your imagination: not just about particular games to facilitate but about the world of childhood and of games in general.

Whenever and however you help children play games, there are several rules you should follow:

- *Make sure that the game environment is reasonably safe.* You cannot prevent every possible accident or problem from occurring, and you will drive kids nuts trying to do so. A certain amount of risk is essential to the enjoyment of any physically active game, not to mention freedom from a lot of extraneous worries. Nevertheless, safety should be your first consideration.

 Before deciding on a game to play, have the players check the game environment for *obvious* hazards: broken glass, slippery mud patches, steep inclines, shallow or rough water, loose area rugs, stumps, or holes. Also consider "situational" problems: proximity to the neighbors, to a dog run, to breakable furniture, to a garden. Determine the game to be played, and how it is to be played, accordingly.

It is always wise to have a first-aid kit handy, as well as water and (when appropriate) sunscreen lotion if the game is being played outdoors. A loud whistle can be invaluable to a facilitator in any emergency: for example, when the game needs to be stopped because of an injury or outside interference.

- *Do what you can with the game environment to enhance the quality of the game.*
  Once you have decided that a particular game is appropriate for the environment, take any easy steps that will make the game more pleasurable to play there. Police the grounds for trash. Make sure all bases, goals, targets, or boundaries are readily identifiable. If the players will be running around outdoors on a hot sunny day, think about shade, sun direction, and wind direction when you are laying out a playing field. If the players want to enjoy a card game indoors, arrange comfortable seating and lighting in an area that is free from distraction.

- *Start with simple games or rules, and work toward more challenging ones.*
  Complicated or physically taxing games or rules may discourage new players, especially if they tend to be shy or uncompetitive by nature. Group dynamics may suffer as individual players with higher skill levels stand out all the more sharply from the others. Therefore, it is best to be conservative when faced with a decision about how challenging a game or a game's rules should be.

  If a group expresses strong interest in a new game or a new set of rules that seems somewhat ambitious for them, you may want to suggest a tryout or practice game first. If this isn't advisable, a familiarity with the contents of this book will help you to suggest similar games or rules that are more compatible with the players' skill levels.

- *Don't intervene unless it is absolutely necessary.*
  Games suffer from too much instruction and interruption. If you hang around the game environment, your presence alone will function well as a general regulating influence. The only things that should directly concern you are unexpected events that threaten the game: What happens if a player is hurt? If a piece of furniture is broken? If a thunderstorm looms? If interest in a particular game starts lagging? In these cases, you will probably want to step in and rescue the situation.

- *Discreetly support fairness and good power management.*
  Human authority in any game situation should rest as much as possible in the players and as little as possible in the facilitator, unless the facilitator is the designated referee. Only in this manner can children learn how to be fair to one another and how to manage interpersonal power issues efficiently. This means that any work you do as a facilitator to ensure that a game will be played honorably, to the satisfaction of *all* players, should be subtle and unobtrusive.

  If you feel in advance that a particular child or subgroup of children might wind up dominating the game, then direct the group toward games that can be played in unison or that involve taking turns. Always engineer consensus decisions regarding what games to play, how to play them, and what to do in a dispute. Engage the entire group in managing problems so that individuals don't shoulder all the blame or abuse. And whenever possible, avoid imposing your real-world adult values on a make-believe children's game: Remember that there *is* a distinct, qualitative difference between **Army** (the game) and war (the scourge of history)—or between appropriate male-female relationships at seven and at twenty-seven.

  Most important, never offer bribes, issue threats, or make demands in an attempt to force a group of children to play well together. If the children really want to play, they will work it out so that they can play, and this almost inevitably involves accommodating one another's needs and desires. Such is the wondrous power of games!

Certain types of games have their own, additional rules of thumb:

- *Party games* should engage every player equally. Choose games in which every player can experience some tangible accomplishment: for example, circle games, **Treasure Hunt,** or **Twenty Questions.** Avoid games where players get eliminated early, or else set up rules so that an "out" player can somehow get reinstated in the game. For children under the age of eight, avoid rewards for winners and punishments for losers: Everyone should get a prize.

- *Indoor games* and *travel games* can sometimes overdominate a child's indoor or travel experience. Take care to foster beneficial solitary activities as well as interpersonal games. For indoor situations, beneficial solitary activities include reading, resting, working on hobbies, or performing chores (some chores *can* be pleasurable). For travel situations, beneficial solitary activities include reading, resting, observing the scenery, or writing postcards or travel diaries. Of course, when traveling by car you can always stop for a break and set up a refreshing game on grass or pavement or in the water!

- *Water games* require that all players be capable of swimming and, in some cases, diving. Purely as a concerned observer, you should ask all players whether they can swim or dive and advise nonswimmers or nondivers not to participate. Perhaps the nonparticipators can keep score instead or play another game out of the water.

  As a water-game facilitator, you should also function as a lifeguard for the play group—so you, too, should be able to swim and dive. If you are not going to be the facilitator, or if you cannot swim or dive, one of the players (preferably the most reliable and/or the best swimmer) should be designated the "referee-lifeguard" for the game, with the understanding that all players should keep alert for any problems or dangers, and no player should perform risky, "lifesaving" stunts without having been trained to do so.

  In a public pool or at a public beach, always check with the professional lifeguard first before playing a group game to see if it poses any difficulties for the players or for the other people using the pool or beach. Never depend solely on the professional lifeguard for the play group's safety.

Games and Creativity

Despite the fact that rules define games, they don't give them life; and it is this "alternative life" quality that makes games so attractive and valuable in a child's world. The very structure of a game provides a lot of room for personal and group inventiveness, involving not only the style of play but also the content. Once kids understand the rules of a specific game, they are free to experiment with them: changing rules to fit the particular mix of players or the available time, environment, and equipment; adding rules to make the game more interesting; eliminating rules that might prove discriminatory or unsafe. Game design can be a game in itself and one that helps children become involved in their game playing more intensely and productively.

Even if children play the same game by the same rules again and again, it will be different each time they play it, thanks to the ongoing individuality of the players, the time-and-space situation of the moment, and blind fate. Thus, games perpetually revive kids and render them better able to deal with the vicissitudes of real life. Most people no longer need games to get in shape for herding sheep or for scouting bad guys, but they do need games to turn their innate playfulness into constructive creativity—the will to imagine and enact that distinguishes thriving from merely surviving.

Games represent real-life situations in miniature. They have their built-in controls, but they are still full of all sorts of personal and social possibilities for knowledge and growth. If children's play is children's work, then games enable a child to work more effectively. As for an adult's work, a highly developed sense of play is becoming more and more of a necessity. Jobs are increasingly more specialized, and a greater and greater premium is placed on exercising one's creativity, both for personal enjoyment and career advancement. Children's games—now as always—prepare children for a successful life as fully realized human beings and remain powerful memories in their minds and hearts throughout their adult years.

Helpful Hints to Get the Ball Rolling

Who is "It"? Which team am I on? Who goes first? These are questions that usually have to be answered before the fun of game playing can begin. In spontaneous play situations, the answers will often be found without much deliberation. The players may call, "Not 'It'!" leaving the role to the slowest caller. Small teams may form naturally among groups of friends. Or the players may flip a coin to see which side goes first.

With large groups and more structured play situations, however, deciding who is "It," who goes first, or how to divide up the teams requires a bit more consideration. The rituals of counting out and choosing sides (frequently involving rhymes and gestures) are important and often enjoyable aspects of play. Here are a few methods for establishing playing order, teams, and who is "It."

Choosing "It"

"It" usually has the most demanding role in a game, as chaser, tagger, seeker, or guesser. Every player who has ever served as "It" knows the fear that he or she will never catch anyone and will be stuck as "It" forever. Since no one ever volunteers to be "It," a number of strategies to choose "It" have been developed.

The most straightforward way to choose an "It" is to determine who is "Not It." When a group of players decides to gather for a game of **Hide-and-Seek** or **Tag,** a quick-witted player will call out, "Not It!" A chorus of "Not Its" will follow, and the last player to call out must be "It."

"Not It" sometimes requires a movement or a gesture to make the decision unequivocal. The first to call, "Not It" may form a circle with the arms. Each player must then put a hand inside this circle while claiming, "Not It." The last player to do so is "It." Or, the first "Not It" caller may touch the ground. The last to do so is "It."

The "Last one is a rotten egg" strategy is similar: One player calls out, "Last one to the tree (or house, or fence) is a rotten egg!" All the players sprint for the goal, and the last one there becomes "It."

A variation of the **Scissors, Paper, Stone** game can be used to discover who is "It" for small groups. In this version, the players gather in a circle. Each holds one hand behind the back. At the count of three, all bring their hands in front of them, in one of three gestures: a V sign with the first two fingers (scissors), an open hand (paper), or a fist (stone). When one player holds out an odd gesture (a fist, for example, when everyone else extends an open hand), that player is eliminated and safe from being "It." This continues until two players are left, at which point the rules of the original game take over: the scissors cut paper; the paper covers stone; and the stone crushes scissors. The loser of this one-on-one shoot-out is "It."

The old method of "drawing straws" is a quick way of choosing who is "It." Different kinds of items can be used: slips of paper, twigs, and so forth. One item is made different from the others. In the case of slips of paper, for example, one slip can be shorter or can be marked with an *X*. The player who unknowingly chooses the exceptional slip is "It." In the case of straws, they can be placed in a bag or box, or held in the hand in a manner that makes them all appear to be of equal length, when in fact one straw is much shorter than all the others. After each player draws a straw, the player who has chosen the shortest straw will serve as "It."

Counting out with rhymes is the most entertaining way of choosing who is "It." Usually, the players gather in a circle. The player who initiates the circle is usually the counter. As the rhyme is chanted, the counter goes around the circle pointing at or tapping each player with every syllable or beat. Sometimes the players hold out one or both fists, and the counter taps each fist with his or her own fist while counting out the rhyme. This is called dipping.

Here is an example of a very old rhyme:

One, two, three,
Out goes she! (or he!)

The player on whom "she" or "he" falls leaves the circle and is not "It." The counter continues (counting himself or herself), until only one player is left.

The most famous of all rhymes is probably "Eeny, Meeny, Miney, Mo" (on the following page):

Eeny, meeny, miney, mo,
Catch a tiger by the toe,
If he hollers, let him go,
Eeeny, meeny, miney, mo.

My mother says to pick this one,
and you are not "It."

For dipping, "One Potato" is also very popular:

One potato, two potato,
Three potato, four,
Five potato, six potato,
Seven potato, more.

Some rhymes require a player to choose a word or number before the rhyme can be continued:

Charlie Chaplin sat on a pin,
How many inches did it go in?
(Answer: Five)
One, two, three, four, five.

or

Engine, engine number nine,
Going down the Chicago line,
If the train falls off the track,
Do you want your money back?
(Answer: Yes)
Y-E-S spells yes and you are not "It."

Who Goes First?

The fastest way to choose who goes first is by flipping a coin and choosing heads or tails. Rhymes can also be used to determine playing order. The order is determined by the sequence in which players are eliminated from the counting-out sequence.

Many games have a built-in method to determine who goes first. Games with sticks or bats, like **Stickball,** use the hand-over-hand system. Here's how it works: One player puts a hand around the bottom of the bat or stick; the next player wraps a hand around the stick immediately above the last; players keep adding hands to the stick until one reaches the top, and that player (or that player's team) goes first.

In card games, play usually begins with the player to the left of the dealer.

For dice games, each player may throw one die before the game. The high roller goes first.

In many ball games, the players "volley" for serve. The ball is put in motion with a throw. It is hit from team to team at least three times for a valid volley, after which time, the team that makes the first error must forfeit the first serve to the other team.

Choosing Sides

An efficient way to determine teams is to count off. The players form a single-file line, and starting at the beginning, call out a number in sequence according to the number of teams. For a game with two teams, the first player in line is "one," the second "two," the third "one," the fourth "two," and so on.

Since games for younger children require less difficult tasks, counting off or simply having an adult divide up the team is sufficient. Games for older players that involve more advanced skill levels may require more elaborate methods to ensure evenly matched teams.

When "captains" are given the chance to choose their own teams, they often form even matches. Selecting captains is difficult in itself. Sometimes players will nominate a particularly skilled player and there will be a general agreement. An adult may randomly choose two players, or winners of a previous game may be given the privilege of serving as captains.

When captains have been chosen, they alternate in selecting players for their teams. This method works best when handled with some diplomacy—no player wants to be the last to be chosen.

These are only a few guidelines to help determine who is "It" and who goes first. Following a few simple rules and guidelines helps children learn many lessons in fairness and good sportsmanship, even before the game gets started!

Selecting the Best Ball for the Game

Many of the following games require some type of ball. While general suggestions are offered, players can often improvise with whatever type of ball is available.

The generic rubber playground ball is usually eight to ten inches in diameter and dull red in color. Most schools use these in gym class because of their durability and versatility, but for the most part, anything that bounces can be used in good cheer.

■ ■ ■

So, now that most of the basics of game playing have been covered . . . let the fun begin!

ONE

Indoor Games for Sunny Days and Rainy Days

Action Spelling

WHERE TO PLAY
Indoors or outdoors

NUMBER OF PLAYERS
4 or more

EQUIPMENT
None

OBJECT OF THE GAME
For players to spell words correctly, substituting motions for some letters

This is a more playful version of the traditional game **Spelling Bee.**

Before the game, the players should select one player to act as the spelling master and then agree on a set of motions that will replace certain letters of the alphabet. *A* could be a jumping jack, *L* a handclap, and *T* a kick.

The number of substitutions made for letters should depend upon the age level of the players. To make the game simpler for younger children, the gestures and letters can correspond: a jumping jack for *J*, a kick for *K* and so on.

The game begins when the spelling master gives the first player a word to spell. That player must correctly spell the word, using the appropriate motions for the letters indicated. A player spelling *pilot* would say "P–I, then clap hands for *L*, say "O," and then kick to represent *T* if a clap signified *L* and a kick *T*.

The next player spells a word given by the spelling master, substituting gestures for letters as needed.

Action Spelling can be played for points or as an elimination game.

VARIATION
Another way to play Action Spelling is to substitute certain motions for vowels and consonants. For example, a hop on one foot could represent a vowel, while a jumping jack might signify a consonant.

Aesop's Mission

WHERE TO PLAY
Anywhere

NUMBER OF PLAYERS
4 or more

EQUIPMENT
None

OBJECT OF THE GAME
To discover the letter that "Aesop" has forbidden before being
eliminated from the game

One player is designated as "Aesop," and the other players are the "animals" of Aesop's fables. Aesop must secretly choose one letter that must be avoided by the players.

Play begins when Aesop asks the first player a question that can require only a one-word answer. A crafty Aesop will try to ask a question that is likely to be answered with a word containing the forbidden letter.

For example, if the forbidden letter is *s,* Aesop might ask, "Which is your favorite season of the year?" hoping the player will respond with "summer" or "spring."

If the player responds to Aesop's question with a word containing the prohibited letter, he or she loses one life. The next player is given a chance to guess the forbidden letter before being asked a question.

After losing three lives, a player is dropped from the game. The players try to discover the taboo letter before using up all three lives. The player who guesses the forbidden letter first becomes the next Aesop.

Animals

WHERE TO PLAY

At a table

NUMBER OF PLAYERS

At least 3

EQUIPMENT

A deck of playing cards

OBJECT OF THE GAME

To win another player's cards by calling out his or her animal noise
before that player calls yours

Shuffle and deal the cards facedown around the table. Next, each player should choose an animal to imitate. When everyone has a different animal, go around the circle a couple of times to practice the appropriate noises.

One player might meow like a cat, another bark like a dog, another hiss like a snake, or moo like a cow, and so forth. All players should try to remember the animals chosen by the others as well as their own.

Play begins at the dealer's left. Everyone around the table discards one card faceup (in sequential order), forming separate discard piles for each player.

When one player lays down a card that is of equal value to another card in someone else's discard pile (two Jacks, for instance), those players with the matching cards try to call out the animal noise of the other.

For example, if the "cow" lays down a 6 that matches the 6 on the pile of the "cat," he or she tries to meow before the "cat" moos. The first of the two players to make the right sound is awarded the discard pile of the other player.

A player who makes a wrong noise, or calls out a noise at the wrong time, must pay the penalty of the top card from his or her discard pile or hand, if there is no discard pile.

The game is continued by the loser of each round, who lays down a new card.

Any player to lose all of his or her cards is eliminated from the game. The player to collect all the cards is the winner.

Playing until final elimination is recommended only for patient players. It might be a better idea to keep track of a predetermined number of rounds and designate the winner as the player with the greatest number of cards at the completion of all the rounds.

Art Consequences

WHERE TO PLAY
Seated at a table

NUMBER OF PLAYERS
3 or more

EQUIPMENT
A few sheets of paper and pencils

OBJECT OF THE GAME
To draw an imaginary figure and create an amusing work of art through group effort

If numbers permit, the players should be divided into groups of three or four. The first player in each group begins by drawing the head and neck of a real or imaginary figure on the top one-third of the paper. When done, he or she folds the paper back so that nothing can be seen of the drawing except a few lines that will allow the next player to continue the figure.

The next player then draws in the shoulders and part of the arms and torso. When done, he or she folds the paper back again so only a bit of the bottom section of the drawing is visible—enough to allow the next player to take up the drawing.

The drawing is passed along and finished by the final player, who then unfolds the paper to reveal the entire figure.

When there are two or more groups of "artists" there can be a competition for the best creation: silliest, scariest, most true to life, etc.

Surrealist artists of the 1930s called this game The Exquisite Corpse and used it to create a number of serious works of art.

Assassin

WHERE TO PLAY
Seated in a circle on the floor or around a table

NUMBER OF PLAYERS
6 or more

EQUIPMENT
Pencil or pen and scraps of paper

OBJECT OF THE GAME
For the "assassin" to eliminate all the other players from the game by
winking at them, while avoiding being caught

Cut up or tear off a small piece of paper for each player. Mark one of these
sheets with an *X,* fold, shuffle, and distribute them among the players. The
players should open them secretly. The player whose paper is marked *X*
will be the assassin.

After all the papers have been checked, the players form a circle around
a table or seat themselves on the floor. Players examine the faces of the
others around the circle, trying to discover who the assassin is. When the
assassin winks at another player, that player must say, "I've been hit" and
must drop out of the game.

If a player catches the assassin in the act of winking, the game is over,
and the sharp-eyed player is the winner. But if the assassin succeeds in
winking at all the players (except the last, who, by process of elimination,
will soon learn who the assassin is), he or she is declared the winner.

Bango

WHERE TO PLAY
At a table

NUMBER OF PLAYERS
At least 3

EQUIPMENT
A deck of playing cards

OBJECT OF THE GAME
To be the first to match your hand to the card values called by the
dealer

This game is a very simplified version of **Bingo,** well suited for children
under eight.

One player shuffles the deck and deals five cards to each player at the table. The players place their cards faceup in front of them.

The dealer then turns over one card at a time from the pile of remaining cards and calls out its value. Any player with a card of matching value can turn that card facedown.

The first player who can turn all five cards facedown shouts, "Bango!" in order to win the round.

Keep track of the number of rounds won by each player if you want to declare a grand winner at the end of the game.

Battleship

WHERE TO PLAY
Best played at a table, but can be played as a travel game if the ride is steady

NUMBER OF PLAYERS
2, or 4 if you want to play with partners

EQUIPMENT
Paper and pencil for each player or team. Graph paper makes playing easier, but it is not essential.

OBJECT OF THE GAME
To sink your opponent's battleships by making successful "hits" on a grid

To prepare for the game, two grids, which represent naval battlefields, need to be drawn on each player's sheet. Each grid should have 10 blocks down and 10 blocks across for a total of 100 blocks. The blocks need not be very big—a quarter of an inch is large enough.

Across the top row of each grid, number the blocks *1* through *10*. Down the left edge of the grids, letter the blocks *A* through *J*. Label one grid for the player and the other for the enemy.

Players then must place battleships on the grid for their respective "sides" by drawing lines through consecutive blocks to indicate their ships' positions. Each player has four ships: an aircraft carrier of four blocks, a cruiser of three blocks, and two destroyers of two blocks apiece.

Players mark their battleships on their grids without letting the enemy see their positions. The blocks must be located on a straight line: horizontally, vertically, or diagonally. A battleship may not be split up.

When the grids are drawn and the battleships are in place, the

(*continued on next page*)

Battleship (*cont.*)

players should determine who fires first. The player chosen to begin gets eleven shots to try to hit the other player's battleships.

That player calls out blocks of the grid according to letter and number: B-10, F-6, and so on, until he or she has used up eleven shots. As the firing player calls out the shots, the defensive player should mark them on his or her own grid with a number *1* to represent shots fired in the first round. The firing player should likewise keep track of his shots fired by marking with *1* the blocks at which shots were fired on his second grid for the enemy.

Then, after all eleven shots have been fired, the defensive player calls out the location of each shot and whether each was a "hit" (if it is one of the blocks on which a battleship is marked) or a "miss" (if it is an empty block). Players should circle the blocks that represent "hits" in order to distinguish them from "misses."

When the first player is done firing, the second player gets the chance to fire eleven shots and is told whether they are "hits" or "misses."

The second round begins with a new group of shots. This time the player is allowed eleven shots minus the number of "hits" that player scored in the previous round. If three "hits" were made in the first round, that player is given eight shots to fire in the second round. Shots are indicated by the number representing that round: Use *1* for shots fired in the first round, *2* for shots fired in the second round, and so on.

Since the object of the game is to sink the other players' ships, shots in rounds following the first should be called in the vicinity of the hits previously made. In order to constitute a sinking ship, all the blocks on which a ship is located must be struck.

Play continues until one player succeeds in sinking all the other's battleships. A player must announce the fact when one of his or her battleships is sunk.

VARIATION

To make the game more challenging, players do not have to reveal that ships have sunk until *all* have been sunk, thereby providing no clues as to the type of boat or number of blocks to be hit. (Battleship was also known humorously as Swiss Navy before it became popularized as a manufactured game.)

Beetle

WHERE TO PLAY
At a table or on the floor

NUMBER OF PLAYERS
2 to 6

EQUIPMENT
One die; pencil and paper for each player

OBJECT OF THE GAME
To be the first player to complete the drawing of a "beetle" after
throwing the correct sequence of numbers

Determine the order of play by rolling the die. The highest roller begins
the game.

The first player rolls the dice, trying to throw a *1*. Each player gets one
roll per turn. The numbers must be earned in order from *1* through *5*.

When a player throws a *1,* he or she begins a beetle by drawing its
body. A *2* is needed next before drawing the head. A *3* is then required to
add three legs on one side of the body, and, on the next turn, another *3*
is needed to add the three remaining legs.

Players who roll a *4* can add one feeler, and a second *4* gets the other
feeler. A *5* allows the player to draw one eye, and the first player to throw
a second *5* and add the other eye may complete his or her beetle to win
the game.

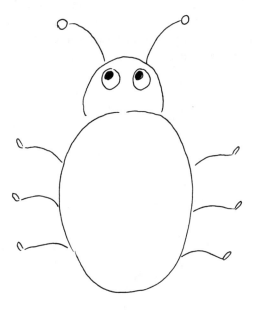

Beggar My Neighbor

WHERE TO PLAY
Anywhere

NUMBER OF PLAYERS
2 to 4

EQUIPMENT
A deck of playing cards for every 2 players

OBJECT OF THE GAME
To win all the cards from your opponent—through chance more than
skill

Shuffle the cards and deal out all of them into piles for each player.

The player at the dealer's left begins the game by laying down the first
card from the top of his or her pile into a center pile, faceup.

If it is anything but a picture or an Ace, the next player follows by
turning over one of his or her cards. If, however, it is a face card or an Ace,
a penalty must be paid by the next player. One card must be paid for a
Jack, two for a Queen, three for a King, and four for an Ace.

The player paying lays out the penalty cards one at a time. If none of
them is a face card or an Ace, the first player may keep all of the cards in
the pile. But, if another face card or Ace turns up, the original debt is
cancelled, and the first player must now pay the appropriate number of
cards to the second player.

Players keep exchanging debt penalties until no more face cards or
Aces are turned up. The game then continues with the next player.

Eventually, players will run out of cards and will be eliminated from the
game. The player who collects all the cards wins.

Bingo

WHERE TO PLAY

At a table

NUMBER OF PLAYERS

3 or more

EQUIPMENT

Paper and pencils; a container for the numbers (a hat, a box, or an envelope are all suitable); a large number of markers (coins, buttons, dried beans, etc.)

OBJECT OF THE GAME

To be the first to fill in a row of 5 numbers—horizontally, vertically, or diagonally

Making the cards to play Bingo takes only a few minutes, while the fun lasts much longer.

First, cut a sheet of paper into 100 small squares and number them *1* through *100*. Place these numbers in a container. A box, a hat, or an envelope are all easy to use.

Each player can make up his or her own game card with a sheet of paper and pencil. Draw a diagram consisting of twenty-five one-inch-square boxes, five across and five down. Fill in the first horizontal line with any five numbers from *1* to *20*, in numerical order (for ease in finding them while the game is played). The second line should be any five numbers from *21* to *40*, the third any five from *41* to *60*, the fourth any five from *61* to *80*, and the bottom row any five from *81* to *100*.

The players should also be given a handful of markers (small enough to fit within the size of the squares), with more available in the center if needed.

One player serves as the caller for the first game. The caller mixes up the numbers and then draws them one at a time. When the caller announces a number, the players check their boards. If they have written that number on their board, they may place a marker on that space.

The caller continues picking numbers until one player has filled in a horizontal, vertical, or diagonal line of five markers. The first player to do so calls, "Bingo" and wins the game.

For a longer game, try to fill up the entire card. Players can also pass their cards around for variety. Make sure everyone who wants a chance to be the caller has one.

(*continued on next page*)

Bingo (*cont.*)

VARIATION

For an even more simplified version, which is great fun to play while traveling, each player needs a sheet of paper and pencil. On the paper, each player draws a small diagram and fills in the numbers on his or her own.

The designated caller should not look at the numbers on the players' cards and should call out numbers at random. Players who have these numbers on their cards blacken out the appropriate squares with pencil, while the caller records all the numbers to avoid repeats. The caller should continue calling out numbers until a player fills a row and calls, "Bingo!"

(Bingo is said to have been invented by a nobleman in Italy, where it is known as "*La Tombola.*" In the age of luxury liners, it was a very popular type of shipboard entertainment known as Housey-Housey.)

Botticelli

WHERE TO PLAY
Anywhere; also a good travel game

NUMBER OF PLAYERS
At least 3

EQUIPMENT
None

OBJECT OF THE GAME
To ask questions that will lead you to discover the identity of a famous person chosen by one of the players

One player selects the identity of a famous person familiar to all the players and informs the other players of the initial of that person's last name.

The other players try to determine the secret identity by asking questions phrased so that the chooser must identify other people with the same initial.

For example, if the initial is *M,* the first question might be, "Are you an Italian artist of the Renaissance?" The chooser must answer with the name of some Italian Renaissance artist whose name begins with *M* or answer a forfeit question.

If the chooser can answer, "No, I am not Michelangelo," then the next player asks a question. However, if the asker stumps the chooser, then he or she has a chance to request more specific information: "Are you male ("No, I am not male") or "Are you alive?" ("No, I am not alive"), for instance. The questions can only be answered by a yes or no.

The chooser continues answering questions: "Are you a Hollywood bombshell?" ("No, I am not Marilyn Monroe"); "Are you in the Baseball Hall of Fame?" ("No, I am not Willie Mays"); and so on, until someone guesses the secret identity.

Of course, players will try to ask more obscure questions in order to stump the choosers and, thus, gain clues.

The first player to guess the identity may choose the individual for the next round.

Boxes

WHERE TO PLAY
Anywhere

NUMBER OF PLAYERS
2 at a time

EQUIPMENT
Paper and pencil

OBJECT OF THE GAME
To connect the dots on a grid to make more boxes than your opponent

Set up the game by drawing a square grid made up of dots. Four dots on each side is a good size to begin with.

•   •   •   •

Choose one player to go first. This player draws a line between any two dots horizontally or vertically. The second player then draws a line connecting two more dots.

Eventually, one of the players will be able to form a box. That player puts his or her initial in the box and is given another turn. He or she may continue adding lines as long as each line forms a new box. If a new box can't be made, the game resumes with the other player taking a turn.

The player with the most boxes when all the dots are connected is declared the winner.

More experienced players will realize how to draw lines strategically to enhance the fun.

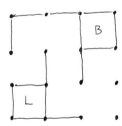

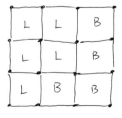

Buzz

WHERE TO PLAY
Anywhere

NUMBER OF PLAYERS
2 or more

EQUIPMENT
None

OBJECT OF THE GAME
To count to 100 while substituting the word *buzz* for the number 7 or its multiples without making any mistakes

---

Players count off to 100 in sequential fashion, replacing 7 and its multiples with *buzz.* For example, players would count out *1* to *14* as follows: "1, 2, 3, 4, 5, 6, buzz, 8, 9, 10, 11, 12, 13, buzz."

When only a few players are involved, there need not be competition, but if a larger group participates, players can be eliminated after two mistakes.

VARIATION
A more difficult version of this game is called Fizz Buzz. In this variation, in addition to replacing 7 and its multiples with *buzz,* the word *fizz* is substituted for the number 5 and its multiples. Some people also like to substitute for double digits of the same number, for example, "1, 2, 3, 4, fizz, 6, buzz, 8, 9, fizz, buzz, 12, 13, buzz."

Cat's Cradle

WHERE TO PLAY
Anywhere

NUMBER OF PLAYERS
1 or 2 at a time

EQUIPMENT
String

OBJECT OF THE GAME
To form shapes by playing with pieces of string

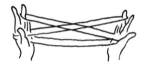

Games with string, like Cat's Cradle, are one of the oldest forms of play—prehistoric children probably created similar shapes from cords of gut. The names given to the game, from Crow's Feet to Barn Doors, reflect what different cultures see in the shapes formed by the string.

There are many ways in which to manipulate a piece of string to form amusing shapes, which are explained in books dedicated to string games. These are a few basic examples.

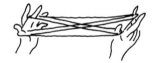

Needed for any Cat's Cradle game is a piece of string, about two feet long, with the ends tightly knotted together to form a single loop.

The simplest Cat's Cradle can be formed by a single player. To begin, hook the loop over the left thumb, draw it across the palm, and hook it again behind the pinky. Repeat this with the right hand so that the loop is stretched between the two hands.

Slide the right index finger under the line of string that stretches horizontally across the left palm and pull it back to the right, making the string taut. Repeat with the left index finger, pulling the string taut again.

This is the basic cradle shape. Turn the hands upside down and it becomes a manger. In some parts of the world, cradle and manger games are associated with the Christmas season.

Witch's Broom and Banana Bunch are two sequential shapes that can also be formed by one player. To begin, start in the same manner as the cradle: hook the loop over the left thumb, draw it across the palm, and hook it again behind the pinky.

This time, instead of repeating with the right hand, let the rest of the loop hang down. Then, take the right index finger, hook it over the line of string that stretches horizontally across the left palm, and pull down, making the string taught. What was originally the bottom of the loop now forms another line across the palm.

Repeat this one more time, so that there are now two smaller loops around the thumb and the pinky. Place the right hand inside the larger loop and open the fingers so this loop lies between the thumb and index finger.

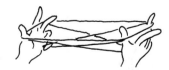

(*continued on next page*)

Cat's Cradle (*cont.*)

Hook the right thumb into the loop around the left thumb, and the right pinky into the loop around the left pinky. Touch the right thumb and right index finger together and draw the string back through the large loop.

Hold the two loops out from the right hand. If you touch the right thumb and right index finger again, it will look as if there are three columns.

Insert the three middle fingers of the left hand in between these strings, one in each column. Drop the loops behind the left hand.

Turn the left hand so the palm faces up. Pull the middle loop straight up and hold it out. This shape is called the Witch's Broom.

Now, carefully pull the left-hand fingers out of the loops and hold them up with the right hand. There will be four loops hanging from one loop—a bunch of bananas, or in some areas, yams.

Ask someone to pick a banana. That person pulls one banana loop down, but it's a trick bunch—the loops will straighten out and all the bananas will disappear!

Cat's Cradle for two differs slightly from the game for one.

The first player wraps the loop in a small loop around one palm (except for the thumb) and then the other. Next, he or she slides the middle finger of the right hand under the string across the left palm, drawing it back.

Repeat on the other side: slip the middle finger of the left hand under the string across the right palm and pull it back. This is the Cat's Cradle.

The second player joins at this point by taking the string off the first player's hands. The second player takes hold of the *X* on one side of the cradle between the left thumb and forefinger, and then the other *X* between the right thumb and forefinger.

He or she then pulls outward and down, bringing the *X*s through into the center section of the loop, pulling the string carefully off the fingers of the first player. The shape formed is called the Soldier's Bed

The first player takes hold of the *X*s, which are now located in the center of the loop, in the same manner, between the thumb and forefinger of each hand, and moves them out, under, and up, pulling them off the second player's hands. The resulting form is called Candles.

To remove Candles from the first player's hands, the second player takes hold of the left string with the right pinky, drawing it back to the right, and then the right string with the left pinky, pulling it back to the left. Holding the string firmly with the pinkies, the second player scoops his or her hands out and under again, bringing them up through the center of the loop. The second player spreads the thumb and index finger on each hand to catch the string and pull it off the first player's hands. The result is a new Cat's Cradle.

Categories

WHERE TO PLAY

Anywhere

NUMBER OF PLAYERS

4 or more

EQUIPMENT

Pencil and paper for each player

OBJECT OF THE GAME

To think of the greatest number of items belonging to a chosen
category within a given time limit

From among the group of players, a list of about twenty categories should
be drawn up. Players can divide up the number of categories to be chosen:
if there are five players, each may select four categories.

Each player writes the names of all the categories at the top of his or
her paper. To begin, one player chooses a letter of the alphabet at random.
(A different player begins the next round by selecting a new letter.)

The players have a given amount of time—usually five or ten minutes,
depending on their abilities—to write down as many words as possible that
start with the chosen letter and correspond to each of the categories. For
example, if the letter *N* is chosen and one of the categories happens to be
States, correct answers would include Nebraska, Nevada, New Hampshire,
New Jersey, New York, North Carolina, and North Dakota.

At the end of the time limit, players should trade lists for scoring. All the
answers are read aloud. For each correct answer a player receives 1 point.
An answer that no one else has thought of receives 2 points.

For another round, a different letter can be picked, and you can either
keep or change the categories.

The player with the most points after a predetermined number of
rounds is the winner.

VARIATION

A less complicated version of this game is First Names First, in which the
only category is first names. Instead of randomly choosing a letter of the
alphabet, a first name is selected. Players must think of more names that
begin with each of the letters in the given name. For example, if Pam is
suggested, other correct answers would be Patricia, Anne, and Mary.

P	*A*	*M*
Patricia	Anne	Mary
Paula	Alice	Michelle
Penny	Alison	Margaret

Charades

WHERE TO PLAY

Anywhere

NUMBER OF PLAYERS

6 or more

EQUIPMENT

Paper and pencils; watch or clock with a second hand

OBJECT OF THE GAME

To guess, in the shortest time possible, the famous phrase or sentence
being acted out by your team members

Two teams are formed; one will start as the actors and the other as the
audience.

Each member of the audience writes down a famous saying or title on
a slip of paper. The phrase should be known to all and should be relatively
short, something like *Gone with the Wind* or *The early bird gets the worm.*

The phrases are shuffled and then distributed to the actors, one to each
player.

One at a time, the actors attempt to convey the phrase to their teammates through pantomime and a series of gestures that are used to clarify
the pantomime:

- Arms crossed over the chest means that the actor will try to mime the
  entire phrase at once.
- A chopping motion signifies that the phrase will be chopped into words
  or syllables. The actor will then hold up one or more fingers to indicate
  which word or syllable he or she is trying to act out at that moment. By
  holding up two fingers and then making a fist, the actor denotes that the
  next two words or syllables should be joined together.
- A hand cupped around the ear means the word "Sounds like . . ." and
  indicates a rhyme word that is somewhat easier to act out.
- A beckoning motion means that the teammates are getting close to the
  right answer. If they are far off the track, the actor makes a pushing
  gesture.
- Looking forward signals future tense, and looking backward means past
  tense.

As the actor pantomimes, his or her teammates call out their guesses,
trying to come up with the correct answer as quickly as possible. Someone
in the audience should time the guesses and write the total time down
when the answer is discovered.

After all the members of the actors' team have had a chance to get their messages across, they exchange roles with the audience team.

The team that has amassed the least total guessing time wins the game.

Cheat

WHERE TO PLAY

At a table

NUMBER OF PLAYERS

3 or more

EQUIPMENT

A deck of playing cards

OBJECT OF THE GAME

To get rid of all your cards by bluffing successfully

Shuffle the deck and deal it out to the players. The player on the dealer's left initiates the game by laying any card from his or her hand facedown in the center of the table, calling out its value at the same time.

The next player aims to follow the last card laid down with the card of the next higher value. If the first card is a 7, for example, the next player wants to put down an 8. This player places the next card facedown without letting anyone see its value and calls out "Eight," regardless of whether it actually is an 8.

It is now up to the rest of the players to decide if indeed an 8 was laid down. If no one wishes to challenge the player, the game continues with the next person, who lays down a card, claiming, "Nine."

If, however, any player believes that something other than the proper card was laid down, he or she calls, "Cheat!" The card is then turned over to see its actual value.

If it is the right card for the sequence (in this case, an 8), the player who made the challenge must add all the cards in the center pile to his or her hand. But if it is not the card it was claimed to be, the player who laid it down has to take all the center cards.

When the game gets heated, disputes may arise as to which player called out "Cheat!" first. A referee can be designated to resolve disputes, or a default system can be used. For example, in case of a dispute, the player nearest to the left of the challenged player will be considered the challenger.

After each round, the game is restarted by the player to the left of the

(*continued on next page*)

Cheat (*cont.*)

challenged player, who lays down a card in the center and calls out its value, as in the beginning of the game.

The first person to discard all of his or her cards is the winner.

VARIATION

A variation of Cheat is called I Doubt It. The rules are basically the same, except that players may claim to have up to four cards to lay down in each round, calling out the values for all of them. For example, if the last card was said to be a *9,* the next player can claim to be discarding two *10*s, when in fact he or she only has one *10.*

If players are not convinced that an opponent has the cards he or she claims to have, instead of calling, "Cheat!" players yell, "I doubt it!"

Clockwise Dice

WHERE TO PLAY
Anywhere

NUMBER OF PLAYERS
2 or more

EQUIPMENT
2 dice; paper and pencil for scorekeeping (optional)

OBJECT OF THE GAME
To be the first player to roll the numbers *1* through *12* in correct sequence

Roll one die to determine the order of play: the high roller goes first. Play continues in a circle from the first player's left or in descending numerical order.

The first player rolls both dice in an attempt to come up with a *1.* If one of the dice is a *1,* he or she has completed the first number in the sequence. If not, he or she must try again for a *1* on the next turn.

Players have one throw per round in which to try for the appropriate number. After one roll, the game continues with the next player.

For numbers *2* through *6,* both dice may be counted in order to earn the needed number. For example, a player trying for *6* may get it in any of these ways: one *6,* two *3*s, a *4* and a *2,* or a *5* and a *1.*

It is also permissible to score two numbers in sequence in one throw of the dice. If a player is trying for *2,* for example, and rolls *2* and *3,* both may be counted as part of the sequence, and he or she will next need a *4.*

Numbers *7* through *12* are scored by adding the spots on both the dice thrown.

The first player to throw numbers *1* through *12* wins the game.

(The game of Dice was played in ancient Greece. According to one story, dice were invented by Palamedes in order to keep his soldiers occupied during the siege of Troy. In another story, they were created by a king of Asia Minor to keep the minds of his people off their hunger during a terrible famine.)

Coffeepot

WHERE TO PLAY
Anywhere

NUMBER OF PLAYERS
3 or more

EQUIPMENT
None

OBJECT OF THE GAME
For "It" to guess the verb known to all the other players by asking questions

One player is chosen to be "It." A second player chooses a verb and whispers it to the remaining players.

When they all know the selected verb, "It" asks a question of each of the players in order to discover the word, substituting "coffeepot" for the unknown verb in the questions.

Take, for example, "ski" as the designated word. In attempting to guess the word, "It" might ask: "Do you 'coffeepot' indoors?" The player would reply "No." "It" might then ask: "Do you 'coffeepot' during the summer?" and so on, until the correct verb is revealed.

A time limit of two or three minutes to discover the word can be set.

The last player to give an answer before the word is guessed must be "It" for the next round.

Colin Maillard
(pronounced "My-yard")

WHERE TO PLAY
Indoors

NUMBER OF PLAYERS
8 or more

EQUIPMENT
Chairs for all players but 2; a scarf or rag to serve as a blindfold

---

OBJECT OF THE GAME
For "Colin Maillard" to guess the identity of the person on whose lap
he or she sits

Before the game begins, one player is chosen to be "Colin Maillard" and
another to be the conductor. The rest of the players sit in the chairs, which
have been arranged in a small circle facing inward.

The conductor blindfolds Colin Maillard, who stands in the center of
the circle. After he or she has been blindfolded, the other players quickly
change places so that Colin will no longer know the seating arrangement.

When the players have all settled into new seats, the conductor announces that they are ready, and Colin Maillard may choose to join one of
them. Colin should begin to move toward someone, aided by verbal
directions from the conductor and a helping hand if necessary. Upon
reaching a player, Colin turns around and sits on that player's knees.

Colin has one guess as to the identity of the player. If the guess is
correct, Colin and that player trade places. (The conductor should also
exchange spots with another player so that all may get to join in the game.)

If Colin guesses incorrectly, the other players indicate the mistake by
clapping. At this point, Colin must move on to another player and continue
guessing until successful. If Colin seems to be in danger of never making
a correct identification, the conductor may give hints to speed up the
game.

(Colin Maillard was a celebrated soldier from Belgium. Though
blinded, he was still successful in battle and was knighted in the year 999.
The king admired his talents so much that he initiated a pageant game that
featured a blindfolded knight, from which this version of **Blindman's
Buff** has descended.)

Concentration

WHERE TO PLAY

At a table or on the floor

NUMBER OF PLAYERS

2 or more

EQUIPMENT

A deck of playing cards

OBJECT OF THE GAME

To gain the greatest number of cards by remembering their locations
after they have been turned facedown

Shuffle the cards and lay them facedown one next to another on the table
or floor in an orderly fashion—perhaps thirteen rows by four rows if you
really want to be neat.

The game begins when the first player turns over any two cards, in
hopes of uncovering a matching pair. If they are of equal value (two
Queens or two 7s, for example), the player may pick them up and keep
them, and guess again.

Cards that don't match must be returned to a facedown position, and it
is then the next player's turn. (Before the cards are turned down again,
players must call upon all their powers of concentration—hence the name
of the game—to fix their locations, which will aid in future guesses.)

The next player flips over two more cards, keeping them if they are a
matched pair and turning them back over if they are not. The game grows
easier as more and more cards are revealed and removed.

When all the cards have been collected, the player with the greatest
number of pairs is the winner.

For younger children, the game can be simplified by limiting the number of pairs available. Separate out ten or so pairs and lay them out, setting
aside the remainder.

Concentration was known as Pelmanism (perhaps after the Pelman
memory course) until the popular TV show brought the game into house-
holds across the country. The TV version was more complex: correct
guesses revealed parts of a rebus beneath the board which also had to be
solved.

Cootie Catcher

WHERE TO PLAY

Anywhere

NUMBER OF PLAYERS

2 or more

EQUIPMENT

A sheet of paper for each player; scissors; something to write with

OBJECT OF THE GAME

To make a "Cootie Catcher" and use it to tell fortunes or make jokes

Begin with a square piece of paper for each player. A nine-by-nine-inch square works well.

Fold each corner over to the opposite corner to make two creases in the square. After making the creases, open the paper flat again. (See step 1)

Next, fold all four corners into the center. This will form a smaller square. (See step 2)

Flip the square over and fold all the corners into the center again, forming an even smaller square. (See step 3)

Flip it back over one more time, and slip one finger into each flap, pressing the center creases in together so that all four fingers bring the flaps to a point in the center. (See step 4)

Number the eight inside flaps, and write fortunes or jokes beneath them.

Have one player choose a number between *1* and *10*. Open and close the flaps of the Cootie Catcher the corresponding number of times. The player should then choose among one of the four numbers displayed on the inside. Open out the flap for the chosen number and read the fortune inside.

VARIATION

Cootie Catcher is also known as Fortune Teller. In this variation, players label the four outer flaps of the Cootie Catcher with colors. On the inside flaps, they inscribe eight different numbers. And, underneath the flaps, they write eight fortunes—anything from *You will marry Billy* to *You will be an astronaut.*

To play with the Cootie Catcher, the fortune teller asks someone to choose one of the four colors. If he or she picks green, for instance, the fortune teller opens and closes the Cootie Catcher five times (determined by the number of letters in the color chosen) while chanting, "G-R-E-E-N."

The fortune teller stops on "N" and leaves the Cootie Catcher open to reveal four numbers inside.

The player must then select a number. While it seems logical to inscribe fairly small numbers here, there's an ingenious rhyme that allows the fortune teller to use any number imaginable. If the player selects *108,* for example, the fortune teller chants, "One, two, skip a few, now it's 108" while opening and shutting the Cootie Catcher 8 times, rather than 108 times.

The player then picks one more number. The corresponding flap is lifted to reveal the fortune underneath.

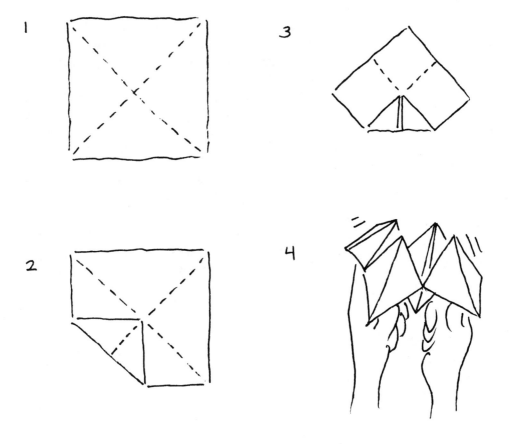

Crambo

WHERE TO PLAY

Anywhere

NUMBER OF PLAYERS

At least 6

EQUIPMENT

None

OBJECT OF GAME

To guess the word that rhymes with the word given by one of the
players

One player is selected to begin the game and choose a word for the other
players to guess. He or she says, "I am thinking of a word that rhymes with
———— ." If the targeted word is *heart,* for example, the player might say
"I am thinking of a word that rhymes with *cart.*"

The rest of the players attempt to discover the mystery word by taking
turns asking questions in which they define words that rhyme with the
word given. For example, if asked, "Is it something you create?" the player
would answer, "No, it is not art." "Is it something sour?" "No, it is not tart,"
and so forth.

If the player who is "It" is unable to respond to the question with an
appropriate rhyming word, the questioner can reveal the desired response
and is given the opportunity to ask a second question. If "It" is stumped
a second time, the questioner reveals once again the desired response, but
this time play moves on to the next questioner in line.

The first player to guess the correct word gets to choose a word for the
next round.

Crazy Eights

WHERE TO PLAY
At a table

NUMBER OF PLAYERS
3 or more

EQUIPMENT
A deck of playing cards

OBJECT OF THE GAME
To be the first to get rid of all your cards

Shuffle the cards and deal seven to each player. Place the remaining cards in a pile in the center of the table. Players examine their cards and sort them by suit, keeping them hidden from their opponents.

The player at the dealer's left initiates the game by laying one card faceup in the center of the table. The next player must follow with a card of the same suit—a club on a club, for example. If a player doesn't have a card with the same suit or wishes to change the suit, then a card of the same value may be laid down, for example, a 6 on a 6, which then changes the suit to the face card.

Eights are "wild," meaning that they can be played at any time. The player putting down an *8,* is allowed to choose a suit for the next player to follow.

When a player is unable to follow with a card of the same suit or rank, or an *8,* he or she must draw a card from the center pile. If the card can be played, it is laid down. If not, the player must continue drawing cards until he or she gets one that can be played.

If a player picks up all the cards in the center pile without finding an appropriate card, he or she calls, "Pass," and the game continues with the next player.

The first player to discard all of his or her cards is the winner.

Crazy Eights can be scored with points if you wish to play a longer game: When one player has gotten rid of all of his or her cards, the other players must tally up the points of the cards remaining in their hands. An *8* is worth 50 points; Jack, Queen, and King are worth 10 points each; Aces are worth 1 point; and the other cards are scored according to their numbers. The player with the lowest score after a predetermined number of rounds wins the game.

Crosswords

WHERE TO PLAY
Anywhere

NUMBER OF PLAYERS
At least 2

EQUIPMENT
Pencil and paper for each player

OBJECT OF THE GAME
To score points by forming words in a crossword diagram

Before beginning, each player draws a crossword diagram (consisting of five boxes across and five down) on a sheet of paper.

The player chosen to go first calls out a letter at random. Each player must place that letter in a square on his or her diagram.

The next player chooses another letter, which all must place in their diagrams, keeping in mind that they are trying to form as many words as possible.

D	O	C	A	T
X	P	A	T	R
W	V	N	T	Y
U	C	O	I	N
F	E	N	C	E

SCORING

ACROSS
   DO   2
   CAT   3
   PAT   3
   COIN   4
   FENCE   5 + 1 BONUS POINT

DOWN
   CANON   5 + 1 BONUS POINT
   NO   2
   ATTIC   5 + 1 BONUS POINT
   TRY   3

35 TOTAL

The players continue selecting letters until all the squares have been filled. When the diagrams are complete, players add up their scores as follows: Horizontal and vertical words score 1 point for each letter. A five-letter word scores a bonus point. Two words may be formed in one line (D-O-C-A-T would score 5 points as *do* and *cat*), but a word that can be split into two separate words (like *canon—can* and *on*) may only be scored once. Remember, however, that if it is a five-letter word, you get a bonus point.

The player with the highest score wins.

Donkey

WHERE TO PLAY
At a table

NUMBER OF PLAYERS
3 or more

EQUIPMENT
A deck of playing cards; pencil and paper for scorekeeping

OBJECT OF THE GAME
To be the first to get 4 cards of equal value and to avoid becoming the "donkey"

One player should be designated the scorekeeper.

In preparation for the game, the dealer should construct a new deck of cards by pulling sets of four-of-a-kind, the number of sets determined by the number of players. For example, if there are three players, the dealer could pull out 3 sets of four-of-a-kind, the 4s, 8s, and kings for example. Set aside the remaining cards—they will not be used.

Shuffle and deal these cards to the players. Each player looks at his or her hand, keeping it secret. Since the object of the game is to get four cards of equal value, each player should examine the hand and choose one to discard. If a player has two Kings, a *4,* and an *8,* the *4* or *8* should be discarded.

Each player places the discarded card facedown on the table. When all have done so, each player should pass the discarded card to the person at his or her left.

Each player then picks up the new card and compares it with his or her hand to see if it will be of use. If it will, then it is added to the hand and another card is discarded. If not, it is placed back down on the table.

The passing of cards should proceed as rapidly as possible; one player will soon have obtained four matching cards. This player quickly places the entire hand on the table and places a finger next to his or her nose.

When the other players notice that the cards have been put down and that another player has given the nose signal, they must hurry to put their fingers next to their noses also.

The last player to imitate the nose signal is designated the "donkey" of that round and is assigned a *D.* The scorekeeper should keep track of the letters as they are given out.

After a player has lost six rounds and has been assigned *D-O-N-K-E-Y,* he or she is the loser.

(*continued on next page*)

Donkey (*cont.*)

VARIATION

Another version of Donkey is called Spoons. It is played in the same manner except that a bunch of spoons (or any objects that are safe and easy to grasp), numbering one fewer than the number of players, is placed in the center of the table.

When a player collects four cards of the same value, instead of using a nose signal, he or she grabs for a spoon. The other players quickly grab the remaining spoons. The player left without a spoon in each round is assigned a letter: *S-P-O-O-N-S.*

The player staying in the game without spelling *SPOONS* is the winner.

Drawing in the Dark

WHERE TO PLAY
Indoors after sunset or in a room that can easily be darkened

NUMBER OF PLAYERS
2 or more

EQUIPMENT
Pencil and paper for each player

OBJECT OF THE GAME
To draw a picture according to a story told by one of the other players, without being able to see the paper

An adult or older child should serve as the storyteller. Give a sheet of paper and a pencil to each of the players. When everyone is prepared, turn the lights out and darken the room.

The storyteller must invent a short tale which will be illustrated by the other players. The story doesn't have to be very elaborate, but it should include a number of different figures and objects which will be drawn by the other players.

For example, the storyteller may begin, "Once there was a girl named Denise. Please draw Denise." All the players should do their best to draw a figure of a girl. After a minute or two, players should finish up their drawings and the story will continue.

For example: "Denise put her dog, Spot, on a leash and took him to a pet show. Now draw Spot and his leash, which Denise holds in her hand. Denise and Spot admired the beautiful trophy that sat on the judges' table.

Now add the trophy and a table to your drawing. Denise and Spot entered Spot in the Pet show. Spot didn't win the trophy, but Denise gave him a bone for being her favorite. Now put the bone in Spot's mouth and finish up your drawings."

When the drawings are complete, turn the lights back on. The illustration that comes closest to resembling the scene described, as determined either by the storyteller or a vote of the group members, is the winner.

Dress Me

WHERE TO PLAY
Anywhere. This is a great icebreaker for a party!

NUMBER OF PLAYERS
At least 4

EQUIPMENT
A big old shirt

OBJECT OF THE GAME
To move the shirt from one player to another while they hold hands

The first player puts on the big shirt and takes the hand of the next player. The rest of the players try to take the shirt off the first player and put it onto the second without breaking their handhold.

The only way that this can be done is to turn the shirt inside out as it goes over the first player's head. Once it is over that player's head and onto the next player, another player joins hands with the player wearing the shirt, and the first player becomes a dresser.

Depending on the number of players, the line can be extended until all the players have had the shirt on and taken off. If there are enough players and shirts available, this can be played in teams as a race.

Drop Dead

WHERE TO PLAY

Anywhere

NUMBER OF PLAYERS

2 or more

EQUIPMENT

5 dice; pencil and paper for scorekeeping

OBJECT OF THE GAME

To score as many points as possible in 5 throws of the dice

SCORE

12

Playing order makes no difference in Drop Dead. Each player is given five throws of all five dice in which to score as many points as possible. The score of each roll is determined by the total number of dots showing.

13

Dice that land with two or five dots showing, however, score nothing. In addition, when a 2 or 5 is thrown, these dice must be set aside and not rolled again. For instance, if on the first roll a player gets *2, 3, 4, 4,* and *5,* he or she must eliminate the *2* and the *5* from the next throw and from then on will have only three dice to roll.

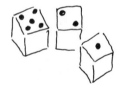

1

The player continues through the five rolls, adding together all dice that reveal one, three, four, and six spots and setting aside the 2s and 5s. It is likely that some players will roll five *2s* and/or *5s* before they get through all five throws. If this happens, this player "drops dead" and is eliminated from the game. The player with the highest score wins. For a longer game, the scores for more than one round can be added together.

3

4

33

Dumb Crambo

WHERE TO PLAY

Anywhere

NUMBER OF PLAYERS

6 or more

EQUIPMENT

None

OBJECT OF THE GAME

To guess the word acted out by another player

Dumb Crambo is a cross between **Crambo** and **Charades.** Like **Crambo,** a rhyme is given as a clue to the word to be guessed, and like **Charades,** the mystery word is acted out before an audience.

The players are divided into two teams: the audience and the actors. The actors leave the room while the audience chooses a word that the actors must guess. When the actors return to the room, they are told, for instance, that they must find a word to rhyme with "fake."

The actors are allowed to consult about their first guess. When ready, they begin miming an action corresponding to their guess. For example, they might pretend to be raking leaves. The audience must call, "Not rake!"

The actors then choose another word. Perhaps this time they will pretend to swim, and the audience will call, "No, not lake!"

Eventually, the actors will discover the word and mime the appropriate actions; in this case, perhaps, taking something out of the oven, putting candles on it and lighting them, blowing them out, and then eating: a cake. The audience and actors then exchange roles.

The team that guesses the words in the fewest number of tries wins the game.

Fifty Points

WHERE TO PLAY
Anywhere

NUMBER OF PLAYERS
2 or more

EQUIPMENT
2 dice; pencil and paper for scorekeeping (optional)

OBJECT OF THE GAME
To be the first player to score 50 points by rolling doubles

Each player should roll one die to determine the order of play. The high roller goes first, followed by the others in descending order, or around the circle from the first player's left.

The first player rolls both dice. He or she scores points only when doubles are thrown. Two *1*s equal 2 points, two *2*s equal 4 points, two *4*s equal 8 points, and two *5*s equal 10 points. However, two *6*s score 25 points, and two *3*s erase a player's total point tally, and he or she must start again from 0.

Play continues in order until one player reaches or surpasses 50 points.

Ghost

WHERE TO PLAY
Anywhere; a good travel game

NUMBER OF PLAYERS
At least 2

EQUIPMENT
None, except pencil and paper if you have a lot of players and want to keep track of their penalty letters

OBJECT OF THE GAME
To continue adding letters to a word being spelled without completing the word by adding the final letter

The first player begins the game by thinking of a word and calling out its first letter, for example, *P,* thinking of *perfect.*

The second player must then add a letter that will continue the word without completing it, perhaps *P-O,* thinking of *poker.*

Each player must add a letter in sequence, avoiding the completion of the word. If the next player can't think of a letter to add, he or she may challenge the player who added the last letter.

For example, a player having difficulty adding to *P-O-N* may challenge the adder of *N.* If that player comes up with *pontoon,* the challenger is assigned a *G,* on the way to collecting the letters to spell *G-H-O-S-T,* which results in elimination.

If the challenged player has bluffed or cannot come up with an acceptable word, he or she gets the *G.*

After someone has been assigned a letter, a new letter is chosen and another word spelled.

The last player remaining in the game after the others have become "Ghosts" is the winner.

VARIATION

In this version, players can add letters in both directions—to the beginning and end of words. Using the previous example, players could add an *O after* the *P,* giving *P-O,* or *before* it, giving *O-P.*

Go Fish

WHERE TO PLAY
At a table

NUMBER OF PLAYERS
2 or more

EQUIPMENT
A deck of playing cards

OBJECT OF THE GAME
To be the first to get rid of all your cards

Shuffle the cards and deal five cards facedown to each player. Each player should examine his or her hand without letting the other players see it. Place the remaining cards, the "fish pile," facedown in the center of the table.

As in **Happy Families,** players try to collect four cards of the same value. Play begins with the person at the left of the dealer, who may ask any other player for a particular card that will help to complete a group of four cards of equal value.

(*continued on next page*)

Go Fish (*cont.*)

That player must give the corresponding card to the asker if he or she has it. The asker is allowed to continue requesting cards until someone doesn't have what he or she asks for.

The player who doesn't have the right card tells the asker to "Go Fish." The asker then must draw the top card from the fish pile and add it to his or her hand.

The player who said, "Go Fish" becomes the next asker. When four cards of equal value are gathered, they are laid on the table in front of their collector.

The first player with no remaining cards in his or her hand wins the game. In case of a tie, the player with the most groups of four wins.

Going to Boston

WHERE TO PLAY
At a table or on the floor

NUMBER OF PLAYERS
3 or more

EQUIPMENT
3 dice; paper and pencil for scorekeeping

OBJECT OF THE GAME
To score the highest number of points by rolling the dice

Each player takes three rolls per turn. Beginning by rolling all three dice at once, the player sets aside the die with the highest score. The other two dice are rolled again, and the die with the highest number is again set aside. The third die is then rolled.

The sum of the three dice equals the player's score for that round. When all players have rolled, a round is complete, and the player with the most points wins the round.

The winner of the game is the player who won the most out of a predetermined number of rounds.

Gossip

WHERE TO PLAY
Anywhere

NUMBER OF PLAYERS
At least 10; this game benefits from having more rather than fewer
players

EQUIPMENT
None

OBJECT OF THE GAME
To pass a message down the line and see how well the original idea
was transmitted

Players form a line or a circle, with one player designated to start a
"rumor." This first player very quickly whispers a statement or story into
the ear of the next player in line. The story is rapidly passed down the line
from ear to ear. The last player to receive the message must recite exactly
what he or she has heard (it will probably have little to do with the
original statement). Then, this new message is compared to the "original"
version.

This game is also called Russian Scandal, Chinese Whispers, Telephone,
and Telephone Operator.

Guess the Number

WHERE TO PLAY
Anywhere; a good travel game

NUMBER OF PLAYERS
2

EQUIPMENT
None

OBJECT OF THE GAME
To guess the number your opponent has chosen

Specify a range of numbers, according to the ages and abilities of the
players: *1* to *100,* or *1* to *1,000,* for example.

(*continued on next page*)

Guess the Number (*cont.*)

The player selected to go first secretly chooses a number within the designated range of numbers. (Players concerned about forgetting their number, or about a cheating opponent, may choose to write down the selected number in each round.)

When the first player indicates that he or she has a number, the second player is allowed to begin guessing the number. The second player makes a guess, and the first player states whether the mystery number is higher or lower than the guess.

Keep track of the number of guesses made by the second player and then the number made by the first player when the positions are reversed. The player who discovered the mystery number in the fewest guesses is the winner.

The way to guess most efficiently is always to choose a number halfway between the given range. For example, if the number is between *1* and *100,* the best first guess is *50.* If the player with the number says "higher," the other knows now to guess *75,* in order to eliminate the largest group of numbers.

Of course, for the most entertainment value, you should allow the players to discover this for themselves, or the game may wear out too quickly!

Guggenheim

WHERE TO PLAY
Wherever there is a flat surface to write on

NUMBER OF PLAYERS
2 or more

EQUIPMENT
Paper and pencils

OBJECT OF THE GAME
To fill in the blanks of the grid with answers for the categories within a certain time period

Each player needs a pencil and a piece of paper. On the paper, draw a grid with six boxes across and six down (thirty-six boxes in total). Choose five categories of items. Use your imagination: flowers, movie stars, baseball teams, etc.

List the categories in the boxes going down the far-left column of the grid, leaving the box in the upper-left corner blank. Next, randomly choose five letters of the alphabet and list them in the top row of boxes going across the grid.

After determining the time limit (usually between two and five minutes, depending on the ages of the participants and the level of difficulty desired), the players should fill in the boxes with names of items that match the categories and begin with the letters designated at the top of the grid.

For example, if the first category is *fruits* and the first letter is *B*, *banana* is a correct answer. When the time limit has passed, the player who has correctly filled the most boxes wins.

Ha, Ha, Ha

WHERE TO PLAY
In any room large enough to accommodate a fairly tight circle of seated players

NUMBER OF PLAYERS
As few as 2, but the more the merrier!

EQUIPMENT
None

OBJECT OF THE GAME
To keep a straight face while the other players try to make you laugh

The players form a circle. One player begins by saying, "Ha"; the next continues, "Ha, Ha"; and the next follows with, "Ha, Ha, Ha"; and so on around the circle, each player adding a "Ha" to the string.

Each player must pronounce the "Ha Ha"s as solemnly as possible, to avoid laughter as long as possible.

Any player who laughs or makes any mistake must drop out of the "Ha Ha" circle. However, he or she now gets to try in any way (except for touching) to make the players remaining in the circle laugh.

The most serious player, by keeping a straight face, wins the game.

Hangman

WHERE TO PLAY
Anywhere

NUMBER OF PLAYERS
2 or more

EQUIPMENT
Pencil and paper

OBJECT OF THE GAME
To guess the secret word before an entire man on the gallows is drawn

---

One player is chosen to be the "hangman." He or she selects a word and records a series of dashes on the paper to represent the letters of the word. If the word is *mystery,* the hangman will draw seven dashes: _ _ _ _ _ _ _ .

The first player tries to guess a letter that might be in the word. If the guess is correct, for example, a *Y,* the hangman fills in the corresponding blanks: _ Y _ _ _ _ Y .

If the player makes a wrong guess, however, the hangman begins to draw the victim on the gallows. For the first incorrect guess, the base is drawn. Subsequent incorrect guesses add the upright, then the arm, the support, the rope, the figure's head, body, right arm, left arm, right leg, and left leg. If the left leg is added to complete the drawing before the word has been discovered, the hangman wins.

When a player makes an incorrect guess, the hangman records the letter so that the other players don't repeat the mistake.

Any player who guesses the word before the figure is completely drawn, beats the hangman.

Phrases as well as single words can be used to increase the level of difficulty.

Happy Families

WHERE TO PLAY
At a table

NUMBER OF PLAYERS
3 or more

EQUIPMENT
A deck of playing cards

OBJECT OF THE GAME
To collect the greatest number of "happy families" (4 cards of equal value)

Shuffle, and deal the entire deck facedown to the players. Don't worry if some players get an extra card.

Players should pick up their cards and look at them in secret, separating them into "families" (i.e., all the cards of the same value should be put together).

The player at the dealer's left starts the game by asking one of the other players for a certain card (a 5 or a Jack, for example) that he or she needs to complete a "family." If that player has the requested card, it must be turned over to the player who asked for it.

A player is allowed to continue asking for cards as long as he or she keeps getting them. When someone doesn't have the requested card, the next player becomes the asker.

When all four cards in a family are gathered by a player, they are laid on the table in front of that player. After all the families have been collected, the player with the most families wins.

Hearts

WHERE TO PLAY
Indoors

NUMBER OF PLAYERS
3 to 6

EQUIPMENT
A deck of playing cards; pencil and paper for scorekeeping

OBJECT OF THE GAME
To score the fewest number of points by avoiding taking tricks with hearts in them

Shuffle the cards and deal them evenly to the players. Any extra cards are placed in the middle of the table, to be taken by the player who wins the first trick. Players should arrange their cards in secret by suit.

The player to the left of the dealer begins the game by placing one card faceup on the table. (Many play that the person with the 2 of clubs begins the game by playing that card first.) The other players must follow with cards from the same suit.

The player who puts down the highest card wins the trick. Players who don't have cards of the correct suit must put down cards of another suit but cannot win that trick.

Since no one wants to collect hearts, the best strategies are to lead with low hearts when you have them (Ace is high) or to dispose of them when you don't have a card to play from the correct suit. Keep high cards of any suit for winning tricks without any hearts in them.

A player may not put down a heart until hearts have been "broken," meaning until someone lays down a heart because he or she does not have a card in the suit that was led.

When all the cards have been played, players count up the number of hearts in their hands and are given 1 point for each heart card.

The player with the fewest number of points wins the round, and the player with the lowest score after a given number of rounds wins the game.

VARIATIONS
There are many ways to make Hearts more challenging.

Black Lady Hearts is scored in the same way as regular Hearts except that the Queen of Spades is worth 13 points rather than 1 point. Some players also play with the Jack of Diamonds scored as negative 10 points.

In Spot Hearts, the heart cards are scored according to their face value, making it imperative that players try to avoid the highest heart cards in particular. For example, a player with a 6 and a Jack of Hearts scores 17 points for the round (6 plus 11 points for the Jack).

In Greek Hearts, players pass three cards they don't want to the player at the left before the game begins. The game is scored like Spot Hearts.

An interesting twist that can be added to any of the spot-scoring games is called Shooting the Moon. If any player manages to capture all the hearts (or, to make it more difficult, all the hearts plus the Queen of Spades), he or she is not penalized. Instead, all the other players are given 150 points.

Hot and Cold

WHERE TO PLAY
In a room where an object can be easily hidden

NUMBER OF PLAYERS
At least 4; good for young children

EQUIPMENT
An object that can be easily hidden; perhaps a small piece of fruit or candy, which will then serve as the prize—you may want to have a prize for each player so that all may enjoy winning the game

OBJECT OF THE GAME
To find the hidden object with the help of the other players

One player is chosen to be the searcher and is sent out of the room. The remaining players hide the chosen object from sight, and the searcher is called back into the room.

As the searcher begins looking for the object, he or she is directed to it through hints given by the other players. If the searcher is far from the object, the others call, "Cold." If the player is near the object, he or she is "warm," then "hot," and "burning" as he or she draws closer. "Freezing," "cool," and other variations in temperature can be used.

How Do You Do, Shoe?

WHERE TO PLAY
Anywhere

NUMBER OF PLAYERS
8 or more

EQUIPMENT
None, except the shoes on your feet

OBJECT OF THE GAME
To pass your shoes around the circle and get them back again

The players remove their shoes and place them in front of them as they sit in a circle on the floor.

At the signal of the leader, all the players pick up their shoes and begin passing them around the circle in one direction as fast as possible.

When the leader calls, "Change!" the shoes should be moved in the other direction. When the leader calls, "Find!" all players should try to get their own shoes as they are passed around. The shoes are kept going around the circle until everyone has their own pair back.

Huckle Buckle Beanstalk

WHERE TO PLAY
In a room that has lots of potential hiding places for a small object

NUMBER OF PLAYERS
At least 5

EQUIPMENT
A small object to hide

OBJECT OF THE GAME
To locate a hidden object as quickly as possible without revealing its whereabouts to the other players

One player is selected to hide the object, while the others leave the room. The object should be hidden so that it is not immediately obvious but can still be partially seen.

The players return when the object has been hidden and begin looking for it with their eyes only—no touching is needed because the object should be at least partially in view.

The first player to spot the hidden object says, "Huckle Buckle Beanstalk" to signify that he or she has seen the object and then sits down without revealing its whereabouts to the other players. One by one, the other players spot the object and call, "Huckle Buckle Beanstalk." When all the players have found the object, the first spotter can hide it for the next round.

Hunt the Key

WHERE TO PLAY
Anywhere

NUMBER OF PLAYERS
8 or more

EQUIPMENT
A small object: a key, a pebble, a coin, etc.

OBJECT OF THE GAME
For the "hunter" to discover who has the key and for the other players to try to conceal the location of the key from the "hunter"

The players form a closely knit circle seated on the ground. One player is chosen to be the "hunter" and must sit in the center of the circle.

While the hunter's eyes are closed, a key (or similarly small object) is given to one of the players in the circle. The players begin passing the key around the circle without actually showing the key, while the hunter watches. At the same time, those players without the key should pretend that they are passing it in order to fool the hunter.

When the hunter suspects someone of having the key, he or she calls the name of that player. The passing stops, and the called player must reveal whether he or she has the key.

If this player has the key, he or she becomes the hunter. If the hunter has guessed incorrectly, the game continues.

I Packed My Bag

WHERE TO PLAY
Anywhere

NUMBER OF PLAYERS
2 or more

EQUIPMENT
None

OBJECT OF THE GAME
To remember a growing verbal list made by the players of all the items packed in a bag

The first player initiates the game by choosing an item to complete the phrase, "I packed my bag and in it I put a(n) ———— ." For example, "I packed my bag and in it I put a toothbrush."

The second player continues the game by repeating what the first person packed in the bag and adding something of his or her own: "I packed my bag and in it I put a toothbrush and a volleyball."

Each player in turn adds another word to the string and repeats the preceding items in order, until it sounds something like, "I packed my bag and in it I put a toothbrush, a volleyball, a comic book, a banana, a deck of cards, a baseball cap, and a tent," and so on.

Any player who forgets an item or recites the list out of order is dropped from the game. The player who remembers the longest string of objects wins.

I Spy

WHERE TO PLAY
In any setting with an assortment of objects

NUMBER OF PLAYERS
4 or more; a favorite of children through the elementary grades

EQUIPMENT
None

OBJECT OF THE GAME
To guess the identity of the item "spied" by another player

One player is chosen to "spy" an object he or she sees in the room or the immediate environment. He or she begins the game by stating, "I spy with my little eye something beginning with *t*" (or any other letter of the alphabet).

The other players call out their guesses, in no particular order. The "spy" tells them whether or not they are correct. "Table?" "No." "Tack?" "No." "Teapot?" "Yes."

The player who first guesses correctly is allowed to "spy" the next object.

Initials

WHERE TO PLAY
Anywhere—great for long car rides!

NUMBER OF PLAYERS
2 or more

EQUIPMENT
None

OBJECT OF THE GAME
To give answers to other players' questions using words beginning with the letters of your own initials

One player is selected as the "questioner" for the first round. The questioner asks each player a question in turn. The players must respond to the question with an answer formed from the initials of his or her own name.

If the questioner asks, "What is your favorite food, Robert Canton?" Robert may reply, "*r*ed *c*herries" or "*r*ich *c*rayfish." If the questioner asks, "How do you like to spend Saturday morning, Sheila Sanders?" Sheila might answer, "*s*leeping *s*oundly" or "*s*elling *s*upermarkets." Answers need not make sense. In fact, ridiculous replies increase the fun!

To play Initials competitively, the questioner queries the other players until they begin dropping out, after hesitating or failing to provide answers, or repeating previously used answers. The last player remaining in the game is the winner and can serve as the questioner for another round.

Letters by Numbers

WHERE TO PLAY

Anywhere

NUMBER OF PLAYERS

3 or more

EQUIPMENT

None

OBJECT OF THE GAME

To be the first to identify which letter of the alphabet corresponds to a number that has been called out

Choose one player to be the caller. He or she begins the game by calling out any number between *1* and *26*. The other players try to be the first to find the corresponding letter of the alphabet. *1* equals *A, 2* equals *B, 10* equals *J,* and so on. To facilitate the determining of correct answers, the caller should write out the alphabet and the corresponding numbers, and keep this list hidden from the other players.

The first player with the correct answer wins a point. Wrong answers mean the loss of a point. The game can be played for time, so that the player with the most points in a given period wins, or it can be played until a given number of points are reached.

VARIATIONS

The game can be reversed for Numbers by Letters: the caller cries out a letter, and the corresponding number must be found. *Z* equals *26, Y* equals *25, M* equals *13,* etc.

To keep players on their toes, the caller can alternate: first a number, then a letter, another letter, a number, and so on.

Magazine Scavenger Hunt

WHERE TO PLAY
Indoors. This could be played on a train or airplane by a small number of children

NUMBER OF PLAYERS
2 or more

EQUIPMENT
Old magazines; pencil and paper for each player or each group

OBJECT OF THE GAME
To find the items on a scavenger-hunt list in a magazine rather than in a house or outdoors

Depending on the number of players, Magazine Scavenger Hunt can be an individual or group activity. If there are more than six players, divide them into groups of two or three. Each group should have pencil and paper to keep track of items as they are found.

Before the game, the party planner should make a list of ten to fifteen items to be searched for within the magazine. In order to be fair, it is best to specify common objects and make sure the articles are appropriate to the magazines available.

Each individual or group has ten to fifteen minutes to leaf through the pages of the magazine in search of the required items. The page number of each discovery should be noted by one of the group members.

If any individual or group finds all the designated objects within a given time period, they win. If time runs out before all the items are located, the individual or team with the most complete list wins.

VARIATION
A simplified scavenger hunt can be also be played with magazines. Instead of designating a list of items, specify a certain letter. Players are given five minutes in which to list all the items they can find beginning with that letter. The player with the most items wins.

Magazine Storytelling

WHERE TO PLAY
Indoors

NUMBER OF PLAYERS
2 or more

EQUIPMENT
Old magazines; scissors; glue; paper

OBJECT OF THE GAME
To write a story using materials cut from magazines

Each player or group is given a set of materials: old magazines, scissors, paper, glue, and crayons or pencils.

Within a given time period—ten or fifteen minutes—the players must compose stories from pictures and words cut from magazine pages. These clippings should be glued to pieces of paper to form a book which can be read when the time is up.

The stories can be judged according to various categories: most clever, best use of pictures, funniest, etc. A topic for the story might be assigned before the story making begins.

Instead of stories, players can also write letters using the magazines: love letters, letters to Santa, the president, etc. Players can even write letters to real people, which can be mailed when the game is finished.

Mathematical Baseball

WHERE TO PLAY
Indoors

NUMBER OF PLAYERS
10 can play at a time. Others may substitute after each inning

EQUIPMENT
None

OBJECT OF THE GAME
To score runs by correctly answering multiplication problems which will advance runners around the bases

Designate a small playing field: four bases in a baseball-field diamond, about six to eight feet on each side. Divide the players into two equal teams. One team takes the "field": there will be a pitcher, a catcher, and first, second, and third basemen. The other team is the "batting" team.

The first batter steps up to home plate. The pitcher calls out a multiplication problem (suited to the ages and abilities of the players)—for example, "Six times two." If the batter answers correctly first, he or she advances to first base. If, however, the catcher has the right answer first, the batter is out.

The next player comes to bat, is given a problem, and is either put out or advances to first base. Any other players on base are also advanced if the batter answers correctly.

The pitcher may attempt to put out players on base by calling a problem their way. If the baseman answers correctly, the runner is out. If the runner has the right answer, he or she is allowed to steal a base.

After three outs, the teams switch places. From inning to inning, players on one team can also exchange roles so that all may have a chance at being the pitcher.

The team with the most runs after a predetermined number of innings wins the game.

Memory Game

WHERE TO PLAY
Anywhere

NUMBER OF PLAYERS
At least 2 (plus a leader)

EQUIPMENT
A large tray and a towel or cloth to cover it; an assortment of about 25 small objects (a marble, a pen, a coin, a ring, etc.); pencil and paper for each player

OBJECT OF THE GAME
To remember as many of the objects seen on the tray as possible

Before beginning, a leader should be chosen. He or she spreads the objects on a tray and covers them with a towel so that no one can see them before the game begins. The tray should be placed in a central position so that all players can see it well. Each player should have a pencil and a sheet of paper.

(*continued on next page*)

Memory Game (*cont.*)

The leader removes the cover from the tray for about one minute. All the players should try to memorize the objects seen. When one minute has elapsed, the leader covers the tray again.

When the tray is covered, the players list all the items they can remember from it on a sheet of paper. Players have three minutes in which to remember and record the objects. The most complete list wins.

VARIATION

An uncomplicated version of Memory Game can be played by two travelers (especially on an airplane).

Select a magazine photograph filled with detail—perhaps a picture of a kitchen or an outdoor scene. Allow the players to study the photograph for a minute, then ask them to list as many objects from the photo as possible. The player with the longest list wins.

Muggins

WHERE TO PLAY
Indoors

NUMBER OF PLAYERS
4 to 8

EQUIPMENT
A deck of playing cards. For more than 4 players, adding another deck lengthens the game.

OBJECT OF THE GAME
To be the first player to get rid of all your cards

Muggins is a Victorian card game that is easily learned and can be played by game lovers of all ages.

Shuffle and deal out four cards, faceup, in the middle of the playing table and then deal an equal number of cards to each player, facedown. Any leftover cards are placed in one of the four center piles.

Starting at the dealer's left, each player turns over the first card in his or her pile. Players are allowed to get rid of a card when it can be played onto a card in one of the middle piles. Cards are playable when they are of a value one card higher or lower than the one in the player's hand: a 9 can go on an *8* or a *10,* a Queen on a King or a Jack, and so forth. Ace is low—it can't be played on a King, nor can a King be played on it.

The first player is limited in that he or she has only the central cards to play onto. If it is possible, he or she plays the card, and then the next player takes a turn.

Whenever a player cannot use the card just turned faceup, it is placed in a faceup pile next to that player's facedown pile. Following players may now put cards onto that pile when possible.

When there are enough piles, players may find it possible to play a card on more than one. Rules of sequence must be followed in this case. A player must first play a card onto a center pile, if possible. If the player can play onto more than one of the other players' piles, he or she must go to the one closest on the left.

Players watch carefully as their opponents play their cards. Anyone spotting another breaking a rule of sequence or playing an incorrect card shouts, "Muggins!" The player caught in error must accept a penalty consisting of taking the top card from all the other players' facedown piles and adding them to his or her own facedown pile.

When a player runs out of facedown cards, he or she turns the faceup pile over and uses that. The first player to get rid of all his or her cards wins the game.

Muggins should be played as fast as possible. Calling out "Muggins!" is the spice of the game, so try to guard against overly careful players by gently prodding them into action.

PLAYER ONE

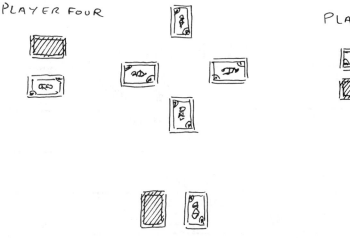

PLAYER FOUR

PLAYER TWO

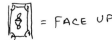 = FACE UP

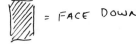 = FACE DOWN

PLAYER THREE

Musical Chairs

WHERE TO PLAY
In a room that can hold enough chairs to accommodate the number of players

NUMBER OF PLAYERS
6 to 20 is most manageable

EQUIPMENT
1 chair for every player except 1 (example: for 10 players, use 9 chairs); music (radios and cassette players are the easiest to use, but record players are also suitable)

OBJECT OF THE GAME
To be the last remaining player sitting in a chair when the music stops.

The chairs should be placed in a straight line with every other chair facing in the opposite direction. (If there is a large group of players, chairs can be placed back to back to save room.)

Before beginning, a leader should be chosen, and the players should distribute themselves evenly around the chairs. When the leader begins the music, the players march in one direction around the chairs.

After a moment, the leader surprises the group by turning the music off. This is a signal to the players to find a seat as quickly as possible and sit down. The player left without a chair is eliminated from the game.

One chair is then removed in order to keep the number of chairs one less than that of players. The leader then starts up the music again, stops it, and the players repeat the dash for seats.

A player and a chair are removed with each round until two players are left to duel for the last chair. The player to capture this final chair wins.

Musical Clapping

WHERE TO PLAY
Anywhere

NUMBER OF PLAYERS
At least 2

EQUIPMENT
None

OBJECT OF THE GAME
To guess the song being clapped out by another player

Choose one player to clap out the first song. The clapper secretly picks a song that he or she thinks will be familiar to all the other players. When everyone is ready, the clapper begins clapping the rhythm to the mystery song.

The other players call out their guesses when they think they recognize the song. The first player to identify the song by its rhythm gets to select and clap out the next song.

VARIATION

Musical Clapping can be played as a team competition if you have enough players and if you can stand the noise! One team claps out the song's rhythm while the other team guesses.

My Ship Sails

WHERE TO PLAY
At a table

NUMBER OF PLAYERS
4 or more

EQUIPMENT
A deck of playing cards

OBJECT OF THE GAME
To be the first to collect 7 cards of the same suit

Shuffle the cards and deal seven, one at a time and facedown, to each player. Set aside the remaining cards—they will not be used. Players should examine their cards in secret and arrange them into groups by suit, being careful to note if they have a concentration of cards in one particular suit.

My Ship Sails begins when each player discards one card. Since the object of the game is to collect seven cards of the same suit (seven diamonds, seven clubs, seven hearts, or seven spades), players should get rid of cards that are useless to them, i.e., of the wrong suit.

After all the players have discarded one card (facedown), they should simultaneously pass this card to the left. When all the cards have been passed, each player picks up the new card, adds it to his or her hand, and discards another. The same card just picked up can be discarded immediately if it is of no use.

(*continued on next page*)

My Ship Sails (*cont.*)

The game continues as players discard and pick up new cards. The first player to collect seven cards of the same suit proclaims, "My ship sails!" in order to win.

VARIATION

Instead of gathering seven cards of the same suit, try to collect a sequence of seven cards, all numbers, or numbers and face cards in combination, regardless of suit. For example, *7-8-9-10*-Jack-Queen-King would be a winning sequence.

Odd Bean

WHERE TO PLAY
In any space large enough to accommodate the group of players comfortably, seated on the floor or around a table

---

NUMBER OF PLAYERS
At least 2

EQUIPMENT
A bag of dried beans, enough so that each player may have 12; small bags to hold the beans

---

OBJECT OF THE GAME
To collect all the beans from the other players

This game is related to *Jan-Ken-Pon* (see **Scissors, Paper, Stone**), but the winner is determined by the number of beans he or she has at the end of the game rather than by a score tallied on paper.

Each player is given a bag filled with twelve beans. The first player hides a number of beans in one fist and asks the next player, "Odds or evens?"

If the next player correctly guesses whether the fist holds an odd or even number of beans, he or she collects those beans from the first player. If the guess is wrong, the second player must forfeit the same number of beans to the first player.

The second player then places a number of beans in his or her hand. He or she turns to the third player and asks, "Odds or evens?" and the game continues.

Any player to lose all of his or her beans must drop out of the game. The winner is the player with the most beans when a set period of time expires, or, if time permits, the player who has collected all the beans.

Old Maid

WHERE TO PLAY
At a table

NUMBER OF PLAYERS
3 or more

EQUIPMENT
A deck of playing cards

OBJECT OF THE GAME
To get rid of all your cards by matching pairs, and to avoid being left with the odd Queen

Remove the Queen of Hearts from the deck. Shuffle the cards and deal the entire deck around the circle of players. Each player examines his or her hand, matches any pairs of equal value (two Jacks, two 6s, etc.), and places them facedown on the table. When all players have gone through their cards, play begins.

The player at the left of the dealer starts by pulling one card from the hand of the player immediately to his or her right (in this case, the dealer).

If the card drawn can be paired with any of the cards already in the players' hand, the two are removed and laid with any previous pairs facedown on the table. If not, play resumes with the next player.

The next player on the left draws a card from the hand of the player on his or her right. Play continues in this manner around the circle until one player is left with the odd Queen. This player is the "Old Maid" and loses the game.

Orchestra

WHERE TO PLAY
Indoors or outdoors

NUMBER OF PLAYERS
5 or more

EQUIPMENT
None

OBJECT OF THE GAME
To follow the motions of the orchestra leader

One player is designated as the conductor. All of the players, including the conductor, choose musical instruments that they will pretend to play.

The players should sit in a circle on the floor with about a foot of space between them. The conductor should be visible to all.

The conductor starts up the orchestra by pretending to play the instrument that he or she has chosen. Once the leader has begun, the other players join in by simulating the motions that their instruments require. Violinists draw their bows, drummers beat out a rhythm, tuba players puff out their cheeks, and so on.

When all the players are motioning musically, the leader switches to the actions for one of the instruments played by another orchestra member. All the players except for the one playing that particular instrument must switch to the same motions as the leader.

The player whose instrument is now being imitated must stop playing and put his or her hands over the ears. For example, if the conductor switches from the flute to the piano, all the players must join in as piano players, while the original piano player sits with hands over ears.

After a few seconds, the conductor returns to his or her own instrument. At this moment, all the other players, including the one with hands over ears, return to their original instruments.

After a while the conductor will change to another instrument, and the other players will follow suit, as described above.

As in **Simon Says,** players are eliminated from the game when they make improper motions. Players who continue with their original instrument after the leader has begun imitating it must leave the game. The same goes for players who forget to switch instruments at the proper time.

The last remaining player in the game wins and can become the conductor if another round is desired.

Pass the Present

WHERE TO PLAY
Anywhere indoors

NUMBER OF PLAYERS
4 or more

EQUIPMENT
A small prize; gift-wrap paper (tissue paper is fine—the wrap need not be fancy); Scotch tape; a radio, record player, or cassette player

OBJECT OF THE GAME
To remove the last layer of gift-wrap and reveal the prize

Before the game, a leader is selected and the prize is wrapped in ten or more layers of paper.

The players sit on the floor in a circle. When the leader starts the music, they pass the gift around the circle as quickly as possible. When the music is stopped, the player holding the present is allowed to remove one layer of paper.

The music starts up again and is stopped, until the gift has been completely unwrapped. The player who is fortunate enough to take off the last layer gets to keep the prize.

Password

WHERE TO PLAY
Anywhere

NUMBER OF PLAYERS
5 at a time. Others can substitute in later rounds.

EQUIPMENT
Paper and pencil (optional)

OBJECT OF THE GAME
To help your partner guess the mystery word by giving him or her synonyms or related words

One player should be designated as the quiz master. The other four players are divided into two sets of partners.

The quiz master chooses a word, which he "passes on" to just one

(*continued on next page*)

Password (*cont.*)

player from each team. The word can be written down on a small slip of paper or can be whispered.

The player chosen to go first is allowed to give his or her partner one clue, which is a synonym for or is related to the mystery word, or he or she can "pass," if the word is too difficult.

For instance, if the word is *lemonade,* the first clue might be *drink.* If the partner guesses *lemonade* correctly, that team is awarded 1 point. If the guess is wrong—*soda* for example—the other team has the chance to offer another clue and guess the word. The next clue might be *citrus.*

When the word is finally guessed, the clue givers and the guessers exchange roles.

The first team to gain a predetermined number of points, or the team with the most points after a given time period, wins. Using short time periods might be a good idea if the quiz master is anxious to join in the guessing.

Questions

WHERE TO PLAY
Anywhere

NUMBER OF PLAYERS
2 or more

EQUIPMENT
None

OBJECT OF THE GAME
To answer every question with a question, until one player forgets or makes a mistake

The game begins when the first player asks a question. The second player must respond with another related question, and then the first player with another question, and so on.

For example, if two players are traveling, the game might begin as follows:

SUSAN: When are we going to get to Boston?
JIMMY: How many miles do we have left?
SUSAN: Do you have an atlas?

JIMMY: Don't you have one?

SUSAN: Why don't you remember to bring it when we travel?

If a player pauses too long between questions, forgets to ask a question, or asks a nonsensical question, he or she is out of the game.

If there are more than two players, determine the order in which players will offer questions before beginning play.

Racetrack

WHERE TO PLAY
Anywhere

NUMBER OF PLAYERS
4 or more

EQUIPMENT
Old magazines; scissors; cardboard; glue; a large sheet of paper or cardboard; pen or pencil; 1 die

OBJECT OF THE GAME
To drive your "car" 100 miles by rolling its way through the diagram

For a fancy version of Racetrack, begin by making a large, roadlike trail of squares numbered *1* to *100,* representing the miles to be covered.

Cut photos of cars from old magazines—one for every player, and two of each make, if possible. For example, if you have four players, clip out two Volkswagens and two Fords. The two players with cars of the same make will be partners. To make the cars more stable as playing pieces, they can be glued to cardboard, but this is not necessary.

Roll the die to determine the order of play, with partners alternating.

The first player throws the die and moves his or her car the number of miles indicated by the die. Play progresses with each player getting one roll each turn.

When a car lands on a square occupied by a car owned by someone other than his or her partner, the car already in the space is sent back to the beginning. Cars belonging to two partners may occupy the same space, however, and as long as they do so, no other car may pass them.

The first car to reach the last space (100 miles) is the winner. This space must be reached with an exact roll of the die.

Rain

WHERE TO PLAY
Anywhere; most effective in a quiet indoor spot

NUMBER OF PLAYERS
At least 3. A large group can whip up a great storm.

EQUIPMENT
None

OBJECT OF THE GAME
To imitate the sound of a rainstorm

The players sit on the floor and begin the game by closing their eyes and becoming absolutely quiet. When all is still, the leader initiates the rainstorm by rubbing his or her palms together. When the player sitting at the leader's left hears this very soft sound, he or she joins in. The player on the left of the second player then joins, until all the players around the circle are producing the same sound.

When everyone is moving their palms together, the leader then makes the storm grow a little louder by snapping his or her fingers. The second player then switches to this sound, and so on around the circle.

After everyone is snapping fingers, the leader changes to slapping the thighs, to make the sound of heavy rain. Thunder can be added by stomping the feet on the floor, until the room is filled with the sound of a furious summer storm.

After the sound reaches its peak, the leader begins to calm the storm by reversing the order of the noises made and returning to a softer sound. (He or she may have to nudge the player at the left in order to get his or her attention in the midst of the peak of the storm—remember, eyes are still closed.)

The group follows the leader back through thigh slapping, finger snapping, and palm rubbing, until the room is returned to complete silence once again.

Rigamarole

WHERE TO PLAY
Anywhere

NUMBER OF PLAYERS
3 or more

EQUIPMENT
None

OBJECT OF THE GAME
To remember a string of alliterative phrases as it goes around the circle

Rigamarole is a memory game that combines mental recall and tongue-twister agility.

The player elected to start begins the game by inventing an alliterative phrase of three words starting with the number *one* and followed by an adjective and a noun each beginning with the letter *o*—"one obnoxious oriole," for example.

The next player must add another phrase following the same guidelines, opening with the number *two,* while repeating the original phrase: "One obnoxious oriole, two tricky teenagers."

The following player attaches a third alliterative saying beginning with *three.* The string of phrases keeps going around the circle of players until ten have been made up.

Rigamarole can be played as an elimination game, but you will doubtless run out of players before you get to ten phrases in a row. It is probably more fun just trying to keep the game going, rather than worrying about finding a winner.

VARIATION
Those who find that they'd like more of a challenge may create phrases in which the length of the phrase (number of words) corresponds to the beginning number (including that number): "Four fussy, frighted finks" (four words).

Rolling Stone

WHERE TO PLAY
Indoors

NUMBER OF PLAYERS
4 to 6

EQUIPMENT
A deck of playing cards

OBJECT OF THE GAME
To be the first player to get rid of all your cards

Before beginning the game, separate some cards from the deck so that there will be only eight cards for each player. For four players, remove the 2s, 3s, 4s, 5s, and 6s. For five players, take out the 2s, 3s, 4s, and 5s and for six players, remove the 2s, 3s, and 4s. Ace is high.

Set aside the removed cards and shuffle the remaining ones. Deal the shuffled cards to the players, one at a time and facedown, so that each player has eight cards. Players secretly examine their cards and arrange them according to suit.

The player at the dealer's left initiates the game by laying a card from his or hand faceup in the center of the table. The next player to the left places a card of the same suit on it if he or she has one, and so on with the following players.

When a player does not have a card of the proper suit, he or she must collect the center pile and add the cards to his or her hand. This player starts the game again by putting a card out for the new center pile.

When all the players have put down a card of the same suit, that pile is set aside and is no longer used in the game. The last player to put down a card may start the new round.

The first player to discard his or her entire hand is the winner.

Scissors, Paper, Stone

(Also known as Rock, Paper, Scissors)

WHERE TO PLAY
Anywhere

NUMBER OF PLAYERS
2 at a time

EQUIPMENT
None

OBJECT OF THE GAME
To anticipate the gesture your opponent is going to make in order to make a gesture that will defeat it; can also be played to determine who will be "It"

Scissors, Paper, Stone is an efficient way to choose who is going to go first or who will be "It" and is also fun when played for its own sake.

The idea of the game is to make a hand gesture representing scissors, paper, or stone that will defeat the gesture made by your opponent.

The three gestures are: two fingers held in a victory sign (scissors), an open hand (paper), and a closed fist (stone). Scissors "beat" paper by cutting, paper overcomes stone by wrapping, and stone conquers scissors by dulling.

Players hide their hands behind their backs and at the count of three, bring them out in front, making one of the gestures. Each round is scored. The first player to reach a specified number of points is the winner.

Scissors, Paper, Stone is often called by its traditional Japanese name, *Jan-Ken-Pon* or *Jan-Kem-Po*.

VARIATION
A game similar to Scissors, Paper, Stone is Odds and Evens. Instead of making gestures to represent objects, the players hold out fingers, numbering from zero (a closed fist), to five (an open hand). One player is odd and the other even. At the count of three, the players reveal a number. If the total of both players' fingers is odd, the odd player wins a point. If the total is even, the even player receives the point.

Or, one player at a time calls out "odd" or "even" as the fingers are revealed. If the number corresponds to the call, that player wins a point.

Seeing Green

WHERE TO PLAY
Indoors

NUMBER OF PLAYERS
Any number

EQUIPMENT
Scissors; glue; bright red construction paper; two sheets of white paper for every player

OBJECT OF THE GAME
To see green shamrocks against a white sheet of paper after staring at red shamrocks

Seeing Green is an optical lesson as well as an amusing St. Patrick's Day activity.

At a table, players cut several shamrocks out of red construction paper and paste them on a larger sheet of white paper. (It is a good idea to have one shamrock already cut out as an example for the players.) Players don't need to spend more than a few minutes on this. Large shamrocks (at least four or five inches high) are most effective.

When all the players have sheets of red shamrocks, they should be instructed to stare at them, eyes fixed on one point, while they slowly count to fifteen: "One shamrock, two shamrock, three shamrock," and so on.

After counting to "fifteen shamrock," the players flip over the papers and now stare at the plain white side of the sheet. After a few seconds, players will see a ghostly image of a green shamrock, rather than a red one.

Since red is the complementary color of green, staring long enough at any red object will produce a green afterimage. (The artist Jasper Johns used this physiological effect in a painting of an American flag. After staring at a flag with green stripes and an orange field of stars, one sees the traditional red, white, and blue flag against a white wall.)

Sentences

WHERE TO PLAY
Anywhere

NUMBER OF PLAYERS
3 or more

EQUIPMENT
If played aloud, no equipment is needed. With paper and pencil, the game can also be played in written form.

OBJECT OF THE GAME
To form as many words as possible beginning with the letters in a given word

---

One player chooses a word (of four to six letters) to be used for the first round.

Each player must create a sentence formed from words that begin with the letters in the original word, in proper order. For example, if the given word is *dream,* an acceptable sentence would be *Don't ride elephants after midnight.*

The next player then chooses a new word, and the game begins anew.

Points are awarded for every sentence formed within a time limit of two or three minutes. The player with the most points after either a predetermined number of words or a given time period wins.

VARIATIONS
More complicated rules can be added to make the game more challenging:

Clever players can try to make the sentence have some relation to the given word. Younger children, however, may prefer nonsensical answers. If nonsensical answers are desired, an extra point can be awarded for the most humorous answer.

Shadow Buff

WHERE TO PLAY

Indoors in a room that can easily be made dark. Great for dark, rainy days!

NUMBER OF PLAYERS

At least 5

EQUIPMENT

A sheet; tacks or tape; a lamp with a strong, high-wattage light bulb; a table; a chair

OBJECT OF THE GAME

To guess the identity of the other players from the shadows they cast upon a backlit sheet

Set up the play area by stretching a sheet tightly between two walls and attaching it with tape or tacks. A few feet behind the sheet, place a strong light (perhaps a lamp without a shade), leaving enough room for one player at a time to pass between the sheet and the light.

Elect one player to be "Buffy." Buffy is seated on a chair on the other side of the sheet. When Buffy is in place, dim the lights.

One by one, the other players pass between the sheet and the lamp, trying to cast shadows upon the sheet. Buffy must attempt to identify the players as they go by, but the players must strive to disguise themselves by making distracting motions or gestures as they move through.

When Buffy guesses the identity of one of the players, they trade places and the game continues. Make sure everyone gets a chance to be Buffy.

Slap Jack

WHERE TO PLAY

At a table (a round one is best but is not essential) or on the floor

NUMBER OF PLAYERS

3 or more

EQUIPMENT

A deck of playing cards

OBJECT OF THE GAME

To capture all the cards in the deck

One player shuffles the deck and deals out all of the cards to the other players in a circle, beginning at his or her left. Players must leave their cards facedown in front of them without looking at them.

The player at the dealer's left begins the game by laying one card faceup in the middle of the group, accessible to all. One by one, in quick succession, the players each lay a card on the center pile.

When a Jack is revealed, the first player to slap that card gets to shuffle the entire pile into his or her own hand. The game is continued by the player to the Jack-slapper's left.

If a player makes a mistake and slaps a card other than a Jack, he or she must forfeit a card to the player who laid down the last card.

A player who has lost all of his or her cards is given one last chance and may remain in the game in an attempt to slap the next Jack and regain a hand. If the attempt is unsuccessful, however, the player must leave the game.

The player who captures all of the cards is declared the winner.

VARIATION

A less physical but no less rowdy version of this game is called Snap. Instead of slapping the Jack, the first player to yell, "Snap!" upon its appearance wins the center pile.

Sneeze

WHERE TO PLAY
Anywhere

NUMBER OF PLAYERS
At least 6 for the best effect; for children under 7

EQUIPMENT
None

OBJECT OF THE GAME
For all the players to call out different syllables at the same time, approximating the sound of a sneeze

The surprise of Sneeze only works the first time the group "sneezes," but younger children will like the noise enough to want to keep sneezing throughout the party.

(*continued on next page*)

Sneeze (*cont.*)

The leader assigns all the players a syllable, explaining to them that it is important to remember their sounds. To make it even more mysterious, the leader may whisper the sound secretly into each player's ear.

The syllables to be assigned are "ash," "ish," "osh," and "choo." When everyone has a sound, the leader asks them all to call their sounds out in unison as loudly as they can at the count of three. When everyone yells, the noise sounds like a very loud sneeze.

Snip Snap Snorum

WHERE TO PLAY
At a table

NUMBER OF PLAYERS
3 or more

EQUIPMENT
A deck of playing cards

OBJECT OF THE GAME
To be the first to get rid of all your cards

Shuffle the deck and deal all the cards facedown. Depending on the number of players, some may get an extra card, but it won't matter. Players should look at their cards while keeping them hidden from each other.

The game begins when the player to the dealer's left selects a card from his or her hand, lays it down faceup in the center of the table and says, "Snip." The player with the card of the next higher value and of the same suit lays that card down on top of the first and calls out, "Snap." Then, once again, the player with the card of the next higher value and of the same suit lays that card down and says, "Snorum." This process continues with the same guidelines, with the fourth player saying, "Hi cockalorum" and the fifth player completing a sequence with the word "Jig."

After a sequence is completed, the player who put down the "jig" card begins another Snip-Snap-Snorum sequence.

The cards range in value from Ace as the lowest to King as the highest. Therefore, if a King is placed down at any point along the sequence, it is considered a "Jig," and a new sequence should begin. In addition, if cards of higher values have already been played, the last card that can be placed down in the pile will count as a "Jig," and a new sequence should begin.

The player to get rid of all of his or her cards first is the winner.

Spelling Bee

WHERE TO PLAY
Anywhere

NUMBER OF PLAYERS
At least 2, but it is more fun with a large group

EQUIPMENT
The game runs most smoothly when someone has prepared a list of words appropriate to the age level of the players beforehand, but it can be played without a list in a pinch. A dictionary is helpful for inspiration and to settle disputes.

OBJECT OF THE GAME
To spell as many words as possible correctly

An adult or mature child should serve as the spelling master.

To begin the game, the spelling master gives the first player an opportunity to spell a word correctly. If the player is correct, a point is awarded. If not, it is the next player's turn, and he or she is given a new word to spell.

The player with the greatest number of points after a predetermined number of rounds is declared the winner.

VARIATIONS
Spelling Bee can also be played as an elimination game. A player leaves the game after incorrectly spelling a word, and the last remaining player wins.

If there are enough players, Spelling Bee can be a team competition and scored or played as an elimination game. When played for points, extra points can be won by correctly spelling a word misspelled by the other team.

Spit

WHERE TO PLAY

Sitting on the floor makes Spit easier to play, but playing at a table is equally fun

NUMBER OF PLAYERS

2

EQUIPMENT

A deck of playing cards

OBJECT OF THE GAME

To be the first to get rid of all your cards

Two players sit on the floor or at a table facing one another. One player shuffles the cards and deals out the deck equally. Each player prepares for the game by laying out a row of cards in the following manner:

First, moving from left to right, place three cards facedown and a fourth card faceup.

Second, again moving from left to right, lay a card facedown on each of the first two cards, and one card faceup on the third.

Next, lay a card facedown on the first pile of cards and a card faceup on the second pile.

Lastly, put one faceup card on the first pile, so that all piles are completed with a faceup card. The remaining cards are placed in a facedown pile at the left of this row.

Both players chant together, "One, two, three, Spit!" At the word "Spit," both players lay the top card from their pile of extra cards side by side and faceup in the center of the playing area.

As quickly as possible, both players try to play cards from their rows on both center cards. A card may be played if it is of a value one higher or one lower than the center card. For example, a *3* or a *5* may be laid on a *4,* and a King or a *2* may be laid on an Ace (suit does not matter).

When a faceup card from one of the piles in a player's row is played, the facedown card beneath it may be turned up and played if possible. Both players will be putting down cards at a breakneck pace, trying to get rid of as many as possible. However, when neither player has another suitable card, the sequence starts again.

The players replenish the cards in the piles in the previously described manner with cards from the extra pile. Then, the players call out, "One, two, three, Spit!" and discard the appropriate cards once again.

As the end of the game nears, players may run out of spare cards altogether and may need a card to "spit." If a player has fewer than the ten cards needed to make a complete row, that's fine—he or she should lay out the available cards and use a faceup card from the leftmost pile as the "spit" card.

Play continues in this manner until one player has discarded all of his or her cards onto the center piles. This player is the winner.

Square Tic-Tac-Toe

WHERE TO PLAY
At a table or on the floor

NUMBER OF PLAYERS
2 at a time

EQUIPMENT
Pencil and paper; 10 coins—5 each of two different types (5 dimes and 5 nickels, for example)

OBJECT OF THE GAME
To place 3 of your coins in a row on a variation of the traditional Tic-Tac-Toe diagram

Each player should have five coins of the same denomination. Choose one player to go first.

With the pencil draw a diagram of a square crossed with four lines.

The two players alternate in placing one coin at a time on the intersection of two or more lines. The first player to place three coins in a row, whether across, up and down, or diagonally, wins the game.

Play Square Tic-Tac-Toe as a "best of" series—best of three, five, or seven games.

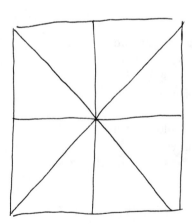
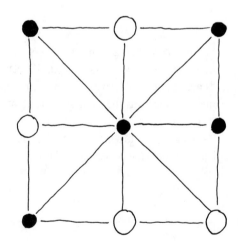

● - DIMES

○ - QUARTERS

Stairway

WHERE TO PLAY
Anywhere

NUMBER OF PLAYERS
2 or more

EQUIPMENT
Pencil and paper for each player

OBJECT OF THE GAME
To form a "stairway" of words of increasing length from a letter chosen at the start of the game

One player selects a letter from which to form the "stairway." Each player should try to form words by adding one letter at a time to the original letter within a given time period of five or ten minutes.

If the given letter is *A*, a stairway might look like this:

A
AT
APE
ACHE
ASPEN
ARTIST
ANIMATE
ADDITION
ACROBATIC
APOSTROPHE

The builder of the longest stairway wins the game.

To avoid frustrated players, it's a good idea to ignore the difficult letters like *Z* and to make sure an easily discovered two-letter word can be found for the chosen letter.

Taste

WHERE TO PLAY
Anywhere

NUMBER OF PLAYERS
3 or more

EQUIPMENT
Paper cups; an assortment of beverages; a scarf or rag to be used as a blindfold; paper and pencil

---

OBJECT OF THE GAME
To identify as many drinks by taste alone as possible

A blindfolded player is given an assortment of different beverages in paper cups to sample and identify. The larger the variety the better—different flavors of soda pop, fruit juices, mineral water, and so on.

Another player records the sampler's guesses. The player who identifies the most (brand names get added points) is the winner.

This is a particularly good, thirst-quenching activity after a more rigorous outdoor game!

Tic-Tac-Toe

WHERE TO PLAY
Anywhere; an easy travel game

NUMBER OF PLAYERS
2 at a time

EQUIPMENT
Pencil and paper

OBJECT OF THE GAME
To place 3 of your marks in a row

Before beginning, draw a simple diagram consisting of two vertical lines crossed by two horizontal lines.

One player takes *X* and the other *O*. Determine which player will go first.

The player to go first marks his *X* or *O* in one of the boxes formed by the diagram. The other player then places his or her mark in one of the boxes. Both players attempt to get a row of *X*s or *O*s, horizontally, vertically, or diagonally.

Continue alternating marks until one player has made a row of three marks, in which case he or she is the winner; or until all the boxes are filled and no one has a row, in which case the game is a draw.

Attentive players will soon learn that there is an advantage to making the first mark and that the center box is always the best choice. Experienced players will eventually reach a point where all games are draws.

VARIATIONS

Play Tic-Tac-Toe so that the first player to get a row of marks is a loser. The diagram can also be increased in size by adding more lines.

Tic-Tac-Toe is also called Noughts and Crosses in England, referring to the *O*s and *X*s.

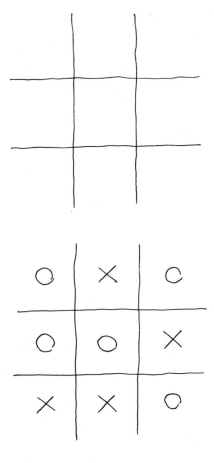

Tip-Tap-Toe

WHERE TO PLAY
Anywhere

NUMBER OF PLAYERS
2 to 6

EQUIPMENT
Pencil and paper

OBJECT OF THE GAME
To tally the highest score by pointing to numbered sections on a diagram; like playing darts on paper

Before beginning the game, a diagram must be drawn. Divide a circle with lines to create ten to twelve pie-shaped wedges. Number the wedges in ascending order around the circle.

A player (with good math skills!) should be appointed scorekeeper.

One by one, the players close their eyes and touch a pencil to the diagram. They are awarded the number of points indicated in the section touched by the pencil. Once a section has been touched, it is crossed out and is no longer worth any points to the following players.

As in darts, players are allowed only one try each turn to score points. If they hit a crossed-out wedge or go outside the circle, they must wait until the next turn. Any player to hit the exact center of the circle automatically wins the game.

When all the sections have been crossed out, the points are tallied and the highest score wins.

Tongue Twisters

WHERE TO PLAY
Anywhere

NUMBER OF PLAYERS
2 or more

EQUIPMENT
A watch with a second hand or a stopwatch

OBJECT OF THE GAME
To repeat the tongue twister as many times as possible without making a mistake

One at a time, the players recite a tongue twister as many times as possible before tripping over their tongues. Whoever recites the most twisters before making a mistake wins!

All the players can be tested with the same twister, or they can try different examples for variety. Here are a few well-known tongue twisters:

Truly rural
Toy boat
Lemon liniment
Red leather, yellow leather
She sells seashells by the seashore
Whistle for the thistle sifter
Six thick thistle sticks
The bootblack brought the black boot back
The sixth sick sheik's sixth sheep's sick
Sarah sits by six sick city slickers
Fresh flesh of fresh fried fish
How much wood would a woodchuck chuck if a woodchuck could chuck wood?

Twenty Questions

WHERE TO PLAY
Anywhere

NUMBER OF PLAYERS
3 or more

EQUIPMENT
None

OBJECT OF THE GAME
To guess the object chosen by 1 player by asking for clues gained from no more than 20 questions—the fewer, the better!

One player is selected to think of an object (secretly). After choosing, he or she tells the others whether it is Animal, Vegetable, or Mineral.

One by one, the other players ask questions requiring yes or no answers that will help them to discover the identity of the object. They are only allowed to ask a total of twenty questions. If a player guesses incorrectly before the twenty questions are asked, he or she is eliminated from the game; however, that guess does not count as a question. If the object is not revealed after the allotted twenty questions, the player who chose the object wins.

VARIATION

Virginia Woolf is another version of Twenty Questions. Instead of choosing an object, the player selects a well-known person. The figure can be from history or from fiction, and can be alive or dead, as long as he or she is famous enough to be known by all those playing the game.

A third variation of Twenty Questions is Where Am I? The first player chooses a place to be and something to do there. For example, he or she might be at an amusement park on the roller coaster, water-skiing on Lake Tahoe, or looking out on Manhattan from the top of the Empire State Building. As in Virginia Woolf, the location should be familiar to all the players. (This version is somewhat trickier since the players are actually trying to uncover two unknowns!)

Up, Jenkins!

WHERE TO PLAY
At a table

NUMBER OF PLAYERS
At least 8

EQUIPMENT
A quarter

OBJECT OF THE GAME
To discover the person who has the quarter

Divide the players into two equal teams and seat the teams on opposite sides of the table. Choose a leader for each team. One side should have possession of the quarter.

At a starting signal, the team with the quarter passes it back and forth with their hands beneath the tabletop.

After counting slowly to ten, the leader of the team without the quarter calls, "Up, Jenkins!" The players of the opposing team must immediately raise their closed fists above the table.

The leader of the other team will then call, "Down, Jenkins!" With this signal the players on the team with the quarter must slap their opened hands down upon the table. The other team should listen carefully for the sound of the quarter hitting the table before it is covered by a hand.

The team without the quarter takes a moment to discuss in secret whom they think might have the coin. They make a guess among themselves and then return to the game.

One by one, the leader calls the names of the players from the other team, trying to eliminate those he or she believes do not have the quarter. Each player must pick up his or her hands from the table when named.

If the quarter appears before the last player is called, the team with the coin may hide it again. If the other team is correct in identifying the player who is hiding the coin, they may now hide it.

Score can be kept according to how many times a team discovers the location of the quarter within a given time limit of ten to fifteen minutes. The leaders can be rotated if other players want to get the chance to call, "Up, Jenkins!"

VARIATION
To add to the challenge, the guessing team should attempt to identify not only the coin holder but under which hand the coin is hidden as well.

War

WHERE TO PLAY

Anywhere. This is a good game to play seated on the floor

NUMBER OF PLAYERS

2 at a time

EQUIPMENT

A deck of playing cards

OBJECT OF THE GAME

To capture all the cards—though no skill is involved

Shuffle the deck and deal the cards evenly between the two players in neat piles, facedown.

The two players simultaneously take the top cards from their piles and lay them faceup in between them. The player who lays down the card of higher value (suit doesn't matter) wins both cards and places them, facedown, at the bottom of his or her pile. Aces have the highest value.

If, however, the cards are of equal value (two 6s, or two Jacks), a "war" is fought. Each player places three cards facedown on his or her original card, chanting "one, two, three," and the fourth faceup, declaring "war!" The player who places the card of the greatest value on the piles wins all the cards in the center. If they are still of equal value, the players repeat the process, laying another card facedown and a second faceup, until one player wins the piles.

Eventually, one player will accumulate all fifty-two cards and win the game. This may take a long time, though. Players anxious to finish can set a time limit to end the game—two or three more minutes of play, for example—before counting cards to determine the winner.

Western Union

WHERE TO PLAY
Anywhere

NUMBER OF PLAYERS
At least 8

EQUIPMENT
None

OBJECT OF THE GAME
To pass a "message" around the circle by squeezing hands without being caught by "It"

The players join hands to form a circle around "It," who stands in the center and covers his or her eyes. One player selects another player in the circle as the recipient of a "telegram" and announces, "I am going to send a telegram to —— [the name of one of the players in the circle]."

With this announcement, he or she squeezes the hand of a player on either side in order to begin the transmission, and "It" opens his or her eyes, hoping to see the message being transmitted by squeeze. If "It" catches someone squeezing, that person must become "It." The direction in which the telegram is being sent can change at any time.

When the player announced as the recipient of the telegram gets the message (in the form of a squeeze), he or she announces so, and the process must begin again until "It" catches someone.

VARIATION
A more continuous version of this game is called Electricity. One player sends a squeezed "shock" that keeps traveling around the circle until "It" discovers it being passed.

What Are We Shouting?

WHERE TO PLAY

Anyplace where shouting won't disturb anyone. Playing this near a
library is not a good idea!

NUMBER OF PLAYERS

10 or more; suggested for younger children

EQUIPMENT

None

OBJECT OF THE GAME

To guess the phrase being shouted by the opposing team

Divide the players into two equal teams. The team elected to shout first
leaves the room to choose something to shout. They should select an
easily recognizable phrase or title from suitable sources such as nursery
rhymes, the names of television shows, or song lyrics. The phrase should
have as many words as the team has players. For example, a team of five
people should choose a five-word phrase. Each player should then be
assigned one word from the phrase to shout.

After picking a phrase, the shouting team should return to the room
where the other team is waiting. At the count of three, each player should
simultaneously shout his or her word.

The opposing team must try to make sense out of the shout and guess
the selected saying. The shout may be repeated once, but then the other
team must attempt to guess. For example, if the chosen phrase is "Mary
had a little lamb," and one player heard "Mary" and another discerned the
word "lamb," the mystery phrase should be easily discovered.

If a team guesses correctly, it is awarded a point and can become the
team that shouts. If it guesses incorrectly, the shouting team gets a point
and is allowed to pick another phrase and begin again. The team with the
greatest number of points after a given time period wins.

Word Lightning

WHERE TO PLAY
Anywhere

NUMBER OF PLAYERS
2 or more

EQUIPMENT
A watch with a second hand or a stopwatch

OBJECT OF THE GAME
To think of as many words as possible beginning with a given letter in 1 minute

One player assigns a second player a letter. The second player has one minute to call out as many words as possible that begin with that letter, while the first player keeps count and watches the clock.

With more than two players, a third person can watch the clock while the other counts the number of words called out.

Play continues until every player has had a turn calling out a list of words. The player who thought of the most words wins.

Yacht

WHERE TO PLAY

Anywhere, even while traveling if the ride is fairly smooth

NUMBER OF PLAYERS

2 or more

EQUIPMENT

5 dice; paper and pencil

OBJECT OF THE GAME

To roll the dice in certain required combinations within 3 rolls

---

Elect a scorekeeper, who should draw a chart of the possible combinations of dice rolls (*1s*, *2s*, *3s*, etc.) and the players' names for ease in recording. The various combinations and corresponding scores are as follows:

1s	Add all the *1s* thrown in three rolls. Highest possible score: 5 points
2s	Add all the *2s* thrown in three rolls. Highest possible score: 10 points
3s	Add all the *3s* thrown in three rolls. Highest possible score: 15 points
4s	Add all the *4s* thrown in three rolls. Highest possible score: 20 points
5s	Add all the *5s* thrown in three rolls. Highest possible score: 25 points
6s	Add all the *6s* thrown in three rolls. Highest possible score: 30 points
Four of a kind	Add all the spots
Full House	Three of a kind plus two of another. Add all the spots
Little Straight	Four numbers in sequence (example: 1, 2, 3, 4). 20 points
Big Straight	Five numbers in sequence. 30 points
Choice	Total spots of all five dice
Yacht	Five of a kind. 50 points

One player begins by rolling all five dice at once, attempting to complete any one of the required combinations from the previous listing within three rolls. After the first roll, the player should examine the dice for the most likely combination to pursue. If a player has two or more of a number, he or she should set those aside and toss the remaining dice, attempting to roll more of the same number.

SAMPLE CHART

	Charlie	Deborah
1s	_____	_____
2s	_____	_____
3s	_____	_____
4s	_____	_____
5s	_____	_____
6s	_____	_____
Four of a Kind	_____	_____
Full House	_____	_____
Little Straight	_____	_____
Big Straight	_____	_____
Choice	_____	_____
Yacht	_____	_____
TOTAL	_____	_____

For example, if the player's first roll yields a *1,* a *3,* two *4,*s and a *6,* that player would be smart to attempt to continue rolling *4s.* He or she would put aside the two *4s* and roll the other three dice again. If another *4* comes up, that would also be put aside, and the player would be given one more roll (with the two remaining dice) to get more *4s.*

Each combination is scored and recorded on the scorekeeper's chart. Once a player has fulfilled a combination, he or she cannot repeat it and must try for the others. After the first players attempt at a combination with three rolls of the dice, it is the next player's turn to roll.

As the end of the game grows nearer, some players may get some scores of zeros, since the more difficult combinations are likely to go unfulfilled.

The player with the highest score when all the combinations have been attempted is declared the winner.

TWO

Games to Play on Grass and Playgrounds

Army

WHERE TO PLAY
On any playground or in a neighborhood wooded area

NUMBER OF PLAYERS
At least 4—the more players, the more adventurous!

EQUIPMENT
Toy guns are not essential. With children's vivid imaginations, a stick can serve many a purpose!

OBJECT OF THE GAME
To win a game of make-believe war and not be hit by the enemy

This game has no hard-and-fast rules but instead is played according to the whims and imaginations of the children playing. Before play begins, players usually create their own war scenarios, including boundaries, how a hit is made, and how a team will be declared the winner.

To begin, players are divided into two teams. These teams each elect a captain who guides the teammates in developing a strategy. Once everyone is ready for battle, play begins!

Once again, this game is best played according to the imaginations of the children, tempered by a reminder that this war play is only a game.

Around Ball

WHERE TO PLAY
Outdoors in an area large enough for 2 circles of players

NUMBER OF PLAYERS
10 or more

EQUIPMENT
2 playground balls of equal size

OBJECT OF THE GAME
To be the first team to pass the ball around the circle 5 times

Divide the players into two equal teams and appoint a captain for each team.

When a starting signal is given, the captain passes the ball to the player on his or her right as quickly as possible. The distance between the players should be determined according to the throwing and catching skills of the players.

The captain calls out, "One" to signify that the ball has been passed successfully around the circle once. He or she counts out each round as it is completed.

Upon calling out, "Five," the captain raises the ball high over his or her head to indicate that the team has finished five rounds. The first team to finish wins the game.

VARIATION

For more skilled players, the methods of passing can be varied with added motions. The first round could be normal passes, the second a pass between the legs, the third could require a bounce and then a pass, and so forth. If a team member makes a mistake in the order of motions, the ball must be returned to the captain and that round begun again.

Baby in the Air

WHERE TO PLAY
In a yard or on a playground

NUMBER OF PLAYERS
8 or more

EQUIPMENT
A rubber playground ball

OBJECT OF THE GAME
To avoid being hit by the ball and remain in the game as long as possible

Players should count off sequentially so that each is assigned a number.

Player number one stands in the center of a circle formed by the other players and throws the ball into the air while calling the number of another player at random.

As the player whose number was called runs to catch the ball, the others run outward from the circle. When the catcher has the ball in hand, he or she yells, "Freeze!" and all the other players must stop in their tracks.

The player with the ball is then allowed three giant steps toward another player of his or her choice, at whom he or she throws the ball.

(*continued on next page*)

Baby in the Air (*cont.*)

Players should be reminded not to throw the ball to hurt a fellow player and that it only has to touch them.

Anytime a player is hit, he or she is assigned a letter, first *B,* then *A, B,* and *Y.* When a player is hit four times and has been given the letters to spell *BABY,* he or she is dropped from the game. Whether or not the player who just threw the ball successfully hits another player, he or she begins play again by tossing the ball into the air and calling another number.

The last remaining player in the game is the winner.

Badminton

WHERE TO PLAY
Outdoors, on grass or pavement

NUMBER OF PLAYERS
2 or 4

EQUIPMENT
A birdie; a net (or a rope to serve as a net); rackets for each player

OBJECT OF THE GAME
To score points by hitting the birdie to your opponent in a way that prevents him or her from returning it over the net

Badminton can be played according to regulation rules or in a more casual manner.

The badminton court measures about forty-five by twenty feet for doubles play and slightly smaller for singles. A service line should be indicated about 3½ feet behind the net on both sides of the court.

For singles, the player to serve first stands behind the service line and hits the birdie underhand with the racket to the opposite side of the opponent's court. If he or she returns the birdie over the net, a volley ensues until the birdie falls to the ground or goes out of bounds.

When it does, if the server is at fault, the serve goes to the other player. If the receiver makes the error, a point is scored for the server, who serves again and continues to do so until he or she makes an error. Points can only be scored by the serving player.

Players may not touch the birdie more than once in succession. If the birdie hits the net, it is still in play as long as it goes over and remains within bounds. Players may not touch the net or reach over it to hit the birdie.

Play continues until one player scores 21 (and wins by at least 2 points).

Doubles play progresses the same way, except that when the first player on a team loses the serve, it goes to his or her partner before going to the other team.

Barnyard Peanut Hunt

WHERE TO PLAY
In a large room or area suitable for hiding peanuts

NUMBER OF PLAYERS
At least 12

EQUIPMENT
1 or 2 pounds of unshelled peanuts, depending on the number of players; a small bag for each team

OBJECT OF THE GAME
To find as many peanuts as possible

Before the game begins, the peanuts are hidden around the playing area.

The players should be divided into an even number of teams with at least three players per group. Each group selects a captain and an animal such as a cat, dog, cow, horse, or bird, whose cry it will imitate.

At the start of an allotted period of time, all players begin searching for peanuts. The captain holds a bag and is the only player allowed to pick up the peanuts. When a noncaptain player finds a peanut, he or she must imitate the sound made by his or her group's animal in order to get the attention of the captain, so he or she will pick up the peanut. If there are many peanuts and many players, the ruckus will suggest a barnyard.

At the end of the search period, the team with the most peanuts wins. Peanuts found can be divided and eaten as a prize.

Baseball

WHERE TO PLAY

On any grassy playground or an already existing baseball field

NUMBER OF PLAYERS

At least 12

EQUIPMENT

Any type of hittable ball; a bat; any objects to serve as bases; baseball mitts, if necessary

OBJECT OF THE GAME

To score as many runs as possible when your team is up to bat and to prevent the other team from scoring when your team is in the field

If a baseball field is not readily available, set up a baseball diamond on any grassy area, as indicated below:

The players are divided into two evenly matched teams, and the players decide among themselves who will serve in each position. One team takes the field, and the other team is up at bat.

The batting team establishes a set batting order for the players to follow. The first batter up stands at home plate and attempts to hit a pitched ball as far as possible and in such a way that it is not easily caught by an opposing fielder. Batters are allowed three strikes before being called out. (A strike is any good pitch not hit.) Batters may strike out, but they cannot foul out (a foul occurs any time a ball is hit out of the diamond). The first two foul balls count as strikes, but a foul cannot count as a third strike to make an out.

When a batter succeeds in hitting the ball, he or she runs to first base as quickly as possible, while the fielder nearest to where the ball was hit attempts to catch it in the air (which would make an out) or field it (pick it up as it is hit along the ground). If fielded, the fielder tries to throw the ball to the first-base player before the batter reaches the plate and the batter attempts to avoid being thrown out by a fielder. If the batter's hit is very good, he or she should decide whether or not it is possible to run to second or third base or home plate without being thrown out and take action depending upon that assessment.

An out is made when a batter makes three strikes, when a hit is caught while in the air, when the first-base player has the ball and tags the base before the runner reaches it, or when a player is tagged by a fielder with the ball while running between bases.

After action has stopped, the second batter takes a turn at bat, and play continues in the same manner. Base runners are advanced when their teammates hit the ball successfully, and players attempt to advance to home plate to score a run.

Each team remains at bat until it has made three outs, at which time it is the other team's turn at bat. After the opposing team has had a chance at bat and has made three outs, an inning is completed.

The winning team is the one that has scored the most runs after a predetermined number of innings.

VARIATION

See **Stickball.**

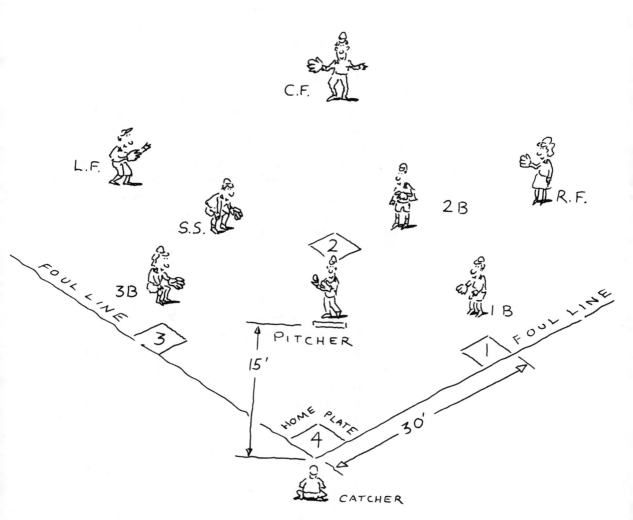

Blindman's Buff

WHERE TO PLAY
Any space large enough to hold a circle formed by the players

NUMBER OF PLAYERS
At least 8. A large group makes the guessing part of the game more challenging.

EQUIPMENT
A blindfold

OBJECT OF THE GAME
For the "blind man" to guess the identity of another player

One player is blindfolded and stands in the center of a circle formed by the other players. Players in the circle join hands and move the circle around in one direction until the signal of three handclaps is given by the "blind man."

When the blind man claps, the circle stops moving, and the blind man points at one of the other players. The blind man then gets one chance to guess the identity of the player he or she has pointed out. If the guess is correct, the blind man and the player exchange places. If the blind man is wrong, the other player must step into the center of the circle.

While still blindfolded, the blind man attempts to tag the other player in the center, who tries to avoid being caught. Once tagged, however, this player must remain still while the blind man tries to identify him or her by touching clothing, facial features, and hair. This player, once identified, is blindfolded for the next round, and the blind man joins the circle.

Blindman's Buff dates back to Ancient Greece, where it was known as Brazen Fly.

VARIATION
The chase sequence can be eliminated for a game that is less active but just as noisy: The players sing a song and circle around the blind man. When the song ends, the blind man points to one player and gives him or her a command involving some use of the voice: "Bark like a dog," "Cry like a baby," etc. The blind man then tries to identify the player. If he or she is successful, they change places. If not, the players begin singing and moving in a circle again.

Bronco Tag

WHERE TO PLAY
In a yard or on a playground

NUMBER OF PLAYERS
At least 10

EQUIPMENT
None

OBJECT OF THE GAME
To join the other players in forming "broncos"

Assuming there are ten players, divide these players into groups of three with one remaining as the chaser. The groups of three form broncos: one player is the "head," and the other two line up behind, holding onto the player in front at the waist; they are the "tails."

After the broncos begin running, the chaser must try to join one of them by getting hold of the waist of a tail player.

If the chaser successfully joins a bronco, the head of the bronco must break off and become the chaser, while the next player in line now becomes the head.

This game has no real winner or loser. The object is simply to elude the chaser if you are part of a bronco and to join a bronco if you are the chaser. The broncos should twist and turn, trying to keep the head facing the chaser in order to avoid getting a new tail.

This game is also called Hook-on Tag.

Brooklyn Bridge

WHERE TO PLAY
On a playground or in a paved driveway

NUMBER OF PLAYERS
6 or more

EQUIPMENT
A ball

OBJECT OF THE GAME
To roll the ball between your opponents' legs

The players are divided into two equal teams. The teams line up facing each other. The two lines should be about fifteen feet apart for six players and farther apart if there are more players. Each player in line stands with his or her feet spread about eighteen inches apart (wide enough for a ball to pass between them).

The teams alternate in trying to roll the ball through the legs of the other team. Players may not move or make any attempt to stop the ball.

If the teams are large, the game can be played for elimination: a player must drop out if the ball goes through his or her "bridge." If the teams are small, the game should be played for points, without the elimination of players.

Buck, Buck

WHERE TO PLAY
Outdoors (on grass) or in shallow water

NUMBER OF PLAYERS
2 at a time

EQUIPMENT
None

OBJECT OF THE GAME
For the player, on whose back sits another player, to guess the number of fingers held up by that player

This game and its variation are potentially rough. Remind all players to go easy on the "horses" and "carriers."

Buck, Buck usually starts quite unexpectedly—when one player runs up to another, jumps on that player's back like a rider jumping onto a horse, and calls out, "Buck, Buck, how many horns do I hold up?"

The "rider" holds up any number of fingers. The "horse" tries to guess the number. The faster the horse comes up with the right number, the faster he or she gets to let the rider down. They can then trade places, the rider becoming the horse and vice versa.

Once someone gets the idea, players will soon be jumping onto one another's backs and calling out, "Buck, Buck," too.

In nineteenth-century England, additional rhymes accompanied the game, which have been forgotten in this century. When a player made an incorrect guess (for example, "five," when the rider held up three fingers), the rider replied, "Five you say, and three there be; Buck, Buck, how many horns do I hold up?"

Upon getting a correct answer, the rider would then chant, "Three you say, and three there be; Buck, Buck, rise up, rise up," and would allow the other player to straighten up.

VARIATION

Another way to play Buck, Buck, also known as Johnny on a Pony and Post and Rider, involves more players.

The players are divided into "jumpers" and "carriers." The first of the carriers stoops over, as in **Leapfrog,** leaning against a wall or a tree for support. He or she can also rest against another player who stands firm at the front of the line.

A second carrier stands behind the first and starts a line behind him or her, leaning over and holding onto the first player's back. The rest of the carriers join the line in the same fashion.

The jumpers line up behind the carriers. The first of the jumpers runs and jumps onto the back of the last carrier in line, then crawls across the backs until he or she is sitting on the back of the first carrier.

The rest of the jumpers follow, each leaping onto the backs of the carriers. If the carriers succeed in supporting the jumpers, they gain a point. If their line is broken, however, the jumpers and carriers exchange roles.

Some carriers will take a cue from the name of the game, Buck, Buck, and will try to shake the jumpers from their backs like bucking broncos.

The team with the most points after a given time period wins the game.

Call Ball

WHERE TO PLAY
On a grassy playground

NUMBER OF PLAYERS
8 or more (a simplified version of **Spud** for children in the primary grades)

EQUIPMENT
A rubber playground ball

OBJECT OF THE GAME
For the player whose name is called to catch the ball

The players make a circle around one person who stands in the middle with a ball. That player tosses the ball straight up, high into the air, and calls the name of one of the other players.

The player whose name was called tries to catch the ball before it bounces more than once. If the catch is good, that player becomes the center person. If not, the player who originally threw the ball begins again.

Capture the Flag

WHERE TO PLAY
Outdoors

NUMBER OF PLAYERS
At least 8

EQUIPMENT
A handkerchief, bandanna, or scarf for every player

OBJECT OF THE GAME
For one team to capture all the handkerchiefs of the opposing team

Designate a play area, about thirty by thirty feet for eight players. A center dividing line should also be established.

Divide the players into two equal teams, each team lining up behind one of the end lines. Both sides place their handkerchiefs just inside the boundary.

At a starting signal, each team rushes for the other team's handkerchiefs. Any players tagged before they have a handkerchief in hand are considered captured and must stand behind the enemy flags.

If a player succeeds in grabbing a handkerchief, he or she is safe from tagging and may run it back behind his or her own team's line.

Players may also free their teammates by tagging them behind the enemy line. They may not, however, free a player and capture a flag in the same run: two separate runs are necessary.

The first team to capture all the other team's flags is the winner. If teams are equally matched, this may take a long time to happen. The game may also be ended after a predetermined period of time, with the team in possession of the greater number of handkerchiefs being the winner.

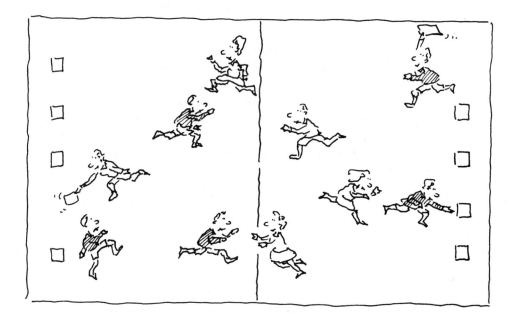

Cat and Mouse

WHERE TO PLAY
Outdoors

NUMBER OF PLAYERS
At least 8

EQUIPMENT
None

OBJECT OF THE GAME
For the "cat" to catch the "mouse"

Before the game begins, designate one player as the "cat" and the other as the "mouse." The rest of the players join hands and form a circle around the mouse, while the cat remains outside the circle.

The mouse starts the game by darting outside the circle and around the players. The cat must try to tag the mouse, while staying on the outside of the circle. The players may lift their arms over the mouse's head in order to help him or her, since they usually sympathize with the mouse. Likewise they will try to block the cat.

When the cat finally tags the mouse, the mouse becomes the new cat, the cat joins the circle, and another player becomes the mouse.

Chimp Race

WHERE TO PLAY
In an area 20 to 25 feet long and wide enough for the racers, on grass, pavement, or indoors, if space permits

NUMBER OF PLAYERS
3 or more

EQUIPMENT
None

OBJECT OF THE GAME
To reach the finish line first despite the awkward "chimpanzee" position

One player is designated as the starter and stands at the finish line. The other players line up at the starting line. When signaled by the starter (who shouts "on your mark, get set"), the players spread their feet apart, bend over, and take hold of their ankles. Then the starter shouts "go!" and they race to the finish line while maintaining a stiff-kneed position: the legs may *not* be bent! If any contestant loses the position, he or she must return to the starting line and begin again.

This can also be conducted as a relay race.

Circle Golf

WHERE TO PLAY
Outdoors, in a backyard or a park

NUMBER OF PLAYERS
2 or more

EQUIPMENT
A golf ball or other small ball; a small golf club, croquet mallet, or stiff yardstick; a plastic cup or jar; a penny; string

OBJECT OF THE GAME
To sink putts from 12 different positions on a circle in the fewest number of strokes

To prepare for the game, mark off a circle about six feet in diameter with string laid on the grass. Choose one spot to represent twelve o'clock, as if the circle were a clock face, and place the penny there. Players will be putting from positions one through twelve. These can also be marked with pennies or coins, or they can be approximated by each player.

If it is your own backyard and the person who does the lawn work won't mind, dig a small hole somewhere near the center of the circle. (Remember to fill in the hole when you are finished playing.)

If the game is played on public property or if you would rather not dig up the lawn, lay a plastic cup on its side, facing the twelve o'clock position, to serve as the hole. The cup will have to be turned toward the player as he or she moves around the circle.

One at a time, the players putt their way clockwise around the circle, beginning at twelve o'clock and progressing through the other eleven spots, after successfully putting at each position. Players should keep track of the number of strokes taken at each position as well. Having all the players count the strokes aloud puts a little more pressure on the putter, keeps everyone interested, and helps the scorekeeping to remain honest.

The player to complete the course in the fewest number of strokes is the winner.

Contrary Children

WHERE TO PLAY

Anywhere

NUMBER OF PLAYERS

At least 6

EQUIPMENT

None

OBJECT OF THE GAME

To do the opposite of the leader's commands, and by doing so correctly, to be the last player remaining in the game

---

Simon Says takes an interesting twist in Contrary Children. Instead of following the leader's commands, players try to do the opposite of what they are told.

For example, if the leader says, "Take three hops toward me," all the players should hop three steps *away* from the leader. When told, "Touch your right foot with your left hand," players are to touch the left foot with the right hand.

Contrary Children requires that the leader be more alert than in **Simon Says.** The leader should not demonstrate any of the movements: he or she should concentrate on watching for players following, rather than opposing, instructions.

Players caught doing what they are told, and not the opposite, must leave the game. The last remaining player is the winner.

Cops and Robbers

WHERE TO PLAY

In any grassy area with places to hide

NUMBER OF PLAYERS

At least 6

EQUIPMENT

None

OBJECT OF THE GAME

For the "robbers" to avoid being caught by the "cops"

The players are divided into two equal teams and players decide among themselves which team will be the "cops" and which will be the "robbers" (after one round the teams will switch roles).

Basically, this is a game of **Hide-and-Seek** with the robbers hiding and the cops seeking. The cops count to 100, while the robbers hide, after which time, the cops set out in search of the criminals.

When a robber is caught, he or she is brought back to "jail" (a designated home base). A captured robber may escape if another robber runs to the jail to rescue a prisoner, without being tagged by a cop. These two robbers sit out for the remainder of the game, until all of the other robbers have either been caught or rescued.

The second round begins with the teams switching roles, and the game continues in the same manner as above. After the second round is completed, the teams count up how many robbers were captured (not including those that escaped) in each round, and the team that "arrested" the most wins the round.

Cowboys and Indians

WHERE TO PLAY
In a flat area large enough to accommodate a circle of running players with at least 5 feet between them

NUMBER OF PLAYERS
10 or more

EQUIPMENT
A whistle makes it easy but is not absolutely necessary.

OBJECT OF THE GAME
To tag the player in front of you, while avoiding being tagged by the player behind you

Starting off, all players are considered "Indians." After one player is designated the leader, the other players should spread out and form a very large circle. Indians should leave at least five feet between each other, and all should face the clockwise direction.

At the leader's signal (a shout or a whistle), all Indians run clockwise around the circle. Each Indian tries to tag the player ahead of him or her before being tagged by the player behind and before the signal to stop is

(*continued on next page*)

Cowboys and Indians (*cont.*)

given by the leader. Players tagged become "cowboys" and must sit in the center of the circle.

After players regroup, the leader gives another signal to start the Indians running around in a circle again. The leader stops the action after approximately ten to twenty seconds, at which point all tagged players (cowboys) must drop out of the game and join the other cowboys in the center of the circle.

This continues until only one Indian escapes being tagged, and this player is the winner! (To make the game more complicated, a signal to change directions can also be added!)

Crossing the Brook

WHERE TO PLAY
On a long strip of grassy land that will allow for safe long jumping

NUMBER OF PLAYERS
5 or more; most suitable for children under 8

EQUIPMENT
Any long objects such as jump ropes or sticks to mark the boundaries of the imaginary brook

OBJECT OF THE GAME
To jump the brook at its widest point

Two markers are laid down a short distance apart (about a foot to begin with) to represent the banks of a brook. The players approach the brook at a run and try to jump across it. Those who fall in are out of the game.

After all players have successfully jumped across the brook, its banks are widened, and the remaining players try to jump over it again. After each round of jumps the brook is made wider until there is only one player left who has stayed out of the water.

Dizzy Izzy

WHERE TO PLAY
In an area free from obstacles. Outside on soft grass is probably best

NUMBER OF PLAYERS
Any number

EQUIPMENT
An umbrella or a sturdy stick about 3 feet long; a bandanna or
handkerchief to serve as a blindfold

OBJECT OF THE GAME
To walk in a straight line after spinning around a stick

A blindfolded player bends over an umbrella or stick, resting the forehead
on his or her hands, which are placed at the top of the stick. The player
pivots around the stick three times in this position and then straightens up
and attempts to walk in a straight line to a finish point located about fifteen
feet away.

Each player should have a spotter to prevent falls or trips. The player
who succeeds in getting closest to the goal wins. This game can also be
run as a race.

Dizzy Izzy remains popular among college rugby players because it is
a blindfolded version of what is known as a "scrum" in rugby.

Drop the Handkerchief

WHERE TO PLAY
Outdoors, on grass or pavement

NUMBER OF PLAYERS
At least 8

EQUIPMENT
A handkerchief or a small piece of folded paper

OBJECT OF THE GAME
For the player with the handkerchief to catch "It" before "It" gets
around the circle and into that player's spot in the circle

One player is designated as "It" and is given a handkerchief or a small
piece of folded paper. The rest of the players form a circle facing in and
hold hands.

(continued on next page)

Drop the Handkerchief (*cont.*)

"It" walks slowly around the outside of the circle, chanting, "A tisket, a tasket, a green and yellow basket, I wrote a letter to my love and on the way I dropped it; a little child picked it up and put in its pocket." Along the way, "It" drops the handkerchief or paper behind one of the players.

When that player realizes that the handkerchief has been dropped behind him or her, he or she must take off at a run in pursuit of "It." "It" tries to get around to the empty spot in the circle before being tagged.

If "It" is tagged before reaching the other player's spot, he or she must continue as "It" and drop the handkerchief again. But if he or she reaches the empty spot, the player left outside the circle becomes the new "It."

Duck Duck Goose

WHERE TO PLAY
On a reasonably flat lawn or other large, smooth, grassy area

NUMBER OF PLAYERS
A minimum of 10 for the most suspense and exercise

EQUIPMENT
None

OBJECT OF THE GAME
For the player who is tapped to catch "It" (or risk becoming "It")

One player is chosen to be "It." This player stands while all others sit cross-legged in a wide circle.

"It" walks around the outside of the circle while tapping each seated player lightly on the head, saying, "Duck" with each tap. He or she eventually taps one player and says, "Goose." This tapped player must quickly stand and try to catch the person who is "It" as he or she runs around the circle, trying to reach the spot abandoned by the "Goose."

If "It" outruns Goose and has taken Goose's place in the circle before being tagged, Goose becomes the new "It." If tagged, "It" must start the process of tapping again.

Egg Toss

WHERE TO PLAY
Outdoors, or you'll risk getting egg on your face, not to mention your home!

NUMBER OF PLAYERS
At least 4

EQUIPMENT
1 raw egg for every 3 players

OBJECT OF THE GAME
To toss the egg the greatest distance without breaking it

Divide the players into partners and line them up facing each other, three feet apart. Players on one side each hold an egg.

At a starting signal, the players with the eggs carefully toss them to their partners. Those who catch the eggs take one step back and with equal care return the eggs with another toss.

With each completed throw, the distance between partners is made wider. The last players to complete a toss without breaking the egg are the champion tossers. These players should see how far apart they can go before the egg is unable to travel the distance without breaking.

Make sure everyone is in play clothes for this game! Have plenty of water on hand to clean up those who don't jump out of the way of smashing eggs quickly enough.

VARIATION
A neater version of Egg Toss can be played with water balloons. These are especially good for parties held on hot summer days when you can put on a swimsuit and when a shower of water from an exploding balloon would feel delightfully refreshing!

Farmer in the Dell

WHERE TO PLAY
Indoors or outdoors

NUMBER OF PLAYERS
At least 6; good for a large group of elementary-school children

EQUIPMENT
None

OBJECT OF THE GAME
To sing "The Farmer in the Dell," accompanied by the choosing of players to represent the characters in the song

Select one player to serve as the farmer. The other players join hands and form a circle around the farmer.

While moving the circle around in one direction, the players sing together "The Farmer in the Dell":

The farmer in the dell,
The farmer in the dell,
Heigh-o, the dairy-o, (or cherry-o)
The farmer in the dell

With the second verse, the farmer chooses a player from the outer circle to represent the wife, while everyone sings:

The farmer takes a wife,
The farmer takes a wife,
Heigh-o, the dairy-o,
The farmer takes a wife.

With each succeeding verse, the appropriate character selects another to join the group in the center of the circle:

The wife takes a child,
The wife takes a child,
Heigh-o, the dairy-o,
The wife takes a child.

The child takes a nurse . . .
The nurse takes a cat . . .
The cat takes a rat . . .
The rat takes the cheese . . .

After the rat has taken the cheese, all the players except the "cheese" re-form the circle again, singing:

The cheese stands alone,
The cheese stands alone,
Heigh-o, the dairy-o,
The cheese stands alone!

With the last "The cheese stands alone," the circle breaks apart, and all the players join in jumping up and down and clapping.

The cheese can serve as the new farmer for another round.

Follow-the-Leader

WHERE TO PLAY
Outdoors, where there are plenty of things to run around, jump over, and climb over, under, and through

NUMBER OF PLAYERS
At least 5

EQUIPMENT
None

OBJECT OF THE GAME
For all the players to follow a difficult course invented by the leader as he or she travels through the play area

Select one player to serve as the leader. Leaders should be careful not to select reckless stunts and should be fair to the abilities of the group. All the other players should line up single file behind the leader.

The leader takes off and all the players follow. The leader's course should be as varied as possible and should challenge the other players to keep up.

Hopping on one foot for ten yards, climbing through a tunnel, running through tires set on the ground, vaulting over small streams—these are the kind of tasks the leader will perform.

Players who have difficulty with a certain stunt can drop from the game or join the end of the line. After a few minutes, change leaders so that everyone has a chance to invent a circuit.

Foul-Play Race

WHERE TO PLAY
Outdoors

NUMBER OF PLAYERS
6 or more

EQUIPMENT
None

OBJECT OF THE GAME
To win the race if you are a fast runner, but to keep your opponents from reaching the finish line if you lose an early heat

Line up the runners at the starting line as in a normal race. For this first heat, everyone runs for the finish line. The player who comes in last, however, is allowed to stand in the path of the race during the next heat.

As the racers come toward the finish line, the player standing in the race path may try to run players out of bounds and into each other, while the racers attempt to avoid any hindrance.

The last runner in the second heat joins the other player in the race path, as do the final runners in succeeding heats. The runner of the last two remaining in the race who manages to get past all the others now standing in the way is the winner!

Frisbee Golf

WHERE TO PLAY
Outdoors, in a large backyard or park, or on a playground

NUMBER OF PLAYERS
2 to 4

EQUIPMENT
This can be played with 1 Frisbee, though it goes a little faster with 2 or more. A pencil and paper are helpful for keeping score

OBJECT OF THE GAME
To complete the Frisbee Golf course with the fewest number of "strokes."

Before the game begins, choose one player to design the first hole. He or she selects a "pin" where the Frisbee should be aimed: at a certain tree, a light pole, a water fountain, or another appropriate object. Holes can be from 50 to 100 feet apart, depending upon the space available.

Hazards along the hole add to the fun—through a tunnel on a playground, over a row of bushes in a backyard, etc. Before beginning the hole, be sure every player understands the requirements.

It doesn't matter who gets to throw first, as long as every player gets a turn. One by one the players throw the Frisbee toward the pin, keeping track of the number of throws it takes them to reach it.

When all players have completed the hole, review all the scores. Then another player gets to devise the next hole, and play continues.

When enough time and space are available, Frisbee Golf can be played like a traditional round of eighteen holes. With some players, it might be best to predetermine the number of holes according to the number of players (for example, six holes for three players so each player gets the chance to plan two holes).

The player completing the course in the fewest number of strokes is the Frisbee Golf champion for the day.

Hat Grab

WHERE TO PLAY
In a yard or on a playground

NUMBER OF PLAYERS
At least 6

EQUIPMENT
Any object that can be easily grabbed, like a hat or a beanbag

OBJECT OF THE GAME
To grab the hat that is placed in the middle of the playing field and escape with it before being tagged by a defender

This game can be decided by keeping score or by elimination. Choose which way to determine the winner before beginning the game.

Define a playing field of approximately forty by forty feet. Establish two end lines on opposite sides of the field, and place the hat in the center of the field.

The players are divided into two equal teams and are assigned roles: one team as "grabbers" and the other as "defenders." The teams should stand behind the opposite end lines.

(continued on next page)

Hat Grab (*cont.*)

To begin the game, one defender steps into the playing field, where he or she must guard the hat. A player from the grabber's team then moves onto the playing field with the intention of stealing the hat and running it off the field before being tagged by the defender.

This sounds easier than it is. A direct approach will probably fail for all but the fastest sprinters. To succeed, the grabber will need to play a bit of cat and mouse: run right, run left, walk a few steps, look bored—anything to confuse the defender and catch him or her off guard. Teammates can join in by trying to distract the defender with shouts or motions, while remaining outside the playing field.

When the game is being played for points rather than elimination, a point is awarded to the successful team. If the grabber manages to get the hat safely off the playing field, his or her team scores a point. If the defender tags the grabber first, the point is awarded to his or her team. To proceed, a new player from each team enters the playing field, and the game begins again.

Continue until each team has had a chance to be both grabbers and defenders. The team with the most points wins. In case of a tie, a tie-breaking round may be necessary.

If the players have chosen to play Hat Grab as an elimination game, players who are tagged while running the hat off the field must drop out. Likewise, defenders who allow the hat to be taken off the field are eliminated.

Continue playing until all players but one have been eliminated. The last remaining player's team wins.

Hide-and-Seek

WHERE TO PLAY
Outdoors where there are plenty of places to hide

NUMBER OF PLAYERS
3 or more; most exciting with lots of players

EQUIPMENT
None

OBJECT OF THE GAME
To come out of hiding and reach home base before being tagged by
"It"

Choose one player to be "It." Establish boundaries for the hiding area and indicate home base. A tree makes an effective home base.

"It" stands at home base, closes his or her eyes, and counts to 100 while the other players scatter around the playing area in search of hiding places. Upon reaching 100, "It" uncovers his or her eyes and announces in a loud voice, "Ready or not, here I come!"

"It" starts roaming the area in search of hiding players. The hiders wait for an opportunity when "It" is looking the other way to sprint for home. Clever players have been known to use tactics such as throwing stones or sticks away from their hiding places in order to fool "It" into thinking they are somewhere else.

When a player feels confident, he or she takes off for home base, calling, "Home free" upon reaching it without being discovered by "It."

If "It" spots a player on the way home, a race to the base ensues. If "It" tags the runner before he or she reaches home, that player is captured and can only be freed by another player racing home and calling, "Home free!"

Since some players may try to hide right next to the base, "It" is allowed to call out, "Anyone around home base is 'It'!"

Likewise, if "It" refuses to wander too far from home base, the first player to run home can proclaim, "Base sticking," which means that "It" must move farther away from home base.

When the last player runs in, the situation must be evaluated to determine who will be the next "It." If the final hider reached home and called, "Home free!" then everyone is free and the same player remains "It."

If the last player caught is the only captured player, he or she becomes "It." If, however, there are others who have not been freed, the first among them to have been caught is "It" for the next round.

VARIATION

A slightly different version of Hide-and-Seek is **I Spy.** When "It" spots a player, he or she calls out the name and location of the hider: "I spy Jeffrey under the slide!" If "It" is correct about both name and location and can reach home base before the hiding player, that player is captured.

Home-Plate Baseball

WHERE TO PLAY
On grass or pavement

NUMBER OF PLAYERS
6 or more

EQUIPMENT
A small ball (perhaps a tennis ball)

OBJECT OF THE GAME
To score runs in a simplified version of baseball

Home-Plate Baseball is similar to **Danish Rounders** but a little less complicated.

Divide the players into two equal teams and decide which will pitch first and which will bat first.

Establish the playing field: a small diamond with sides of eight to ten feet. Designate home plate and a pitcher's mound about five feet from the plate.

One player from the pitching team stands on the pitcher's mound, while another player from that team serves as catcher. One player from the "batting" team steps up to the plate. All the other players remain on the sidelines.

The game begins with a slow underhand pitch to the batter. The pitcher keeps throwing balls to the batter until he or she successfully hits the ball with a hand.

The batter then runs to first base as the pitcher attempts to field the ball. The catcher does not get involved in fielding—he or she serves only to return balls that have been pitched but not hit. The pitcher attempts to touch the ball to home plate before the runner reaches first base. If this happens, the runner is out. If not, the runner is safe.

Before beginning again, the pitching team rotates. A new player steps in to be the pitcher, the pitcher becomes the catcher, and the catcher joins the line of players waiting to pitch. A new batter then steps up to home plate, and the ball is pitched again.

Runners score when they are advanced around the bases by the hits of their teammates. Outs can be made only by touching home plate. No stealing of bases is permitted.

After three outs, the pitching and batting teams exchange roles. As in real baseball, three outs for each team complete an inning. The team with the most runs after a predetermined number of innings wins the game.

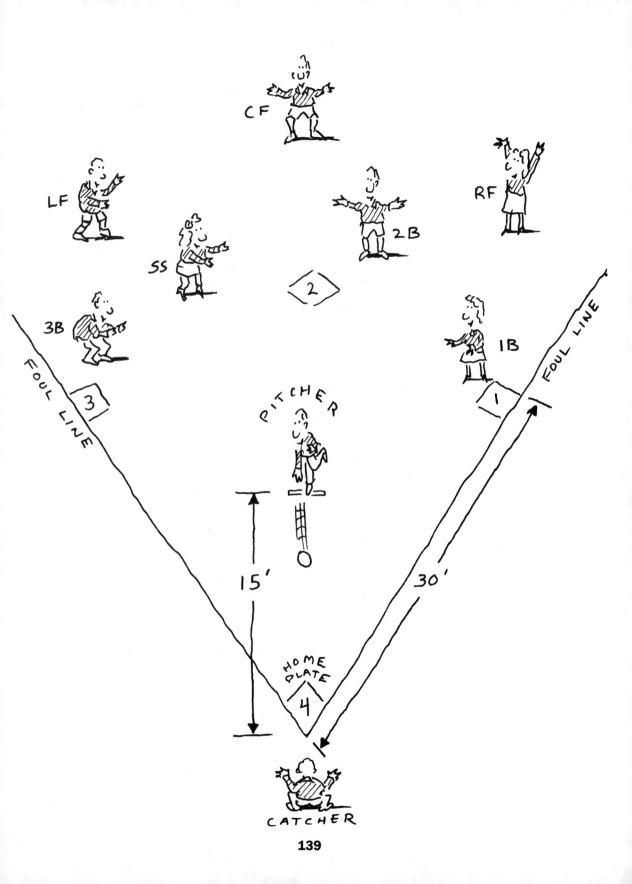

CF

LF

RF

SS

2B

3B

1B

FOUL LINE

2

FOUL LINE

3

PITCHER

1

15'

30'

HOME
PLATE

4

CATCHER

139

Hot Potato

WHERE TO PLAY

In an area large enough for the players to form a circle that will allow for a good game of catch. Make sure all breakable objects are safely put away or out of range.

NUMBER OF PLAYERS

6 or more

EQUIPMENT

A small object to toss: traditionally a potato, but a tennis ball could also be used

OBJECT OF THE GAME

To catch and throw the "hot potato" as quickly as possible in order to avoid being caught holding it

The players gather in a circle, seated on the ground. They all face the leader, who is seated in the center.

The leader begins the game by tossing the potato to one of the other players. The leader then closes his or her eyes while the other players continue to pass the potato within the circle at random, keeping it in their possession for as short a time as possible, as if the potato were steaming hot, right out of the oven.

After a short period, the leader calls out, "Hot!" The player caught holding the hot potato is eliminated, and the leader begins the toss again.

The game continues until all players but one have been ousted from the circle. This player is declared the winner.

VARIATIONS

To minimize the danger of flying objects, the potato can be passed around the circle in sequential order rather than tossed across it.

Hot Potato can also be played with music. The leader stops the music instead of yelling, "Hot" in order to catch one of the players with the potato.

Human Hurdle

WHERE TO PLAY
On dry ground

NUMBER OF PLAYERS
At least 10

EQUIPMENT
None

OBJECT OF THE GAME
To be the first team to complete a series of human hurdles

Divide the players into two equal teams. Both teams should assign their players numbers (for example, *1* through *6* if there are six players on a team).

Each team forms a large circle according to a numerical order. Players should lie on their backs with heads toward the center of the circle and feet pointing out.

At a starting signal, player number 1 from each team jumps up and runs around the circle, vaulting players 2, 3, 4, and so on, until reaching his or her original starting place. Player number 1 then lies back down.

Once player number 1 is back in place, player number 2 stands and continues the hurdling, over player 3 and the rest in succession, until returning to the starting point.

Each player in succession leaps over all the other players. When the last player has completed the circuit and has returned to position, his or her team shouts to indicate that they are done. The first team to finish wins.

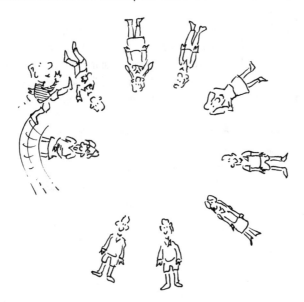

I Draw a Snake Upon Your Back

WHERE TO PLAY
In an area that permits both running and hiding

NUMBER OF PLAYERS
At least 5

EQUIPMENT
None

OBJECT OF THE GAME
The same as that of **Hide-and-Seek**, but with a fancy method of determining who will be "It"

One player is chosen to turn his or her back on the other players.

Another player traces a squiggly line down the first player's back with a finger, while saying, "I draw a snake upon your back. Who will put in the eye?"

A third player then steps forward and "puts in the eye" by poking the first player in the back.

After allowing a few seconds for that player to step back, the first player turns around and will make a guess as to who put in the eye. Before he or she makes a guess, however, the first player invents a forfeit.

If the first player guesses the poker's identity correctly, the poker will have to perform this forfeit. If the first player makes an incorrect guess, however, he or she will have to perform the forfeit. (This ensures that the first player won't choose anything too nasty, since there is always the possibility of guessing incorrectly and having to perform the forfeit him- or herself.)

The first player announces the forfeit, something like, "Run to that tree and back" or, "Say 'she sells seashells by the seashore' twenty times." After the forfeit is set, the first player makes a guess at the identity of the poker.

If the first player is correct, the poker will be "It" for a game of **Hide-and-Seek.** If the first player makes a wrong guess, however, he or she will be "It."

Instead of counting to 100 while the others hide, "It" performs the forfeit. At the same time that "It" is running to the tree or tripping over a tongue twister, the other players scatter and hide.

When "It" has completed the forfeit, he or she yells, "Ready or not, here I come," and a game of regular **Hide-and-Seek** ensues.

Ice Cubes

WHERE TO PLAY
Outdoors, on a warm day

NUMBER OF PLAYERS
At least 8

EQUIPMENT
An ice cube for each team

OBJECT OF THE GAME
To melt an ice cube by passing it from team member to team member

Divide the players into two equal teams. At a starting signal, each team picks up an ice cube and tries to melt it as quickly as possible.

Players can rub it between their hands or against their clothes, but they aren't allowed to put it in their mouths. While they are trying to melt the ice cube, it should be passed around the team frequently—no player should keep it for more than a few seconds at a time. Players should keep it off the ground, too.

The first team to melt its ice cube wins. On a really hot day, you may want to play more than one round of this game!

Jack Be Nimble

WHERE TO PLAY
Outdoors, or indoors in a large room cleared of obstacles

NUMBER OF PLAYERS
At least 8 (best for children in the early grades)

EQUIPMENT
A block of wood or an old hardcover book, about 8 to 12 inches high

OBJECT OF THE GAME
To jump over the article representing the candlestick while reciting the "Jack Be Nimble" rhyme

Set an object—a block of wood, a book, or something similar—upright in the middle of the play area. The players should line up in single file about fifteen feet from the object.

(*continued on next page*)

Jack Be Nimble (*cont.*)

One at a time, the players run toward the object and jump over it, while reciting, "Jack be nimble, Jack be quick, Jack jump over the candlestick."

Players successfully clearing the object join the end of the line, while players knocking it over leave the game. The most nimble "Jack" wins the game.

Johnny-Jump-Ups

WHERE TO PLAY
In any grassy space large enough to accommodate the group with room for each player to jump up

NUMBER OF PLAYERS
10 or more (younger children will love this!)

EQUIPMENT
None

OBJECT OF THE GAME
The players pretend to be flower seeds, awaiting a sign from "Spring" to sprout and grow. The players jump at the proper signal.

This game is a simple but energetic version of **Simon Says.** It can be played in two ways: as a team competition or as an individual elimination game.

One player should be selected to be "Spring," who will be the leader. The rest of the players, the "seeds," count off into two teams. Each player should remember his or her assigned number, 1 or 2.

All the seeds spread out over the play area and crouch down. Spring gives the signal to sprout by clapping.

When Spring claps once, all the seeds on team 1 should jump up. When Spring claps twice, the seeds on team 2 leap up. If Spring claps three times, all seeds must jump up at once.

If played as a team competition, penalty points are given to the team each time a player jumps at the incorrect signal. The team with fewer points after a given number of rounds wins.

If played as an individual elimination game, each player leaves the game after an incorrect jump. The last remaining player wins.

Kick the Can

WHERE TO PLAY

Outdoors

NUMBER OF PLAYERS

At least 5

EQUIPMENT

An aluminum can, the bigger the better

OBJECT OF THE GAME

To avoid being tagged by "It" in a version of **Hide-and-Seek**

Kick the Can is the city kid's favorite form of **Hide-and-Seek.** The clatter of the rolling can adds another sound to the usual urban din.

The player selected to be "It" has the pleasure of kicking the can as far as possible to signal the start of the game. When the can starts to roll, the other players bolt for their hiding places.

"It" then runs after the can, replaces it in its original spot (home base), and counts (with eyes closed) to 50 or 100 to give the other players a little more time to hide.

After "It" has finished counting, he or she proclaims, "Ready or not, here I come!" and sets out in search of the hiding players.

When "It" spots a player, he or she calls out the hider's name and rushes to beat that player back to the can. If "It" gets there first, the hider is captured.

Captured players can be freed by a hiding player who gets to the can without being spied by "It" and kicks the can, yelling, "Home free!" Everyone can then hide again.

Kickball

(Also known as Kick Soccer)

WHERE TO PLAY

Outdoors

NUMBER OF PLAYERS

6 or more

EQUIPMENT

A large rubber ball

OBJECT OF THE GAME

To score runs in a game similar to **Stickball** by kicking a large rubber ball rather than hitting a small one

---

Kickball is similar to **Stickball** and is well loved by younger children who have not yet developed the hitting skills necessary for a good game of **Stickball.** It is more difficult to strike out in Kickball, except by kicking foul balls.

First, set up a baseball-type diamond as the playing field, with twenty to thirty feet between the bases. Mark the bases so that all the players will know where they are.

Divide the players into two teams. Arrange one on the field in the various positions and line up the other team to kick.

The pitcher rolls the large rubber ball to the kicker, who stands at home plate. The first two foul balls kicked by each player are considered to be strikes, but a third foul cannot count as a third strike. Three strikes are an out, though most players won't strike out.

When a player succeeds in kicking the ball, he or she dashes for first base. The fielders try to gain control of the ball and may put the runner out in one of four ways: by catching a fly ball (a ball hit in the air); by throwing the ball to the first-base player, who will then touch the base before the kicker reaches the plate; by tagging the runner with the ball; or by hitting the runner with the ball (hits on the head are not outs and should be avoided when possible).

As in baseball, throwing the ball to first base before the runner arrives is a "force" out, but the runner must be tagged when it is not a force.

Since the big rubber ball will not travel very far when kicked high into the air and will make for an easy fly out, the best kind of kick in Kickball is hard and straight through a gap between fielders.

Three outs is half an inning; the teams then switch kicking and fielding positions.

The team scoring the greatest number of runs after a given number of innings wins the game.

King of the Hill

WHERE TO PLAY

In any area that has a hill or a mound that a "King" can defend

NUMBER OF PLAYERS

3 or more

EQUIPMENT

None

OBJECT OF THE GAME

For the "King" to remain in possession of a defined area of turf and for the other players to try to become the "King"

Because this game has the potential to get very physical, some ground rules should be established to make sure it is played in an orderly manner. (Only gentle pushing and pulling should be allowed, and no tripping, kicking, tickling, or similar roughhousing should be permitted.)

To start off, one person is designated the "King," and he or she stands on the top of a small hill or mound, ready to guard against attacks from the other players. The other players try to push or pull the King down from the hill so that they can take over the "kingdom."

This game results in a continual turnover in who rules as the "King of the Hill," because players are constantly dethroning each other.

Kitty Wants a Corner

WHERE TO PLAY

In any area that has easily identifiable landmarks to serve as "corners": trees, buildings, playground equipment, and so on

NUMBER OF PLAYERS

At least 5

EQUIPMENT

None

OBJECT OF THE GAME

To get from one corner to another before all the corners are filled

The player chosen to be the "Kitty" stands at the center of a designated playing area. The other players stand near landmarks that have been

(*continued on next page*)

Kitty Wants a Corner (*cont.*)

agreed upon as the "corners": trees, corners of buildings, slides, see-saws, etc. The number of landmarks will always be one less than the number of players.

To begin the game, the Kitty meows and calls, "Kitty wants a corner!" All the players, including the Kitty, leave their spots in search of a new corner. The player who doesn't find a corner becomes the new Kitty.

Leapfrog

WHERE TO PLAY
Outdoors, preferably on soft, dry grass

NUMBER OF PLAYERS
At least 6, of similar size

EQUIPMENT
None

OBJECT OF THE GAME
To "leapfrog" from the starting line to the finish line faster than the other team

Establish starting and finish lines, 50 to 100 feet apart, depending on the number of players. Split the players into two equal teams. One player from each team should squat down on the starting line, tucking in his or her

head and shoulder. The other players on each team line up single file about ten feet behind the stooped-over player.

At the starting signal, the first player in line runs up to the stooped-over player and "leapfrogs" over him or her, placing his or her hands on the player's shoulders and vaulting over them, legs apart.

Once over the first player, the second player joins the line in a stooped position a few feet in front of the first player. The third player then runs and leapfrogs over both of the players, one at a time. When all of the players have leapfrogged and are hunched over in a row, the first player to have been leaped over gets up and leaps over the line of players, keeping the pattern going. Once he or she is over the player in front of him or her, that player gets up and begins leaping also.

This continues until one of the teams leapfrogs all of its players over the finish line and is declared the winner of the race.

Lemonade

WHERE TO PLAY
In a yard, park, or playground with room to run

NUMBER OF PLAYERS
At least 8

EQUIPMENT
None

OBJECT OF THE GAME
To guess the actions of the other team and then join in a quick game of
Tag

The players are divided into two teams. The teams line up at opposite sides of a playing area, which is clearly defined before play begins.

One team is selected to go first. The members huddle and secretly choose two things: a place to be from (any city, state, or country) and some action to perform (washing dishes, playing basketball, painting a picture, etc.).

The "acting" team moves to the center of the playing area, saying, "Here we come." The other team asks, "Where from?" The first team replies with the place they have chosen. The second team then asks, "What's your trade?" and the first team replies, "Lemonade!"

(*continued on next page*)

Lemonade (*cont.*)

After the first team says, "Lemonade," they begin to perform the action chosen earlier. The other team tries to identify the activity, yelling out its guesses.

When someone on the second team calls out a correct guess, a game of **Tag** begins; the first team turns and runs back to their starting line as the second team tries to catch them.

After both sides have had the chance to act out their trade, the team that has tagged the most players can be declared the winning team.

Log Roll

WHERE TO PLAY
In any grassy area

NUMBER OF PLAYERS
At least 8

EQUIPMENT
None

OBJECT OF THE GAME
To ride across a line of rolling "logs"

All the players but one lie side by side on the floor on their stomachs. The remaining player (the first rider) gently climbs on top of this row of "logs," resting on his or her stomach across the upper portion of the backs of the logs.

When all of the players are in place, the line of logs begins to roll in one direction. The rider will be taken along with them until he or she goes over the last log. When this happens, the rider joins the logs, and another player becomes the rider. With practice, the log roll can go on indefinitely.

(It may be easier to get younger children to play this game, but it's known to have been used as a freshman-orientation activity at some colleges!)

London Bridge

WHERE TO PLAY
Outdoors on soft, dry grass

NUMBER OF PLAYERS
At least 8

EQUIPMENT
None

OBJECT OF THE GAME
To march under "London Bridge" while singing the song, ending in a
Tug-of-War

Two players are chosen to form the bridge. Between the two of them, they secretly decide that one will represent gold and the other silver. They face each other, raise their arms above their heads, and join hands.

The other players form a single-file line at one side of the bridge. Together all the players sing:

London bridge is falling down,
Falling down, falling down,
London bridge is falling down,
My fair lady.

While singing, the players march through the arch formed by the bridge players. At the words "My fair lady," the arch players lower their arms over the player who happens to be standing underneath, taking him or her "prisoner."

The bridge players whisper to the prisoner to choose gold or silver and place him or her on the gold or silver side of the bridge according to that choice.

The players march again through the succeeding verses of the song. A player is imprisoned with every "My fair lady."

Additional verses are:

Build it up with iron bars . . .
Iron bars will rust away . . .
Build it up with steel and stone . . .
Steel and stone will bend and break . . .
Build it up with gold and silver . . .
Gold and silver will be stolen away . . .
Get a man to watch all night . . .
Suppose the man should fall asleep? . . .

(continued on next page)

London Bridge (*cont.*)

Get a dog to bark all night . . .
Suppose the dog should find a bone? . . .
Get a lion to roar all night . . .
Suppose the lion should see a mouse? . . .
Here's a prisoner we have found . . .
What's the prisoner done to you . . .
Stole my hat and lost my keys . . .

Use as many verses as you have players.
    When only one player is left, the final verse is:

Off to prison he [or she] must go,
He must go, he must go,
Off to prison he must go,
My Fair Lady.

    The last prisoner is then captured and chooses a side, gold or silver. The gold and silver teams line up behind their respective leaders, the bridge players. These two grasp hands at waist height. Their teammates link up behind them, each player holding onto the waist of the player in front.
    An informal **Tug-of-War** is held between the gold and silver teams, with each team trying to topple the other. The team that remains standing is victorious.

Maypole

WHERE TO PLAY
Outdoors

NUMBER OF PLAYERS
4 or more

EQUIPMENT
A long pole (a broomstick will do); paper streamers or ribbons; colored tissue paper; tape

OBJECT OF THE GAME
To twist around the Maypole

For centuries around the world, the coming of spring has been celebrated with May Day festivities. The beautiful Maypole, decorated with luxurious ribbons and fresh flowers, has been the centerpiece of May Day celebrations.

To make a modern-day replica of the Maypole, begin with a long stick or pole. An old broom or mop handle will serve well.

Cut a piece of ribbon or streamer about ten feet long for each player. Players can decorate these with flowers made from tissue paper. Wrap extra streamers around the pole and then attach the streamers trimmed by the players to the top. To make the pole even lovelier, crown it with more tissue-paper flowers.

The simplest Maypole activity is to march with it. One person holds the pole aloft while the other players hold the ends of their streamers and walk alongside it. Dances can also be invented.

Players can also twist their streamers around the Maypole in traditional fashion. Everyone should gather around the Maypole, holding their streamers out, and count off until everyone is either a *1* or a *2*.

The *1*s pass the *2*s on the outside, holding their streamers over those of the *2*s. The *2*s then move in the other direction, passing their streamers over those of the *1*s. The *1*s and *2*s keep alternating until the streamers are woven around the Maypole, and then they can unwind them.

The Maypole was very popular at the turn of the twentieth century, when May Day was declared a play holiday for all schoolchildren. The artist Maurice Prendergast painted a wonderful series of children dancing around Maypoles in Central Park during the first few years of the century.

Some believe that May Day celebrations date back to the tree worship of the Druids in England, Ireland, and France. Others believe these rituals go back to the spring festivals of ancient Egypt and India.

Moving Statues

WHERE TO PLAY
On the grass, playground, or sidewalk

NUMBER OF PLAYERS
At least 4; it is more fun with more players!

EQUIPMENT
None

OBJECT OF THE GAME
To reach the finish line without being caught moving by the caller

Establish a starting line and a finish line about fifty feet apart. The player chosen to be the caller stands at the finish and the other players line up at the start.

The caller turns his or her back to the other players and begins counting to ten. The other players rush toward the finish line quickly but carefully, because they must be motionless, like "statues," when the caller finishes counting and turns around to face them.

Any player caught moving by the caller must return to the starting line. The first player to the finish line becomes the caller for the next game.

Mulberry Bush

WHERE TO PLAY
In a park, on a playground, or indoors if there is enough room

NUMBER OF PLAYERS
At least 4—this is wonderful for younger children!

EQUIPMENT
None

OBJECT OF THE GAME
To sing and perform the actions mentioned in the song

The players form a circle and sing this familiar children's rhyme, while acting out the motions described in the verses:

Here we go 'round the mulberry bush,
The mulberry bush, the mulberry bush,
Here we go 'round the mulberry bush,
So early in the morning.

(Walk around the circle.)

This is the way we wash our clothes,
Wash our clothes, wash our clothes,
This is the way we wash our clothes,
So early in the morning.

(Make clothes-washing motions.)

This is the way we iron our clothes,
Iron our clothes, iron our clothes,
This is the way we iron our clothes,
So early in the morning.

(Kneel on the ground and make ironing motions.)

This is the way we mend our clothes,
Mend our clothes, mend our clothes,
This is the way we mend our clothes,
So early in the morning.

(Pretend to sew.)

This is the way we sweep our floors,
Sweep our floors, sweep our floors,
This is the way we sweep our floors,
So early in the morning.

(Pretend to sweep the floor with a broom.)

A song leader can be chosen to come up with new verses for the group to sing, or players can take turns thinking of their own verses to add to the string.

Newcomb

WHERE TO PLAY
Outdoors, on grass or pavement

NUMBER OF PLAYERS
8 or more

EQUIPMENT
A volleyball or a similar type of ball; a net or rope

OBJECT OF THE GAME
To score points by causing the other team to fail to return the ball

Newcomb is a much simplified version of **Volleyball** that requires only the ability to catch and throw rather than a series of ball-handling skills.

If you already have a volleyball or tennis net in place, Newcomb requires no preparation except the designating of boundaries. Depending upon the number of players and their ages, a court can be set up from twenty by forty feet to thirty by sixty feet.

Instead of an official volleyball or tennis net, Newcomb can be played over a rope stretched between two trees or fence posts. The older the average age of the players, the higher the rope should be.

Divide the players into two equal teams and put them on opposite sides of the net. (See illustration for guidance on how the players should be arranged.)

Flip a coin to determine which side goes first. Any member of the team with the ball can begin play by throwing the ball over the net, hoping that it will fall to the ground before the other team can catch it. If the ball does hit the ground, the team that threw it scores a point.

If it is caught and returned, the ball remains in play until it drops on one side or another. If it falls on the serving team's side, the serve goes to the other team.

The ball is out of play if it hits the rope or net, goes under the rope, or goes out of bounds before being touched by a player. A point is scored or the serve changes teams according to which team last hit the ball and is responsible for the foul.

The first team to score 21 points (and win by at least 2 points) wins the game. Newcomb makes a good best-of-three-games series, with teams switching sides after every game.

Obstacle Course

WHERE TO PLAY
On a playground or in a park

NUMBER OF PLAYERS
2 or more

EQUIPMENT
This depends on the materials at hand and the location of the course. You can make do with natural obstacles and the man-made features of an area or add your own for difficulty. If you are going to race for time, a watch is needed.

OBJECT OF THE GAME
To complete the course in the shortest period of time

An obstacle course can be as simple or as complicated as you like, depending upon the materials available and/or the abilities of the players.

On a playground, incorporate the equipment already set up, by crawling through a tunnel, swinging across the monkey bars, hopping through a row of tires, and so forth. In a park, you can leap over logs, crawl under bushes, somersault along the grass, and so forth.

Obstacles can also be created. For example, you could tie a string between two trees for a low hurdle; place a jump rope on the ground and assign each player twenty jumps; lay down a piece of lumber to be used

(continued on next page)

Obstacle Course (*cont.*)

as a balance beam; place a towel on the ground to represent a pool to leap over—anything that is challenging but also safe.

Before beginning the race, establish the course by walking through it with all the players, and demonstrate how to play each of the obstacles. When everyone understands the course, let each player run it alone while being timed.

If a player fails to complete an obstacle correctly, he or she must try again until it is done properly. The runner with the fastest time is the winner.

VARIATION

The obstacle race can also be held simultaneously between two players if two identical courses are set up. For instance, a course might consist of a low hurdle, twenty-five jumps with a rope, two somersaults, throwing a ball into a basket, and then a sprint back to the beginning. If there are enough players, two teams can be formed and a relay race held.

Obstacle People

WHERE TO PLAY
On a soft, dry patch of grass or indoors in a large open room, free of breakable objects

NUMBER OF PLAYERS
At least 6 (best for younger children)

EQUIPMENT
None

OBJECT OF THE GAME
To be an obstacle in an obstacle course, and to climb over all the other obstacles

Some of the players will be obstacles and some will be climbers. The divisions need not be strict, as long as all players get a chance to be both.

The players who are obstacles scatter themselves about the play area and form themselves into shapes to be climbed over, through, around, or under: bridges, logs, roadblocks, and the like. In addition, players can work alone or in pairs to create obstacles.

The remaining players go through the obstacles as they are instructed by the obstacles themselves. The obstacles and climbers should switch periodically.

Octopus

WHERE TO PLAY
On a grassy playing field

NUMBER OF PLAYERS
At least 8

EQUIPMENT
None

OBJECT OF THE GAME
To avoid being caught by the "octopus"

One player is designated the "octopus" and roams freely in the "ocean"—the play area. The other players are "fish." When the octopus yells, "Cross!" the fish attempt to move from one side of the ocean to the other without being tagged by the octopus.

Any fish who is caught by the octopus becomes a "tentacle" and helps the octopus catch other fish as they try to cross the ocean again. The tentacles can be required to stand still, using only their arms to tag fish, or they can be allowed to move freely, like the octopus, for a livelier game!

Pom Pom Pull Away

WHERE TO PLAY
Outdoors

NUMBER OF PLAYERS
At least 8

EQUIPMENT
None

OBJECT OF THE GAME
To run from one side of the play area to the other without being tagged by "It"

(continued on next page)

Pom Pom Pull Away (*cont.*)

This is a simple version of **Red Rover.**

Mark out a playing area, approximating a twenty-five-by-twenty-five-foot square. Designate one player as "It." He or she stands in the middle of the play area while the other players line up on one side of the play square.

When "It" yells, "Pom Pom pull away, run away, catch away!" all the players in line sprint for the opposite side of the square, while trying to avoid "It."

Players tagged must join "It" in the center of the square and try to catch other players after calling, "Pom Pom pull away" again, this time in unison. Any player who runs outside the play area must also become a tagger.

The last player who remains untagged wins the game.

VARIATION

Pom Pom Pull Away is also played as Hill Dill. The rhyme called out in this version is, "Hill Dill, come over the hill, or else I'll catch you standing still."

Prince Tiptoe

WHERE TO PLAY
Anywhere

NUMBER OF PLAYERS
6 or more; best for children from 4 to 6 years old

EQUIPMENT
None

OBJECT OF THE GAME
To follow "Prince Tiptoe" in tiptoeing around the play area

Prince Tiptoe is effective as a transition from noisy, active games to quieter periods for young children.

Designate one player as "Prince Tiptoe" (or "Princess Tiptoe," if so desired). Let the other players spread out over the play area.

Prince Tiptoe begins by putting a finger to his lips and whispering, "Ssh! Here comes Prince Tiptoe." When all the players are silent, the Prince begins slowly tiptoeing around the room. Players are tapped by Prince Tiptoe and join in line behind the Prince, tiptoeing at the same speed.

When all the players are in line, Prince Tiptoe moves faster, still on tiptoe. After leading the players around the area in snaky patterns at a good pace, the Prince slows the movement.

Turning to the player directly behind him, the Prince signals another "Ssh." The player behind should quickly tiptoe back to his or her original spot and be seated.

This continues until all of the players have returned to their seats, after which Prince Tiptoe also settles down, and the game is complete.

Rabbit

WHERE TO PLAY
Outdoors, where there is plenty of room to run

NUMBER OF PLAYERS
8 or more

EQUIPMENT
None

OBJECT OF THE GAME
To catch the "rabbit" if you are the "hunter," and to evade the "hunter" if you are the "rabbit"

Before the game begins, one player should be chosen to be the first running "rabbit" and another to be the "hunter."

The rest of the players divide into groups of three. Within these groups, two hold hands to form a "rabbit hutch," and the third plays a rabbit, standing enclosed in their circle.

The game begins when the hunter starts to chase the rabbit without a home. After a bit of chase, the rabbit can decide to hide in a hutch, and he or she can trade places with one of the rabbits inside a hutch. The rabbit that had been safely tucked inside the hutch must then avoid being tagged by the hunter and find a new hutch.

If the hunter catches the rabbit, they switch roles and the chase begins again.

There are really no winners or losers in this game; it should be played until everyone gets tired of the chase. Rabbits and the players who hold hands should trade places fairly frequently so everyone gets the chance to join the action.

Races and Relays

WHERE TO PLAY
Outdoors

NUMBER OF PLAYERS
2 or more

EQUIPMENT
See "Variations"

OBJECT OF THE GAME
To be the first team to reach the finish line after completing the
required motions

There is a wide assortment of fun and exciting races and relays to play—
and, with just a little imagination, anyone can develop new racing challenges to add to these.

Races are run individually by all the players competing at once. Racers
are lined up at the start and head as quickly as possible toward the finish
line.

Relays involve teams and can be set up in a variety of ways. In the most
traditional form, each team is arranged in a line so that everyone moves
only in a forward direction.

For party givers, a more practical arrangement is a setup with each team
divided into two lines about twenty-five feet apart. Races go from the first
line to the second, then turn around and head back to the start. Or, when
racers reach the second line, they go to the end of the line, and the first
teammate in that line takes off.

Here are a few tried-and-true examples of races and relays:

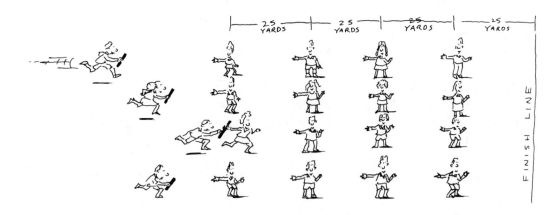

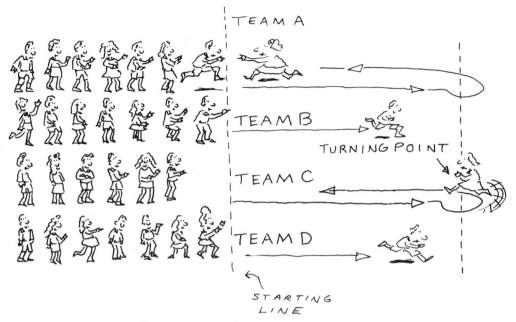

CLASSIC RELAY RACE

In the Classic Relay Race, all you need is a starting line, a finish line, and something to serve as a baton to be passed from player to player (a stick will suffice).

Divide the players into an equal number of teams, with three or four runners per team. Line the runners from each team along the race route. If there are four on each team, place one at the start, one twenty-five yards ahead, another twenty-five yards beyond, and the last twenty-five yards beyond that (which should be twenty-five yards before the finish line).

At the starting signal, the first runner in line on each team, clutching his or her baton, sprints to the second player in line. Upon reaching that runner, he or she passes the baton, and the second runner dashes for the third, who then passes it to the fourth. The fourth runner heads for the finish line.

The first team to reach the finish without dropping the baton wins.

GOSSIP RELAY

Instead of passing a baton, in the Gossip Relay players pass along a message. Before the race begins, the starter whispers a phrase to the first runner from each team. The runners must whisper into the ear of the next runner in line. The first team to reach the finish line *and* call out the correct phrase wins the race.

(*continued on next page*)

Races and Relays (*cont.*)

CRAB RELAY

For the Crab Relay, line up each team's runners behind the start. At the signal, the players crawl backward on all fours from the first to the second line, where they can stand up and run back to the start. At the start, they tag the next runner in line, who follows the same pattern. The first team to complete the pattern successfully and cross the finish line first, wins!

KANGAROO RELAY

Runners in the Kangaroo Relay hop from the first line to the second, where they turn around and hop back, then tag the next runner.

ONE-FOOT RELAY

For the One-Foot Relay, runners are required to hop to the second line on one foot, then switch feet and hop back on the other.

LEGS CROSSED RELAY

Runners in the Legs Crossed Relay cross the left leg in front of the right all the way to the second line, then cross the right leg in front of the left for the return trip.

MIXED RELAY

In the Mixed Relay, the runners on each team have to move in different ways. For a team with four runners, for example, the first might hop on two feet, the second on one foot, the third run backward, and the fourth run normally.

For a longer version of the Mixed Relay, all the players on each team must run all four ways.

If there is pavement nearby and you have a few balls, another good Mixed Relay involves ball-handling skills. For the first round, players dribble the ball to the end of the line and back, then they pass it through the legs, then roll it toward the line and race ahead of it to pick it up, etc.

THREE-LEGGED RACE

Rags or scarves are needed for the Three-Legged Race. Each player needs a partner. The partners stand side by side, and their inside legs are loosely tied together with a rag or scarf. At the starting signal, the partners hobble off to the finish line together. (This should always be played on grass, as racers inevitably stumble!)

PIGGY-BACK RACE

One partner climbs on the back of another partner for the Piggy-Back Race. Make sure you switch so both partners have a chance to get a ride.

WHEELBARROW RACE

Another partners race is the Wheelbarrow Race. The partner to serve as the wheelbarrow gets down on hands and knees at the starting line. At the signal, the other partner picks up the legs of the "wheelbarrow," and they move together toward the finish—the wheelbarrow moving his or her hands as fast as possible. Players are likely to fall but may continue from where they land. Run the race again so that the wheelbarrow and driver can change roles.

SACK RELAY

Sack Races might be easier to run as relays—that way you don't need as many sacks or old pillowcases. The first runner on each team lines up before the starting line while standing in the sack or case. At the starting signal, he or she hops to the second line and back. At the starting line, he or she climbs out of the sack and passes it to the next runner in line.

POTATO RELAY

After dividing the players into equal teams, place piles of potatoes behind the second line, one for every player on each team. The first runner in each line sprints for the potatoes with a plastic spoon in hand.

Upon reaching the potatoes, he or she picks one up with the spoon and must walk it back to the start, keeping it balanced on the spoon. At the start, the spoon is passed to the next player. The first team to get all of its potatoes back to the start wins.

WILLIAM TELL RELAY

The first runner on each team is given an apple. The player must keep the apple balanced on his or her head and walk to the second line. Once there, he or she may take hold of the apple and run back with it, passing it on to the next player at the start.

OASIS RELAY

Each team is given a plastic or paper cup full of water. Players must jump to the second line and back, trying to spill as little water as possible, and

(*continued on next page*)

Races and Relays (*cont.*)

pass the cup to the next teammate in line. The team with most water in its cup at the end of the race wins.

FIREFIGHTERS' RACE

Buckets, bowls, or other containers filled with five or six cups of water are set up at each line, two for each team. The first runner scoops a plastic or paper cup of water from the bowl at the start and runs it to an empty bowl at the second line, trying to avoid spillage.

He or she pours the water from the cup into the bowl and sprints back to the beginning. The next player repeats the process, until one team has succeeded in transferring all of its water from the first bowl to the second.

NEWSPAPER RACE

Each player (or team) is given two sheets of newsprint. At the starting signal, players lay one sheet down in front of them and step onto it. Then they lay down the other sheet, step onto that, and turn around and pick up the sheet left behind. Players may move to the finish line only by stepping from sheet to sheet.

SUITCASE RELAY

If you have small suitcases for this game, it is more authentic, but paper bags work just as well. Before the party, fill each bag with a number of folded items (keeping the number and type of items in each suitcase similar): an old T-shirt, a pair of pajamas, some socks, etc.

Set a suitcase or bag down for each team at the starting line, and remove the contents, placing them next to the suitcase.

At the starting signal, the first runners pack the case or bag with the objects, pick it up, and run to the second line and back again. They then unpack, and the next player packs and runs. The fastest packers and travelers win the relay.

A variation on this relay is to divide each team in half and have one half stand at one end of the playing area and the other half twenty-five yards away. The race begins with first player opening up the suitcase, putting on its contents, shutting the suitcase, and running with it to the teammates lined up across the playing area.

Having reached the opposite teammates, the player should take off those clothes, while the first player in line packs them up and then sprints back to the first line. This pattern continues until each player has been both dresser and packer.

PEANUT RACE

The Peanut Race is best run indoors and on carpet. Players are each given a peanut (still in the shell), and they all line up behind the starting line on hands and knees. The first player to push the peanut to the finish line (about ten feet away) with his or her nose wins the race.

CRACKER RACE

The Cracker Race can be held indoors and does not require any running at all. Each player is given two or three saltine crackers. The first to finish eating the crackers and successfully whistle a tune ("Yankee Doodle" or something else familiar) wins.

Red Rover

WHERE TO PLAY
On a grassy area

NUMBER OF PLAYERS
At least 10; 20 players make for more adventure!

EQUIPMENT
None

OBJECT OF THE GAME
To break through a line of players in order to capture a member of the opposition for your own team

Two equal teams, each with a captain, are formed. One team lines up, holding hands.

The captain of the team now holding hands designates a member of the other team by calling out, "Red rover, red rover, let _____ come over."

The player whose name was called runs over to the line and tries to break through the line of arms and hands. If he or she is successful, a member of the team holding hands must be forfeited to the other team. If he or she is unsuccessful, that player must join the team he or she just tried to break through.

The other team now lines up and the process is repeated. The team with the most players after a given amount of playing time wins.

Ring-Around-the-Rosy

WHERE TO PLAY

Outdoors on a soft, dry area of grass

NUMBER OF PLAYERS

2 or more

EQUIPMENT

None

OBJECT OF THE GAME

A sing-along for young children

The players stand in a circle and join hands. They sing the traditional rhyme in one of its many forms and fall to the ground as they sing the last line.

Ring around the rosy,
Pocket full of posies,
Ashes, ashes, we all fall down.

Or . . . A-tishoo, a-tishoo, we all fall down.
Or . . . Last one down is a red, red rosy.

Ring-a-Levio

WHERE TO PLAY

In an area that provides ample hiding places, such as a park or playground with trees and shrubbery

---

NUMBER OF PLAYERS

10 or more; larger groups are more challenging!

EQUIPMENT

None

OBJECT OF THE GAME

For one team to capture all members of the opposing team

A "den" about five feet square should be designated in the middle of the playing area. A wider "danger area" of approximately thirty square feet should also be established.

Players should be divided into two equal teams and a "den warden" chosen for each team. One team, with its den warden, stands inside the den, while the other team runs for various hiding places. When they are all hidden, their den warden shouts, "Ready!"

When those in the den hear the "Ready!" call, they try to discover the hiding members of the other team, catch them, and bring them back to the den for safekeeping.

Meanwhile, the warden watches all prisoners in the den. Members of the hiding team can attempt to free one imprisoned group member at a time by getting both feet into the den, shouting, "Ring-a-levio," and running out again.

The den warden can recapture them within the limits of the danger area, but if they safely cross the boundary, they are free!

The game ends when one team has captured all the members of the opposing team. Then a new round can begin with each team switching roles.

Run for Your Supper

WHERE TO PLAY
In any area with plenty of room for running

NUMBER OF PLAYERS
At least 10 (works best with lots of players!)

EQUIPMENT
None

OBJECT OF THE GAME
To run around the circle fast enough to get to an empty space

One player is designated as "It," while the others join hands in a circle. "It" remains outside the circle.

As "It" walks around the circle, he or she chooses two players who are next to each other and pulls their joined hands apart, calling, "Run for your supper!" These two players run in opposite directions around the outside of the circle in a race back to their original spot.

"It" takes one of the vacated places. The first runner to return and slap the outstretched hands of "It" completes the circle. The player left outside the circle becomes the next "It."

VARIATION
Instead of running for their suppers, players can also hop, skip, crawl, march, and so forth.

Sardines

WHERE TO PLAY

Outdoors where hiding places are easy to find, or in a big house that
has lots of places to hide

NUMBER OF PLAYERS

At least 6

EQUIPMENT

None

OBJECT OF THE GAME

To join all the other hiding players in one hiding space

This game is like a reverse **Hide-and-Seek**. The player who has been
chosen to go first leaves the other players (who have their backs to the
playing area) in search of a hiding place. The first player has a minute to
hide and should attempt to find a spot in which all players will be able to
fit—but just barely.

After a minute has passed, a second player has a minute to search for
and find the first and then joins him or her in the chosen spot. The third
player goes in search of the others after another minute has passed, and
so on with each of the players. If any player is unsuccessful in finding the
hidden players within a minute's time, they are out of the game.

The game ends when the final player discovers the hiding spot into
which the other players are packed like sardines. The real challenge in this
game is for the tightly packed hiders (sardines) to refrain from laughing
or talking, thus giving away their location.

Sewing Up the Gap

WHERE TO PLAY

In a large area suitable for running

NUMBER OF PLAYERS

At least 10—larger groups make it more challenging!

EQUIPMENT

None

OBJECT OF THE GAME

For the chased player to close all the gaps in the circle before being
tagged by the chaser

The group forms a circle, standing arm's distance apart, with two players—the chaser and the chased—remaining on the outside. The two outside players stand on opposite sides of the circle.

When given a signal to go, the chaser begins chasing the other player around the circle. The chased player begins to weave in and out of the circle.

When the chased player passes from the outside of the circle to the inside through two players, they join hands in order to "sew up the gap." The player being chased aims to sew up all the gaps so he or she is safely on the inside and therefore cannot be tagged by the chaser. If he or she is caught by the chaser, they exchange roles.

Simon Says

WHERE TO PLAY
In an area large enough to allow each player enough space to perform vigorous physical tasks

NUMBER OF PLAYERS
5 or more

EQUIPMENT
None

OBJECT OF THE GAME
To follow the commands of the leader correctly and remain in the game as long as possible

One player is chosen to be the leader, "Simon." The leader faces the group, issues a command "Simon says do this . . ." while demonstrating an action.

The group must perform the activity commanded *only* if the leader states *"Simon says* do this . . ." If the leader simply says, "Do this" without the words, "Simon says," the group is not to copy him or her. For example, if the leader says, "Do this," and jumps in the air, any player who also jumps in the air must drop out, because the leader didn't say, "Simon says." In addition, if the leader moves to perform a jumping jack and a player does not properly imitate the movement, that player is eliminated.

Simon should try to confuse the other players by giving commands

(*continued on next page*)

Simon Says (*cont.*)

rapidly and trying to slip in a "Do this" order to fool others into following.

The last player remaining wins and become Simon for the next round.

VARIATION

This game can also be played indoors if Simon gives more restrained commands, like clapping, touching the top of the head, or rubbing the stomach. It can also be played simply with hand gestures: thumbs up, thumbs down, right, and left.

Spud

WHERE TO PLAY
On grass or a paved play area

NUMBER OF PLAYERS
8 or more

EQUIPMENT
A rubber playground ball

OBJECT OF THE GAME
To avoid being hit by the ball and remain in the game as long as possible

One player is selected to toss the ball first. The other players gather around while he or she throws the ball into the air and calls the name of one of the players.

As the player whose name was called runs to catch the ball, the others run away from him or her as quickly as possible. When the catcher has the ball in hand, he or she yells, "Freeze!" and all the runners must stop in their tracks.

The player with the ball aims it at a player of his or her choice, usually the closest player, so he or she has the best chance of making a hit. Players should throw the ball gently at the targeted player and never so hard that it would hurt a fellow player.

Anytime a player is hit, he or she is assigned a letter, first *S,* then *P, U,* and *D.* When a player is hit four times and has been given the letters to spell *SPUD,* he or she drops out of the game.

If the thrower fails to hit the player at whom the ball was aimed, he or she is assigned a letter, and the targeted player is allowed to recover the ball and throw it at another player.

The throwing continues until another miss is made. The last player at whom the ball was thrown picks it up, tosses it in the air, and calls the name of another player to start the game again.

The last remaining player in the game is the winner.

VARIATIONS

In Buddy Spud, players need buddies (partners). The game progresses in the same way as regular Spud, except that when the player whose name was called catches the ball, he or she may pass the ball to another buddy, if the buddy is in a better position to hit another player.

If the buddy doesn't catch his or her partner's throw, or misses the player at whom he or she aims the ball, the partners are assigned a letter. When the partners get *SPUD* (i.e., four misses) between the two of them, they are out of the game.

Baby in the Air is similar to Spud, with numbers rather than names called out. Players should count off sequentially so that each is assigned a number.

Player number 1 stands in the center of a circle formed by the other players and throws the ball into the air while calling one of the numbers of the other players at random.

The player whose name was called is allowed three giant steps toward the nearest player before trying to hit him or her with the ball. When players are hit, they are assigned letters: *B-A-B-Y.*

(An old name for Spud is Burly Whush. Instead of calling "Freeze!" the player with the ball cried, "Burly Whush!" and was allowed to "burly whush"—throw the ball at—any player.)

Here is another variation. The player who catches the ball is allowed to take seven giant steps toward the player nearest him or the player of his choice before trying to hit him or her with the ball. (Kids can run far when a ball is thrown into the air as high as a person can throw.)

Or, the person whose name is called screams "freeze" after retrieving or catching the ball. Then he or she says "S-P-U-D-period-question mark-comma," and takes a giant step with every chant. This version is, perhaps, more suitable for older players.

Statues

WHERE TO PLAY

On a grassy area or playground

NUMBER OF PLAYERS

More than 4

EQUIPMENT

None

OBJECT OF THE GAME

To pose as the best "statue"

One player is chosen to be the "sculptor" and the others will be the "statues."

The sculptor takes each player by the hand and twirls him or her around twice, then lets go. The twirled player freezes into a statue form.

The statue can be funny, elegant, athletic—anything the player wants. The statues must hold their positions until all the players have been twirled. The sculptor then chooses a favorite statue, who becomes the next sculptor.

VARIATION

The sculptor can assign statue types to the players before they are twirled. For example, he or she might require that the players strike animal-like poses. All can try for the same look, or every statue can be of a different variety.

Tag

WHERE TO PLAY

Outdoors

NUMBER OF PLAYERS

6 or more

EQUIPMENT

See "Variations"

OBJECT OF THE GAME

To be the only player to avoid being tagged by "It"

Tag in its simplest form is a matter of selecting "It," defining the boundaries of the play area, and giving chase until one player is left and is declared the winner, or all are caught, in which case "It" triumphs. When all players have been caught, the first one tagged becomes "It" for the next game.

Other games of Tag are endless—the player tagged becomes the new "It" until he or she can tag another player. Tagging the player who just tagged you is cheating!

Adding complications varies the game. Here are a few ideas:

ANKLE TAG

When a player is approached by "It," he or she can become safe by grabbing the ankle of another player. The player whose ankle is being held may be tagged by "It" unless he or she can in turn grab the ankle of a player (other than the one already holding on).

BALL TAG

In Ball Tag "It" tags other players by hitting them with a soft rubber ball rather than by touching them.

CROSS TAG

Select one player to serve as the first "It," and define the play area. "It" begins the game by calling the name of one player, and chasing after him.

"It" keeps after that particular player until another player crosses between them. The crossing player then becomes the object of "It's" chase. The other players will join in trying to help the chased player to avoid being tagged by distracting "It," but many will keep from crossing between them.

FLASHLIGHT TAG

Flashlight Tag is a nighttime version of traditional tag. Players are caught when "It" shines a flashlight on them.

FREEZE TAG

In Freeze Tag, players tagged must stand motionless until touched by another player who is still free. "It" wins if he or she can freeze everyone.

JAPANESE TAG

"It" in Japanese Tag must chase the other players while holding one hand on the spot where he or she was tagged until someone new can be touched.

(*continued on next page*)

Tag (*cont.*)

PIGGY-BACK TAG

When "It" draws near, players can gain safety by riding one another piggy-back. No two players may get together twice in a row, though.

PRAYER TAG

Players in Prayer Tag are safe from "It" if they drop to their knees and clasp their hands in an attitude of prayer when "It" approaches. "It" will back up five yards, during which time the player on his or her knees must get up and run or risk being tagged.

SKUNK TAG

A player is safe when he or she puts an arm under the knee and holds the nose. The player must then hop ten steps and start running again.

TOUCH WOOD TAG

Any player touching wood when "It" draws near is safe.

TV TAG

In order to be saved from tagging, players must answer correctly a TV question asked by "It": "Who's the star of . . . ?" "Who played the lead role in 'I Love Lucy'?"

Tetherball

WHERE TO PLAY
Outdoors

NUMBER OF PLAYERS
2 to 6

EQUIPMENT
A regulation tetherball; hanging by its cord from a pole

OBJECT OF THE GAME
To wrap the ball on its rope completely around the pole by batting it with the hand

The ball is different from other playground balls in that it is equipped to be attached to a strong cord which is hung from a pole. A court can be established by marking a circle about five feet in diameter around the pole. Divide the circle into two halves and extend the line a few feet outside the circle on each side.

A team may consist of one to three players. The team members line up outside the circle but on their side of the court. Players must stay on their own side of the court; failure to do so constitutes a foul.

Stepping into the circle is also a foul, unless the ball is almost completely wrapped around the pole and can only be reached from inside the circle.

The player chosen to hit first may bat the ball with the hand either to the left or to the right. The opposing player or team attempts to bat the ball back in the opposite direction.

The two teams continue hitting the ball back and forth until one team succeeds in wrapping the rope and ball completely around the pole. That team scores a point, and the other team is given the ball to start the new round.

The player or team earning the greatest number of points in a given amount of time, or scoring 10 points first, wins.

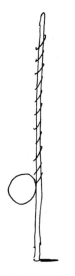

THE WINNING
POSITION

Threading Grandmother's Needle

WHERE TO PLAY

Outdoors

NUMBER OF PLAYERS

At least 8; best for children in the primary grades

EQUIPMENT

None

OBJECT OF THE GAME

To keep running under bridges formed by the players' arms

To play Threading Grandmother's Needle, the players should form two equal lines facing each other. The players at the ends of each of the two lines chant in unison, "Grandmother's eyes have grown so dim, the needle she can't fill."

The two players at the other end of the lines then respond, "Our eyes are very bright and good, thread it for her now we will." At this signal, each player grasps the hands of the player directly across in line, raising them above head level.

The two players who have offered to "thread grandmother's needle" run through the tunnel of upraised arms, taking a new position at the front of the line.

They initiate the action again by calling, "Grandmother's eyes have grown so dim, the needle she can't fill." The two players now at the end of the line call out the response and run under the bridges again.

Players keep forming bridges and running under them until everyone has returned to their original positions, or they can keep going until they get tired of the game. Running through the tunnel may prove so much fun that the rhyme will be dispensed with and the players will get the line moving very quickly.

Tiger and Leopard

WHERE TO PLAY
Outdoors, on soft grass

NUMBER OF PLAYERS
10 or more

EQUIPMENT
None

OBJECT OF THE GAME
For the "leopards" to jump over the "tigers" and avoid being caught by them

Establish a starting line and a finish line, about fifteen feet apart.

Divide the players into two teams: the "tigers" and "leopards." The tigers stand along the starting line with a leopard behind each tiger.

Together the players chant, "A tiger, a leopard / A leopard, a tiger / One of them crouches / The other jumps over."

When the players first say, "A tiger," the tigers drop to their knees. At "One of them crouches," the leopards step up and put their hands on the tigers' shoulders.

After saying, "The other jumps over," the leopards leap over the tigers' backs (as in **Leapfrog**) and run for the finish line. The leopards then turn around and run back to the starting line, trying to avoid being caught by the tigers.

Tigers who catch leopards become leopards, and leopards who are caught become tigers. The rhyme is chanted again, and the jump-and-chase sequence continues until all the players are either leopards or tigers.

Toesies

WHERE TO PLAY
On soft grass or a cushiony carpet

NUMBER OF PLAYERS
2 or more (wonderful for younger children!)

EQUIPMENT
None

OBJECT OF THE GAME
For 2 children to roll across the floor while keeping their toes touching

Two players lie on the floor with their feet touching and try to roll across the grass or the room together, keeping their toes in touch.

With four or more players, this can be a race.

Touch Football

WHERE TO PLAY
Outdoors, on grass

NUMBER OF PLAYERS
At least 4

EQUIPMENT
A football

OBJECT OF THE GAME
To score touchdowns in a modified version of tackle football

Like other games that are based upon regulation sports, Touch Football can be played according to strict rules or free-form, depending on the players, their level of experience, and the mood of the game.

A regulation football field is 100 yards long and 53⅓ yard wide, but for Touch Football, a much smaller field is desirable, depending on the number of players and the passing abilities of the quarterbacks. For five players on a side, a 40-yard field will probably be sufficient. If the field is too long, no one may ever score!

Divide the players into two equal teams and select a quarterback for each side. The other positions need not be fixed (running back, fullback, etc.). Flip a coin to determine which team will have the ball first.

Decide what type of "touch" will be used to signify a tackle. One-hand or two-hand touches can be used, or players can tuck bandannas or handkerchiefs into their clothing, which will be pulled to signal a tackle. Even Touch Football can get rough—watch that players aren't taking the touch as an opportunity for a good slap or an unnecessary shove.

Start the game with a kickoff if you have someone with a good kicking leg on the team. If everyone's barefoot, the kick-off can be a pass. The kicking team lines up at its goal line, while the receiving team stays behind the "50-yard" line (midfield). The kicker boots the ball as far down field as possible. (If kicking proves to be difficult, start the game at the "fifty" with the first down.)

Someone on the receiving team catches the ball and attempts to run it back to their opponent's goal line. The runner is "tackled" when he or she is touched by a member of the opposing team.

The receiving team then has four tries, or "downs," to attempt to move the ball to the opposite goal line and score. For each down, the team in possession huddles to determine the next play. One of the players is chosen to receive the ball, in a hand-off or a pass play.

After discussing the play, the team with the ball returns to the line of scrimmage (the spot where the last team member with the ball was "tackled") and lines up to begin the play. The defensive team stands on the other side of the line.

At the quarterback's signal ("Hike!"), the players go into motion. The quarterback attempts to get the ball to the chosen player. Defensive players will attempt to get to the ball carrier for the tackle. Offensive players may block: they will try to keep the defensive players away from the ball carrier by bumping them lightly or getting in their way while running.

If the team with the ball manages to get it over the opponent's goal, a touchdown, worth 6 points, is scored. More often, however, the team will fail, and the ball must be turned over to the other team. They must put the ball down on the spot where they gained possession of it and attempt to get down the field in the other direction.

When good kickers are involved, punting is allowed. On the fourth down, if a team feels that it won't be able to score, it may choose to kick the ball down the field in order to put the other team as far from the goal line as possible.

A team may also gain possession of the ball when the other team fumbles, or if they intercept a pass.

If kicking is part of the game, you might also want to add field goals, and points after the touchdown. If a team nears the goal line but feels that another running or passing play will not get them a goal, they may choose to have the kicker boot the ball over the end of line to score 3 points. After

(*continued on next page*)

Touch Football (*cont.*)

a regular touchdown is scored, the kicker is given one play in which to kick the ball over the goal line to score 1 point.

A regulation football game has four quarters of fifteen minutes each. For Touch Football, you can play according to these rules, set your own time limit, play to a predetermined score, or simply play until everyone is exhausted or has to go home.

Tug-of-War

WHERE TO PLAY
Outside, on soft, dry grass

NUMBER OF PLAYERS
6 or more

EQUIPMENT
A long, smooth, sturdy rope; a bandanna or rag

OBJECT OF THE GAME
To pull the opposing team over the center line

For young children, dividing the teams can be done randomly since players will be fairly equal in strength. For older players, however, it might be best to have captains choose teams, since groups of matched strength add drama to the game.

Establish a center line in the pulling area. The teams should line up single file on either side of this line. Tie a rag or bandanna around the center of the tugging rope to mark it, and hold the rope with this marker over the center line.

Each player should hold onto the rope, with three or four feet between players, and with players alternating on each side of the rope. A particularly strong team member can be positioned at the end of the line as an "anchor."

At a signal, both teams attempt to pull the first member of the other team over the center line with the rope. The game may end when that player steps over the line but more likely will finish with a bang as all the players go sprawling across!

Twine the Garland

WHERE TO PLAY
Outdoors, or indoors if there is enough room

NUMBER OF PLAYERS
At least 8 (best for younger children)

EQUIPMENT
None

OBJECT OF THE GAME
For a line of players to wrap into a knot and then unwrap the knot

---

The players form a line and grasp hands, forming a "garland." A player on one end is designated to stand still, while the garland wraps around him or her.

(*continued on next page*)

Twine the Garland (*cont.*)

While the players sing to the tune of "Yankee Doodle," "Twine the garland, girls and boys, twine the garland, girls; twine the garland, girls and boys, twine the garland, boys," the line dances around, finally wrapping itself around the stationary player.

When everyone is tightly twined, the line then unwraps itself, the players now singing, "Untwine the garland, girls and boys, untwine the garland, girls; untwine the garland, girls and boys, untwine the garland, boys."

All the players will probably want a chance to be the center of the "twine of garland."

Ultimate Frisbee

WHERE TO PLAY
On a large grassy field

NUMBER OF PLAYERS
At least 6

EQUIPMENT
A Frisbee

OBJECT OF THE GAME
To score goals by throwing the Frisbee downfield and eventually to a teammate standing behind the goal line

Ultimate Frisbee is a fast-paced variation on football.

The Ultimate Frisbee field should be about 180 feet long and 90 feet wide, depending on the number of players and their throwing abilities.

Form two equal teams and decide which will "receive" the Frisbee first. Each team lines up behind its own goal line to begin the game.

The game starts when the other (i.e., "throwing") team tosses the Frisbee to the receiving team. The receiving team may catch it and start moving it downfield or let it land untouched, and then pick it up and move it.

If any member of the throwing team is fast enough to intercept it, however, or to touch a player about to catch the Frisbee before he or she does so, the throwing team may take possession of the Frisbee.

The Frisbee may only be moved by passing—no walking or running with it is allowed. Players may pivot on one foot while trying to find a teammate to throw to. Players caught moving with the Frisbee forfeit possession to the other team .

Unlike football, in Ultimate Frisbee there are no downs. The Frisbee is kept in motion as long as possible, only coming to rest when it falls to the ground or an error is committed.

The Frisbee can be intercepted at any time. If a teammate fails to catch a pass obviously aimed at him or her, and the Frisbee falls to the ground, the other team is given possession.

To score, the Frisbee must be thrown by one teammate inside the field to another teammate outside the goal line. If the pass is not caught, possession goes to the other team.

Each goal in Ultimate Frisbee is worth 1 point. Play to a predetermined number of points or within a time limit.

Volleyball

WHERE TO PLAY
Outdoors

NUMBER OF PLAYERS
In regulation Volleyball, there are 6 players to a side, but for informal play, a team can accommodate up to 9 players on a side. Players can also be rotated in order to give the greatest number the opportunity to participate without crowding the court.

EQUIPMENT
A net; a volleyball

OBJECT OF THE GAME
To score points by causing the other team to fail to return the ball over the net

For regulation Volleyball, it is best to play on a standard court with a net already in place. For more casual play, however, stretch a rope or net (seven to nine feet high) between two poles or trees and establish a court from thirty to sixty feet long and fifteen to twenty-five feet wide. (This game can be modified to suit the ages and playing abilities of the children involved.)

In formal Volleyball games, there are six players on each side. This is also the ideal number when players are highly skilled. If there are more than six players on a side, but you want only six on the court at a time, use a rotation system: every time the serve changes teams, the last player to

(*continued on page 187*)

SERVER

30 TO 60 FEET

15 to 25 FEET

SERVER

186

Volleyball (*cont.*)

have served goes out and a new player comes in to serve. For informal Volleyball games, up to nine players can be on one side of the court at a time.

After deciding which team will serve first, the teams should take their places on the court as shown below:

The server for the first team stands behind the boundary line at the right in the back row and hits the ball over the net, either underhand or overhand, using the palm or the fist. If the ball hits the net, fails to go over, or goes out of bounds, the serve is given to the other team.

If the serve is successful, the receiving team is allowed three hits to return it over the net. Players may touch the ball with any part of the body above the waist but may not hold or carry it. Players may not touch the net at any time.

If the ball touches the net but goes over, it is still in play (except on the serve). Balls hit into the net can also be hit out over and over, as long as only three hits are taken by the team.

Different types of hits may be used to get the ball back over the net. For the *bump,* players turn their palms up and place one hand inside the other, forming a flat surface with the forearms. When the ball nears, the player bends his or her knees to get under the ball and "bumps" it up into the air on this flat surface.

The *set* is used to place the ball near the net so that it will be in a better position for another teammate to hit it over. When the ball approaches, it is hit back into the air with all ten fingertips.

The *spike* is a hard slam of the ball with the fist or palm. The spiker tries to aim the ball into an empty spot on the opponent's side of the court.

Experienced Volleyball players will learn how to control the ball by making full use of all three allowed hits and different techniques for hitting. Casual players will have just as much fun trying to get the ball over in every possible (and legal) manner.

The ball is volleyed back and forth across the net until one side fails to return it. If the receiving team errs, the serving team scores a point. The serving team keeps the service until they make an error. Then, the service is given to the other team. A team can only score when it is serving.

The first team to score 21 points wins the game. Best of three- or five-game series can be played, with the teams exchanging courts after every game.

Water-Balloon Ball

WHERE TO PLAY
Outdoors!

NUMBER OF PLAYERS
6 or more

EQUIPMENT
Lots of water balloons

OBJECT OF THE GAME
To play your favorite ball games, with water balloons instead of balls

Instead of playing games like **Newcomb** and **Basketball** with regular balls, try them with water balloons.

For example, play Water-Balloon Basketball: Set up a fairly small court, depending upon the number of players. Ten by twenty feet is good for six players. Place buckets at each end of the court to serve as baskets.

Instead of dribbling, throw the ball around as quickly as possible—only two steps are allowed when you have possession of the balloon. Two points are scored for each basket. If it is a really hot day and you have plenty of balloons, you might make it a three-pointer if you can burst the balloon at the same time that you score a basket.

Try Water-Balloon Newcomb: Stretch a string across the playing area and see how long you can pass the balloon across the net before breaking it.

Wink

WHERE TO PLAY
In an area large enough to contain a circle of chairs

NUMBER OF PLAYERS
15 is ideal. There must be an uneven number of players.

EQUIPMENT
1 chair for every 2 players, and another for "It"

OBJECT OF THE GAME
To change chairs when winked at before being caught by your partner

Arrange the chairs in a circle, leaving plenty of room between each chair and in the center of the circle. The players should arrange themselves around the circle with one player behind and one player seated in each chair. One chair will remain empty; this is "It's" chair.

"It" stands behind his or her chair and initiates the game by winking as secretively as possible at a seated player. The seated player must then jump up and try to get into the empty chair in front of "It" before being tagged by the person standing behind him or her (this player must act quickly to try to tag the winked-at player from his or her position as this player is not allowed to move from behind the chair).

If the winked-at player succeeds in reaching the new chair (without having been tagged), the abandoned partner with the empty chair becomes "It" and must wink at another seated player in order to find a new partner. If the winked-at player is tagged by his or her partner, he or she remains seated, and "It" must wink again.

Wrestling Games

WHERE TO PLAY
Arm Wrestling and Thumb Wrestling can be played anywhere. For Hand Wrestling and One-Legged Wrestling, an outdoor setting on soft, dry grass is preferable.

NUMBER OF PLAYERS
2 at a time

EQUIPMENT
None

OBJECT OF THE GAME
To defeat your opponent a demonstration of strength or balance

ARM WRESTLING

Arm Wrestling is most fun for players who are closely matched in strength.

The two players should be seated at a table across from one another. They place their right elbows on the table and clasp hands.

At a signal (or after counting to three), each player attempts to push the other's hand to the tabletop. The first player to touch his or her opponent's arm and hand to the table, while keeping elbows on the table, is the winner. Play a best-of-three series.

THUMB WRESTLING

Thumb Wrestling is a modified version of Arm Wrestling that can be played by any two people, regardless of arm strength.

(continued on next page)

Wrestling Games (*cont.*)

The two players set down their right hands perpendicular to the table, pinkies against the table and thumbs on top. They link hands by curving the fingers and forming a hook.

To begin the match, the players count to three while motioning with their thumbs: One (lift the thumb and put it back down), Two (lift the thumb, cross it over or under the other player's thumb, Three (touch the thumb back to its original position and then lift it to begin the attack). After the count of three, the match starts.

The object is to pin the opponent's thumb to his or her hand. Play a best-of-five or -seven series for Thumb Wrestling.

HAND WRESTLING

Hand Wrestling is like Arm Wrestling but uses the whole body.

The two players line up facing one other. They brace their right feet together in front of them and grasp right hands firmly. The left foot is placed far behind and planted firmly to provide balance.

At a signal, the players try to cause one another to lose balance. The player who first makes his or her opponent touch any part of the body, except the feet, to the ground is the winner.

ONE-LEGGED HAND WRESTLING

One-Legged Hand Wrestling is similar to Hand Wrestling, with an added difficulty: players are allowed to stand on only one leg.

The opponents face one another. Each holds the left leg behind by grasping the foot with the left hand and keeping the knee bent.

The players link right hands and try to disrupt one another's balance. The first player to cause the opponent to touch some part of the body other than the right foot to the ground, or force him or her to let go of the left leg, is the winner.

THREE

Games to Play on Pavement, Steps, and Stoops

Ball Punch

WHERE TO PLAY
Outdoors, on grass or pavement

NUMBER OF PLAYERS
At least 8

EQUIPMENT
A large rubber ball

OBJECT OF THE GAME
For "It" to punch the ball into the circle as it is passed from player to player

One player is elected to be "It." The others form a large circle facing inward, with three or four feet between players. "It" must remain outside the circle.

The player with the ball initiates the game by passing it quickly to the player directly on his or her left or right. The ball may not be passed across the circle or skip players in its movement around the circle.

"It" chases the ball as it moves around, trying to punch it into the center of the circle while it is between players. Players can use faking movements to fool "It" into running in the wrong direction.

If the ball falls to the ground, the last player to touch it may pick it up and start it moving again.

When "It" succeeds in punching the ball, the last player to touch it becomes the new "It."

Basketball Games

WHERE TO PLAY
Anywhere you find a basketball hoop: on a playground, in a park, or in your own driveway

NUMBER OF PLAYERS
2 or more

EQUIPMENT
A basketball; a hoop

OBJECT OF THE GAME
See "Variations"

In addition to regulation basketball, pick-up games, and one-on-one, there are many other basketball games that test ball-handling and shooting skills.

HORSE

Horse is probably the most famous of all the basketball shooting games. Two players decide between themselves which one will go first.

The game begins when the first shooter takes a shot from anywhere on the court. If he or she sinks it, the second player must attempt the same type of shot from the same location. Be it a hook shot from the right base line, or a long, long throw from half-court—if the first player makes it, the second player is challenged to match it.

If the second player makes the shot, the first shooter makes a different attempt. But if the second player misses, he or she is assigned an *H*.

When the first player misses a shot, the second player gets an opportunity to make a shot which must be imitated.

The privilege of the first shot passes back and forth between the two players as they make and miss baskets. The letters *H-O-R-S-E* are assigned to players as they miss successive shots.

The first player to collect *HORSE* loses the game.

AROUND THE WORLD

Players attempt to sink baskets from seven spots in a semicircular pattern around the hoop in Around the World. The player chosen to go first shoots from position one. If the ball goes in, the player goes on to the next position, and so forth, until he or she misses.

If a player misses, he or she will take up at the same position at the next turn, but for the time being, the ball goes to the second player, who begins at position one also.

(*continued on next page*)

Basketball Games (*cont.*)

The first player to make shots one through seven and then back (from seven through one) wins.

FOUL SHOOTING

Anyone who watches college basketball quickly learns that foul shots often mean the difference between a win and a loss. Foul Shooting contests simulate game-time pressure.

For a simple Foul Shooting game, each player takes twenty-one consecutive shots from the foul line. The other player is encouraged to distract the foul shooter verbally, as the crowd is apt to do in a game situation. The player to sink the most shots wins.

TWENTY-ONE

Twenty-One combines foul shooting with lay-up practice. One player stands at the foul line and takes a shot. The other waits underneath the boards. If the basket is good, the ball is returned to the foul shooter, who earns 2 points.

If the shot misses, the player beneath the hoop may rebound the ball and attempt a lay-up. If the ball goes in, he or she earns a point, and the players switch positions. But if the rebounder misses, the ball is passed back to the foul shooter.

The first player to reach 21 wins the game. However, 21 must be scored exactly. Therefore, a player at the foul line with 20 points will deliberately miss the shot, hoping to be able to score the winning point on a rebound after the other player's foul shot. The score of a player who goes over 21 is completely wiped out.

3-2-1

In 3-2-1, players also aim to score 21. The player selected to shoot first attempts to sink a foul shot. If it goes in, he or she scores 5 points, and the ball goes to the other player.

If the foul shot misses, the shooter rebounds it and must shoot from the site of the rebound. This shot, if made, earns 3 points, and the ball is given to the other player.

When the 3-pointer is missed, the shooter has one more rebound and shot, for 1 point. After all three shots have been taken, the other player takes a turn.

If a player has built up a point total and then misses three shots in a row in one turn, he or she loses all those points and must start again.

The first player to score 21 points wins the game. It is okay to go over 21.

GREEDY

Greedy is played with two players, each of whom has a basketball. One basketball should be marked with an *X* of masking tape in order to distinguish one ball from the other.

The two players begin shooting simultaneously. Each player may only shoot with his or her own ball—players shooting with the wrong ball are automatic losers.

The first player to score ten baskets is "greedy" and wins.

STEAL THE DRIBBLE

Ball-handling skills are tested in Steal the Dribble—no shooting is involved. Players take turns dribbling the ball from the foul line to a spot underneath the basket. The other (i.e., nondribbling) player serves as the defender and attempts to hit the ball away, steal it, or force a double dribble or walk.

A player who makes it from the foul line to the basket earns a point; a defender who forces an error also earns a point. Players alternate as dribbler and defender. The first to score 21 points is the winner.

Battleball

WHERE TO PLAY
On grass or pavement

NUMBER OF PLAYERS
10 or more

EQUIPMENT
A large rubber ball

OBJECT OF THE GAME
To be the first team to score 21 points by hitting members of the opposing team with the ball

---

Battleball is like a one-on-one game of **Dodge Ball,** though scored as a team competition.

Before beginning, mark out a playing field—a twenty-by-twenty-foot square is good for ten players—and place the ball in the center of the square.

One player should be designated as the referee. The remaining players are divided into two equal teams. Each team counts off consecutively so that every player has a number. The teams should line up in numerical order on opposite sides of the square.

(*continued on next page*)

Battleball (*cont.*)

The referee starts the game by calling a number. The two players from the opposing teams who share that number sprint for the ball at the centerof the square.

The first player to reach the ball must remain in the center of the square, while the other is allowed to roam around the rest of the square.

The player with the ball tries to hit his or her opponent with the ball. If he or she is successful, or if the other player steps outside the square while trying to dodge the ball, the thrower's team gains a point. (Players should be reminded not to get carried away and throw the ball too hard.)

If the player at whom the ball is thrown catches it, a point is scored for his or her team.

If the ball misses the player at whom it was thrown, no point is scored.

If the ball bounces before going out of the square or touching the player at whom it was thrown, that player can throw it back if he or she can gain control of it before it leaves the square.

Play progresses when the referee calls a new number.

The first team to score 21 points wins.

Beanbag Toss

WHERE TO PLAY
Outdoors on pavement or indoors, if space permits

NUMBER OF PLAYERS
2 or more

EQUIPMENT
At least 1 beanbag; paper, pen, and tape to make an indoor target, or chalk to mark an outdoor target; paper and pencil for scorekeeping

OBJECT OF THE GAME
To score the most points by throwing your beanbag onto the target

If you are going to play indoors, draw a target on a large sheet of paper and tape it to the floor; if outdoors, mark the target on the pavement with chalk. Here are a few suggestions for target designs:

One at a time, the players take turns tossing the beanbag onto the target. Only beanbags that are completely within a marked space can earn points.

Scoring can be done in a variety of ways. One method is to establish a number of players to reach by adding up the points from tosses—for example, the first player to reach 200 points wins. To make it more difficult, the player could be required to total exactly 200 points. Alternatively, the player to score the highest total in a given number of tosses is the winner.

For a more intricate game, play Beanbag Toss like darts: players aim to hit each number and the bull's eye three times in order to win the game.

Alternate designs for targets.

Bombardment

WHERE TO PLAY
On pavement or grass

NUMBER OF PLAYERS
At least 10

EQUIPMENT
A rubber playground ball

OBJECT OF THE GAME
To eliminate the opposing team by hitting its members with the ball

Delineate a playing field for Bombardment, about thirty by thirty feet for ten players. Divide the court into two equal halves.

Form two teams, each one located in one half of the field. Select a team to throw the first ball.

As in **Dodge Ball,** players throw the ball at the other team, attempting to strike opponents and "get them out" or catch thrown balls in order to put the thrower out. And as in all games involving hitting players with the ball, players should be reminded not to throw the ball too hard.

Like Prison Dodge Ball (see **Dodge Ball**), a player who is hit must leave the court. In this game, however, that player goes to stand behind the opposite team's base line. From this position, players may attempt to catch balls thrown by their own teammates that were missed or dodged by the "enemy."

A player who catches one of his or her own teammate's throws may rejoin the team. Savvy players will throw balls directly at their teammates behind enemy lines if they think they can avoid interception. The first team to eliminate the opposing team wins the game.

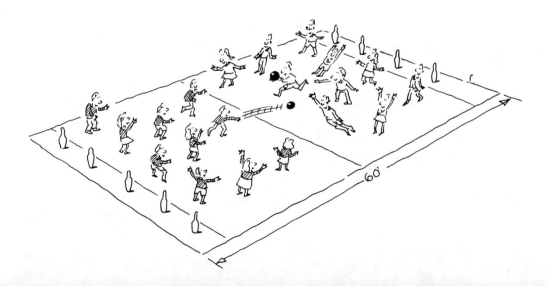

VARIATION

Bombardment can also be played with eight to ten Indian clubs or pins from a toy bowling set. Instead of sending hit players behind enemy lines, the clubs or pins are placed in this area.

Each team tries to knock over the pins behind the opposing team rather than hit the players. Players attempt to defend their own pins at the same time.

The game can be played with more than one ball at a time if so desired. The ball may be passed or dribbled between players to distract the other team. The first team to knock down all the other team's pins wins.

Bounce Ball

WHERE TO PLAY
On pavement

NUMBER OF PLAYERS
At least 4

EQUIPMENT
A tennis ball; chalk

OBJECT OF THE GAME
To get your opponents out by hitting them with a ball, which must bounce once before making contact

The boundaries of the play area are important for Bounce Ball. Lines should be marked with chalk on pavement to form a rectangle or square. The size of the play area depends on the number of players—for four players, sides of about thirty feet will serve well. Enlarge the play area if more players are involved.

Players step into the rectangle. Bounce Ball is started when one player throws the tennis ball high into the air. The first player to gain control of the ball attempts to get another player out by bouncing it toward him or her.

If the ball hits that player after bouncing once, the hit player is eliminated. Players are free to run to avoid the ball, but they must not step outside the boundaries of the play area.

If the ball completely misses all other players before bouncing again, anyone may grab it and try the next bounce.

(*continued on next page*)

Bounce Ball (*cont.*)

If the ball is thrown and hits a player without bouncing, both the player who was hit and the player who threw the ball are out. To begin play again, one of the eliminated players should toss the ball into the air.

The last player remaining in the game is the winner.

VARIATION

Bounce Ball is slightly different when played with a volleyball-sized ball rather than a tennis ball. Instead of being free to run away from the ball, once one player gains control of the ball, all the others must freeze in place. Players are allowed to pivot on one foot in order to avoid being hit, but anyone moving the pivot foot is also eliminated.

Circle Dodge Ball

WHERE TO PLAY
Outdoors, on pavement or grass

NUMBER OF PLAYERS
At least 10

EQUIPMENT
A rubber playground ball

OBJECT OF THE GAME
To be the last player remaining in the center of the circle who has not been hit by the ball

Divide the players into two teams. One team forms a loose circle, while the other team spreads out within this circle.

The players on the circle's edge throw the ball at the players in the center, who dodge to avoid being hit. Unlike other versions of **Dodge Ball,** in this game players *may not catch the ball.*

If the ball stops moving within the circle, it may be rolled out by one of the center players without penalty. When more than one player is hit by the same throw, only the first to be hit is out.

Players who are hit join the circle and become throwers. The last remaining player in the circle wins the game.

For the next round, the players who originally formed the outer circle become the center group, and the original center players become the circle of throwers.

Cross-Over Dodge Ball

WHERE TO PLAY
On a playground or in a park or backyard

NUMBER OF PLAYERS
At least 10

EQUIPMENT
4 playground balls for every 10 players

OBJECT OF THE GAME
To get all players on one side

This is like regular **Dodge Ball,** but in this variation, no one gets eliminated.

(continued on next page)

Cross-Over Dodge Ball (*cont.*)

Players are divided into two equal teams, and the balls are divided between the teams. When a player is hit with a ball, he or she must quickly cross the center line to join the other team. The game involves more constant motion than regular **Dodge Ball.** Eventually, all the players should end up on one side.

Danish Rounders

WHERE TO PLAY
On a playground, in an area about half the size of a tennis court

---

NUMBER OF PLAYERS
At least 8

EQUIPMENT
A tennis ball; a piece of chalk

OBJECT OF THE GAME
To score runs in a simplified game of baseball

Designate a playing area by drawing with chalk a square about half the size of a tennis court (fifteen to twenty feet). In the corners of the square, draw boxes (about three feet on each side), to represent bases like those in a traditional baseball diamond. Make a circle in the center of the playing area (about four feet in diameter) to serve as the pitcher's mound.

The players should be divided into two equal teams and the first team to hit determined. The fielding team places one player on the pitcher's mound and one behind home plate. The other players should scatter evenly around the play area, for everyone is an outfielder; there are no base players. The first player from the hitting team steps up to home plate, also known as the hitter's box. The pitcher throws the tennis ball above the head of the "batter," who must hit it with one hand and then run to the first square. Hitters get one chance to hit a pitch successfully. Even if they are unsuccessful in hitting, or if the pitch is bad, they run to the first square.

The fielders try to catch the ball and get it back to the pitcher as quickly as possible. The pitcher, upon receiving the ball, touches it to the ground inside the pitcher's circle and calls, "Down!"

Any runner who is not on a square when the ball is "down" is out. If the ball is caught in the air before bouncing, the hitter is also out, and any other players running between squares are out. Each inning, as in base-

PITCHERS MOUND

HOME PLATE

ball, is made up of three outs, after which the batting and fielding teams exchange places.

When a player succeeds in running around all four squares, a run is scored.

There is no limit to the number of players who may be in a square at one time, and running does not have to occur in consecutive order. Players don't have to run every time the ball is hit, but they must also remember that they can't score any runs if they refuse to move from a safe base.

After all the players have been to the bases once, batting order is determined by the order in which players returned to home, regardless of whether this was the result of a run or an out.

If there is only one player left waiting to bat, he or she may have three separate tries at hitting, in hopes that another player will either score a run or be put out, and therefore be able to bat again. The batter must run to the first square each time and can be put out.

The team with the most runs after a predetermined number of innings wins. Danish Rounders can also be played for individual points, coming to an end after a designated time period.

Dodge Ball

WHERE TO PLAY

On grass or pavement

NUMBER OF PLAYERS

At least 10; large groups are the most fun

EQUIPMENT

A rubber playground ball

OBJECT OF THE GAME

To get all your opponents out by hitting them with the ball

Define the Dodge Ball court by making a square, about thirty by thirty feet, depending on the number of players. Divide the court into two halves with a center line.

Form two equal teams and choose which one will throw the first ball. Each team takes position on opposite sides of the court.

One of the players from the team elected to go first starts the game by throwing the ball at a player on the opposing team. If the ball hits a player who fails to catch it, the hit player is out and must leave the court.

If the player catches the ball, the thrower is out of the game, and the catcher throws it back across the center line, trying to hit an opponent.

After the ball hits a player or bounces without being caught or hitting anyone, the first player to get to it throws it again.

Anyone stepping over the center line or out of bounds while trying to dodge the ball is out.

The first team to eliminate all its opponents wins.

PRISON DODGE BALL

Prison Dodge Ball takes longer than regular Dodge Ball and may have to be decided by stopping the game and counting to see who has the greatest number of players left. It has the advantage of keeping players sent outside the court interested in the game, since at any moment they may be called back in.

Play proceeds in Prison Dodge Ball as in regular Dodge Ball, except that when a player is out, he or she joins a line of players at the side of the court waiting to return to the game.

When a player catches a ball, not only is the thrower out, but the catcher's first teammate in line on the sidelines is allowed to rejoin his or her team.

Prison Dodge Ball is best with twenty or more players. Using two or three balls at a time keeps the players moving quickly in and out of the game.

Errors

WHERE TO PLAY

Outdoors, on pavement

NUMBER OF PLAYERS

2 at a time

EQUIPMENT

A rubber playground ball

OBJECT OF THE GAME

To field the ball with as few errors as possible

Errors is an adaptation of fielding drills for baseball players, with a scoring system added.

The two players stand about twenty or thirty feet apart. They take turns rolling the ball to one another. The fielder must pick up the ball as quickly and cleanly as possible and roll it immediately back to the thrower, as if trying to get a runner out.

A player making a fielding error or a bad roll back to his or her opponent is given 1 point. The first player to score 21 points loses.

Since the game is scored for errors, players will often do what they can to force their opponents into making fielding mistakes. They will throw the ball hard, put a spin on it, and even try curve balls and sliders if they have some familiarity with different baseball pitches.

Firing-Squad Dodge Ball

WHERE TO PLAY

Against a wall—find one without windows

NUMBER OF PLAYERS

10 or more

EQUIPMENT

A rubber playground ball; chalk

OBJECT OF THE GAME

To eliminate all the players on the other team by striking them with the ball, or catching balls thrown

Divide the players into two equal teams. The team serving as the firing squad lines up facing the wall, about fifteen feet in front of it.

(*continued on next page*)

Firing-Squad Dodge Ball (*cont.*)

The other team stands a couple of feet in front of the wall, facing out, with two or three feet between players. Mark boundaries two or three feet from the players on each end of the line against the wall so players may not move too far out of the line of fire while dodging the ball.

Members of the firing squad take turns throwing the ball at the players against the wall. When a player against the wall is hit, he or she must leave the game. If a player against the wall catches a ball, the thrower is out.

The team with the last remaining player wins. After the first round, the teams should switch places.

Four Square

WHERE TO PLAY
On pavement

NUMBER OF PLAYERS
4 at a time. More can substitute in, if desired.

EQUIPMENT
A rubber playground ball; chalk

OBJECT OF THE GAME
To progress to the server's square and remain there as long as possible

Four Square is an expanded version of **Two Square:** more players, a bigger ball, and a larger court.

Mark out a square for the court with chalk. The size of the court depends on the ages and skill levels of the players, ranging from eight by eight feet for elementary-school players to sixteen by sixteen feet for junior high students. Divide the court into four equal squares and label them *A, B, C,* and *D. A* is the server's square, and a diagonal serving line can be drawn across that square if desired.

One player stands in the far corner of each square in order to be best prepared for any ball hit to them. In which square the players begin can be decided fairly by counting off or drawing lots, but more likely, someone will call, "Four Square!" and the first four players into the court will start the game where they choose.

The server initiates the game by bouncing it once behind the serving line and then batting it with an open hand into one of the other squares.

The player receiving the serve must let it bounce once and then hit it

into another square. Any balls that land on lines or leave the court are considered to be out.

When a player commits a fault (steps over the line while serving, misses a serve, hits a line, hits a ball out of bounds, fails to return a hit, uses a fist or an overhand motion to hit the ball, or is hit by the ball on any part of the body except the hands), the players shift around the diagram.

If the server (A), is at fault, he or she moves to square D, D moves to C, C moves to B, and B becomes the next server. The idea is to move up a square after each fault and eventually reach the server's box.

When there are more than four players, the one who commits a fault leaves the court and joins the line of players waiting to get back into the game. A player from the line moves into square D, and the other four players move up one square.

If there are only four players, the one who committed a fault moves to square D, and the others rotate to fill in empty squares.

There isn't really a winner in Four Square—the players keep rotating until they grow tired of the game or (more likely) they have to leave. The most proficient players are rewarded with the greatest amount of playing time since they make the fewest mistakes.

Four Square is also called Beggar, Jack, Queen, King. Instead of labeling the squares A, B, C, and D, they are marked B, J, Q, and K. The King serves, and players move from Beggar to King as quickly as possible.

Fox and Geese

WHERE TO PLAY
On a large paved playing area

NUMBER OF PLAYERS
At least 4

EQUIPMENT
A piece of chalk

OBJECT OF THE GAME
To play a game of tag while remaining on the designated lines of a diagram drawn on the pavement

---

To prepare for the game, draw a large circle (twenty to fifty feet in diameter, depending on the number of players and space available) on the pavement. Divide the circle into eight sections, like pieces of pie.

One player is chosen to be "It." To begin the game, "It" stands at the center of the circle and the players line up on the circle's outer edge.

As in **Tag,** upon the signal given by "It," the players run to avoid being tagged. However, all players, including "It," may only run along the lines drawn on the pavement. A player becomes the new "It" when tagged or if he or she runs *off* the lines.

Fox and Geese makes a great winter game for children in snowbelt areas. Simply mark off the paths of the circle by stamping the snow down. In the snowy state of Minnesota, this game is called Cut the Pie. Fox and Geese is also known as Wheel Tag.

German

WHERE TO PLAY
On a sidewalk, against a wall or stoop

NUMBER OF PLAYERS
4 to 6

EQUIPMENT
A small, hard rubber ball (like the balls used for handball, racquetball or tennis); chalk

OBJECT OF THE GAME
To score runs by throwing the ball against a wall

Draw a court for German on the sidewalk or pavement with chalk. The court should border against a playable wall and be about four feet wide and twenty feet long, and divided into five boxes.

The box closest to the wall is the batter's box. Moving toward the end of the court, the boxes represent baseball hits: single, double, triple, and home run.

(*continued on next page*)

German (*cont.*)

The players form two equal teams, two or three on a side. One team is designated to bat first and the other to field. The fielding team takes position in the boxes. If there are three team members, one stands in each of the single, double, and triple boxes. If there are only two, one stands between single and double, and the other between triple and home run.

Play begins when the first batter steps into the batting box and tosses the ball against the wall. The fielders must attempt to catch the ball, but only after it bounces at least once.

The value of the hit is determined according to which fielder gains control of the ball—if the first catches it, the hit is a single, the second, a double, and the third, a triple. If the ball gets past all the fielders, the batter earns a home run.

As in baseball, players are advanced (move from base to base) and score according to hits of the following batters. If the first player has hit a single, a double by the second batter will advance the first to third base, and a single by the next hitter will score a run. If the batter up is on base, he or she may leave the base to hit, but must keep track of how he or she would be advanced and score as though still on base.

There are no outs in German—an inning is over after all the players on both teams have had two times at bat.

The team with the greatest number of runs after a predetermined number of innings wins the game.

Goal Kickers

WHERE TO PLAY
On a playground

NUMBER OF PLAYERS
4 to 6 players per team

EQUIPMENT
A rubber playground ball; chalk

OBJECT OF THE GAME
To score goals by kicking the ball through the opponents' territory

Divide the players into two equal teams and select a captain for each team.

Outline the playing area by drawing a rectangle in chalk on the pavement. The size of the playing area depends on the number and ages of the players (half the size of a tennis court—fifteen to twenty feet—is best for elementary players). Split the rectangular court into two halves by drawing a line across the center. The two back boundaries serve as goal lines.

A basketball-style tip-off begins Goal Kickers. Each team spreads out over one half of the court. A player tosses the ball up between the captains, who jump to control it with a tap. The ball can be tapped forward or backward, but after the tip-off, the ball may only be controlled with the feet.

Players try to kick the ball through their opponents' half of the court and over their goal line in order to score. The team to score more points within a given time period, or to reach a certain goal total first, wins.

Greek Ball Game

WHERE TO PLAY
On a paved parking area

NUMBER OF PLAYERS
10 or more

EQUIPMENT
A rubber playground ball and a piece of chalk

OBJECT OF THE GAME
To be the first to reach the ball in the center of the court and throw it over the base line of the other team

Designate a square playing area by drawing its sides with chalk, if possible. The size of the area depends on the number of players. For a game with ten players, a square of about fifteen feet on each side is needed. The size of the playing area should also be determined by the throwing abilities and ages of the players.

Divide the players into two equal teams. The teams line up evenly along two opposite sides of the square. The ball is placed in the center of the court. One player from each team is chosen to be the first runner. These two players stand in opposite corners of the square.

When a signal is given, the two runners sprint to the center of the play area in order to grab the ball. The player who gets to the ball first picks it up and attempts to throw it over the base line of the opposing team.

If the runner succeeds in getting the ball over the base line, his or her team gains a point. The other team may try to prevent the ball from going over by catching it or bumping it. If the runner's first throw isn't success-

ful, the ball is kept in play, with both sides trying to get the ball over the other team's base line.

When one team succeeds in throwing the ball over the opposing team's base line, the game is set up again. The original runners go to the end of the line, and two new players become runners.

The game is scored by striving for a predetermined point total or by adding up the total number of points made by each team after all the players have had the chance to be runners.

Handball

WHERE TO PLAY
On pavement, against a wall

NUMBER OF PLAYERS
2 or 4 at a time

EQUIPMENT
A hardball or tennis ball; chalk if you need to mark your own court

OBJECT OF THE GAME
To score points in a game like tennis, except that the ball is hit against a wall rather than over a net

Many urban playgrounds feature walls built just for Handball. The game can also be played against any wall adjacent to a paved surface, as long as there is no danger of breaking windows.

A regulation handball court is twenty feet wide and thirty-four feet deep, with a serving line sixteen feet from the wall. This size can be adjusted according to the space available if you are marking your own court with chalk.

For singles play, determine which player will serve first. Both players stand in the middle of the court, facing the wall. The server initiates the game by bouncing the ball once against the pavement and hitting it, when it comes up, at the wall. The ball must bounce back out over the serving line to be considered good. The server has two tries to make a good serve.

The other player tries to hit the served ball back against the wall. The ball can be hit after one bounce or while still on the fly.

The ball is hit back and forth continuously between players until one fails to hit it, or hits it over the wall or out of bounds. If the receiver makes the mistake, the server scores a point. But if the server makes the error, the serve goes to the other player. Players can only score points when they

(*continued on next page*)

Handball (*cont.*)

are serving. Sometimes one player will get in the way of the other as he or she goes for the ball. This is a foul and means that the serve must be repeated if the receiver committed the foul, or that the serve will go to the receiver if it was the server's error.

The first player to score 21 points is the winner.

Doubles play is basically the same. Only the partner closest to the ball may return it. Only the serving partner may be in the court while serving, but his or her partner may run back in as soon as the serve is hit.

Handball Tennis

WHERE TO PLAY
On pavement

NUMBER OF PLAYERS
8 or more

EQUIPMENT
A handball or tennis ball; chalk

OBJECT OF THE GAME
To score the most points in a game resembling tennis but played without rackets

Establish the boundaries of a court, about fifty by twenty-five feet, with chalk. Draw a dividing line through the center of the court.

Divide the players into two equal teams. Each team should then count

out, to determine the order in which players will serve. The teams spread out over opposite sides of the court.

The team elected to go first serves the ball from any point on its half of the court. The server bounces the ball once, then hits it with the palm into the other side of the court.

The other team should attempt to return the ball by bouncing it back over the center line by hitting it with the palm. The ball may bounce more than once before being returned to the other court.

The ball is still in play as long as it is bouncing. If the ball stops or goes out of bounds in the receiver's court, a point is scored by the serving team. If it stops or goes out in the server's court, the serve is given over to the receiving team.

The first team to score 21 points wins the game.

THE MARKER

Hopscotch

WHERE TO PLAY
On pavement

NUMBER OF PLAYERS
2 or more

EQUIPMENT
Chalk; a marker for each player (a stone, a bottle cap, etc.)

OBJECT OF THE GAME
To hop through a diagram drawn on pavement, stepping on as few lines as possible

There are as many Hopscotch diagrams and sets of rules as there are cities and countries where the game is played! Below is but a small sampling of the many varieties.

(*continued on next page*)

Hopscotch (*cont.*)

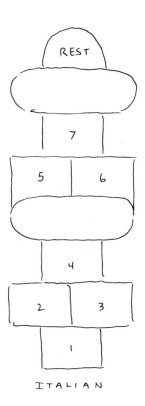

ITALIAN

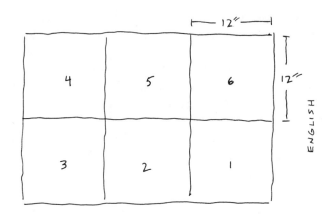

ENGLISH

For a basic game, mark the diagram (see American Hopscotch) on the pavement in chalk and determine the order of players.

The first player stands outside the court and tosses a marker into the space labeled *1*. The marker must land completely within the intended space—if it touches any lines, the player forfeits a turn.

When the marker lands correctly, the player hops into the diagram. When there are two spaces side by side, the player straddles them, one foot on each side. For single spaces, the player hops on one foot.

In the court shown in illustration #1, the player would hop through, straddling *1* and *2,* landing on one foot on *3,* straddling *4* and *5,* and landing on one foot in spaces *6* through *10.* After *10,* he or she would then work backward through the diagram, stopping to pick up the marker on the way back.

The rest of the players would follow, all trying to get through all the spaces without stepping on any lines. Stepping on a line sends you back to the beginning to repeat that space.

When all the players have had a turn, the first player now throws the marker into space *2* and hops through the diagram accordingly.

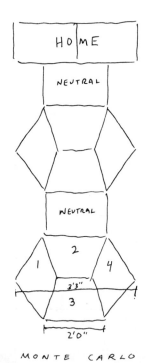

MONTE CARLO

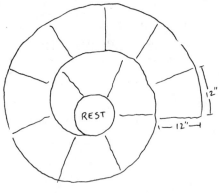

SNAIL

The first player to navigate all the spaces successfully wins the game.

For any diagram that contains rest spaces, a player may land in these spaces with two feet (for example see Italian Hopscotch).

In some versions, players must jump *over* the space in which the marker rests, and in another variety, the marker is *kicked* through the court rather than tossed.

Once the players have been through the court once, another round is begun. Every time a player gets through the court successfully, he or she initials the space in which the marker rests. Other players may no longer step in that space, but the player to whom it belongs may stand in it on both feet.

For English Hopscotch (see illustration), the player must hold the marker between the feet while jumping through the diagram. Only one jump is permitted to reach a space.

Hunter and Rabbits

WHERE TO PLAY
On pavement, in a playground or on a driveway

NUMBER OF PLAYERS
At least 8

EQUIPMENT
A rubber playground ball

OBJECT OF THE GAME
To avoid being hit with the ball by a "hunter" if you are a "rabbit"

Basic boundaries for the playing field should be established so that the rabbits cannot run too far from the hunter. One player is elected to be the first "hunter," while all the others are "rabbits." The hunter has the ball.

At a starting signal, the hunter tries to hit rabbits with the ball as they run. Hunters should only throw the ball gently at the rabbits. The hunter is allowed to move toward the rabbits, but only while bouncing the ball (like dribbling in basketball). Rabbits are allowed to deflect shots with their hands and forearms, thereby avoiding a real "hit," so the hunter should try to fake out the rabbits as much as possible.

When the hunter succeeds in hitting a rabbit with the ball, that rabbit becomes a hunter. When there is more than one hunter, they may no longer dribble the ball but instead must pass it to one another in order to get near the rabbits.

Eventually, all players but one will be hunters. The lone surviving rabbit is the winner.

Jacks

WHERE TO PLAY
Outdoors, on smooth and flat pavement, or indoors, on a smooth floor

NUMBER OF PLAYERS
1 or 2 at a time

EQUIPMENT
A jacks set (jacks and a ball)

OBJECT OF THE GAME
To bounce the ball and pick up jacks according to the rules of the various Jacks games

Jacks players grow proficient by practicing alone, then hone their skills by competing with others.

Games begin with a flip of the jacks to see who goes first. Each player takes the jacks in one hand, throws them a few inches into the air, flips over the hand, and tries to catch as many on the back of the hand as possible. The player to catch the most gets to go first.

The simplest Jacks game involves picking the jacks up in series, adding one jack with every bounce. The first player scatters the jacks on the ground or floor. Then, he or she tosses the ball into the air, picks up one jack, and catches the ball after one bounce.

He or she then bounces the ball again, picks up another jack (keeping the first one in the hand), lets the ball bounce once, and catches another jack, continuing in this way until all the jacks have been scooped up. When a player misses a jack or the ball, his or her turn is over, and the other player begins.

For added difficulty, players can pick up two jacks at a time on the second throw, three at a time on the third, and so forth.

Another version of the basic game involves successfully picking up jacks as prescribed by the guidelines of the round number (onesies, twosies, threesies, foursies, etc.) For example, in onesies, players pick up one jack at a time, with one toss, bounce, and catch of the ball. After successfully picking up all ten (one by one) while making sure not to touch any other jacks in the pick-up motion, the player moves on to twosies. In this round, the player picks up jacks two by two until all ten have been scooped up. In any round with leftover jacks, players should pick them up in one final scoop.

As long as the player continues to pick up the jacks without moving any neighboring jacks, or dropping the ball or any jacks, he or she may continue through each successive level. The first player to make it successfully through tensies—picking up all ten jacks at once—wins!

Sweeps is similar to the basic game, but instead of picking up the jacks, the players sweep them close to the body.

In Eggs in the Basket, players toss the ball, pick up a jack, then put it into the left hand before catching the ball.

In Flying Dutchman, the player throws the ball, picks up a jack, catches the ball then tosses it again, throws the jack from one hand to the other, and catches the ball after only one bounce. This is one of the most difficult Jacks games. Play progresses through rounds of onesies, twosies, threesies, etc.

In Double Bounce, players let the ball bounce twice before catching it.

Crack the Eggs requires players to "crack" or tap each jack on the ground with the right hand before putting it in the left hand.

Jump Rope

WHERE TO PLAY
Outdoors, on pavement

NUMBER OF PLAYERS
At least 3

EQUIPMENT
A jump rope (approximately 12 feet long)

OBJECT OF THE GAME
To jump over the turning rope while performing stunts or reciting rhymes, without making an error

In the most basic form of Jump Rope, two players hold opposite ends of the rope and spin it in a big circle, while a third player stands between them and jumps over the rope as it swings underfoot.

When played competitively, the players often count the number of completed jumps. When a player misses a jump, he or she becomes a turner, and a new jumper begins.

More advanced jumpers can try other stunts:

- Use a double hop (a second jump added while the rope is still overhead). It requires a steadier rhythm but can be maintained longer than the single hop.
- Jump on one foot, and then the other.

(*continued on next page*)

Jump Rope (*cont.*)

- Jump very high, while the turners spin the rope fast enough to pass twice under the jumper's feet before he or she lands.
- Jump while rocking: place one foot ahead of the other, jumping first on the front foot and then on the back foot.
- Jump while bouncing a ball at the same time; this is known as Rock the Boat.
- Play Salt and Pepper: the turners alternate spinning tempos, turning the rope slowly (Salt), then speeding it up (Pepper), and so on.
- After jumping, set a stick or stone onto the ground, then pick it back up after the next jump, set it back down again, and so forth.

Jump Rope rhymes are also very popular. Rhymes help players keep rhythm, start their jump counts, describe stunts to be performed, and are even used to predict the future.

Simple counting rhymes often go like this:

Cookies, candy in the dish;
How many pieces do you wish?
1-2-3-4 . . .

Prediction games usually involve a love interest:

Ice cream soda, lemonade, punch;
Spell the initials of my [your] honey bunch.
A-B-C-D . . .

The initial on which the player misses is considered to predict the first initial of the jumper's sweetheart. The rhyme is repeated to discover the last initial.

Another rhyme resembles "He loves me, he loves me not":

One I love, Two I love,
Three I love I say;
Four I love with all my heart,
Five I cast away;
Six he loves, Seven she loves,
Eight both love;
Nine he comes, Ten he tarries,
Eleven he courts, Twelve he marries.

The number on which the player misses reveals the true state of the romance!

Some rhymes are used to introduce stunts. In "Policeman, Policeman," the jumper is given the opportunity to invent a stunt after reciting the last line and before jumping out:

Policeman, policeman, do your duty,
Here comes [the name of the next jumper]
And she's a cutie;
She can jump, she can twist,
But I bet she can't do this.

To make it more difficult, have the next jumper repeat the stunt before going on to his or her own invention.

Another stunt favorite is "Teddy Bear":

Teddy bear, teddy bear, turn around [player turns around],
Teddy bear, teddy bear, touch the ground [player touches ground],
Teddy bear, teddy bear, tie your shoes [player touches shoe]
Teddy bear, teddy bear, read the news [player imitates reading paper].
Teddy bear, teddy bear, go upstairs [player lifts knees high as if climbing stairs],
Teddy bear, teddy bear, say your prayers [player puts hands together in an attitude of prayer],
Teddy bear, teddy bear, turn out the light [player reaches up to click off the light],
Teddy bear, teddy bear, say good night! [player says good night and jumps out].

(More verses can be added to "Teddy Bear.")

A Jump Rope game that requires and thinking and jumping at the same time is " 'A' My Name Is . . ." The first jumper begins with *A:*

A, my name is *Alfred*,
My wife's name is *Angela*,
We grow *artichokes*
In *Atlanta*.

The next jumper begins with *"B*, my name is *Brenda*," and so on. The jumpers alternate with letters. When players make mistakes, they are eliminated. The last remaining jumper is the winner.

London

WHERE TO PLAY

On pavement

NUMBER OF PLAYERS

2 or more

EQUIPMENT

A marker for each player (a small, smooth stone, a bottle cap, a checker, etc.); chalk

---

OBJECT OF THE GAME

To be the first to draw three men in one square of the London board

Draw a London diagram on the pavement with chalk. The board should be about three feet across and five feet deep and should be divided into seven steps. At the "top" of the diagram, add a curved line to top it off and label the space within this line *London*.

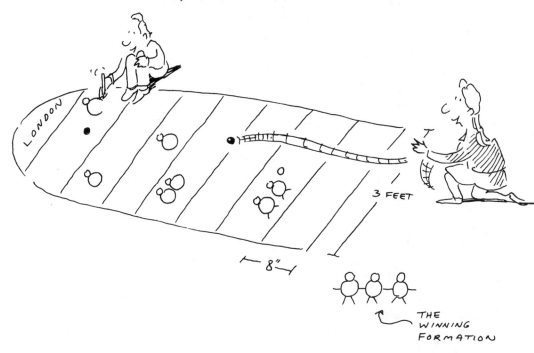

THE WINNING FORMATION

The first player stands at the other end of the diagram and slides a marker into the board. He or she must draw a man's head in the space in which the marker has come to rest. Players should write their initial in the circle that represents the head in order to keep everyone's men separate.

The other players each take a turn, drawing heads in the spaces in which their markers land. More than one player may have a head in one space. Players are allowed to add to their own men only. If a marker comes to rest on a line, the player is not allowed to draw in that turn.

In following rounds, if a player's marker lands in a space in which he or she has already drawn a head, he or she may add a body to that head. With succeeding turns, he or she will draw one leg, and then another leg.

When the marker comes to rest in a space in which he or she has not yet drawn a head, one must be added. If the marker lands in the space marked *London* at any time, that player is allowed to draw one head in every space or add the next appropriate mark to a man already started in each space.

When a player completes a man in one space, he or she begins on a new man next to the first. At the point where a player has three men in one space, complete except for arms, he or she concentrates on landing the marker in that space once more.

Upon putting the marker in the right space, the player can draw a straight line through all three men, adding their arms, linking them together, and winning the game.

Marbles

WHERE TO PLAY

On a paved surface or a patch of hard dirt, neither of which should be perfectly smooth: the more bumps and ridges, the more challenging!

NUMBER OF PLAYERS

2 or more

EQUIPMENT

Marbles

OBJECT OF THE GAME

To "win" marbles from your opponents by hitting their marbles in various ways

In their heyday, marbles were fantastically made and colored—players could easily identify their own by their distinctive markings. Today's marbles are usually mass-produced and are difficult to distinguish. To avoid

(*continued on next page*)

Marbles (*cont.*)

arguments, if you're playing for keeps, make sure everyone understands that provision before the game begins.

If you don't want to play for keeps, make sure everyone can identify their own marbles. Or, if they are similar enough so that it doesn't matter who gets which marbles, make sure everyone remembers how many they brought into the game.

Traditionally, the most frequently used types of marbles are *alleys* (small stone or glass balls) and *taws* or *shooters* (much larger balls, usually made of stone). If you don't have a real shooter, you can pick out any of your other marbles to use as one.

RING GAME

A basic marble game is played by drawing a large circle (about two to three feet across). Each player places the same number of marbles (four to six) anywhere within the circle.

One at a time, the players pitch their shooters in from outside the circle, attempting to knock the interior marbles out of the circle. A player is allowed to keep any marbles knocked out of the circle. Depending on the age or skill level of the players, shooters can either be rolled or pitched. A marble is pitched when it is resting between the thumb nail and index finger and the thumb flicks it out of its resting position.

He or she should try to make sure that the shooter rolls out of the circle, for any shooter that stops within it may be hit by another player. Any

player who hits another player's shooter when it is inside the circle may claim all the alleys won by that player up to that point in the game.

A player continues with a turn until he or she fails to hit a marble to the outside of the circle. Play resumes with the next person.

The player with the most marbles when all have been hit out of the circle is the winner.

In another version of the Ring Game, a smaller circle (about six inches across) is inscribed inside the large circle.

Each player puts the same number of marbles (four to six) inside the smaller circle. One at a time, the players take their shooters and aim at the marbles in the small circle, trying to knock them outside the outer circle.

In this game, the shooter must remain inside the large (outer) circle. A player continues a turn as long as he or she continues hitting marbles outside the circle, with the shooter remaining inside the larger circle, taking shots from the spot at which the shooter has stopped.

The turn goes on to the next player when a player fails to hit a marble outside the circle, or when his or her shooter leaves the circle.

The player with the most marbles at the end of the game is the winner.

PYRAMID GAME

A smaller circle, about a foot across, is drawn for the Pyramid or Castle game. The first player places three marbles together to form a base and one marble on top of them to make a pyramid.

The next player is allowed to take a shot at the pyramid in order to knock it down. If successful, he or she collects all the marbles from the pyramid. (To make the game more difficult, allow the shooter to take only those marbles that roll outside the circle.)

If the shooter fails to knock down the pyramid, however, the pyramid "builder" claims one of the shooter's marbles.

The shooter then sets up a new pyramid for the next player. The player who collects all the marbles is the winner.

SHOOTING GALLERY GAME

For Shooting Gallery, a straight line two or three feet long is marked in the dirt. The first player shoots one marble over the line.

The next player tries to hit that marble with his or her own, shooting from behind the line. If the marble is hit, that player claims both marbles. If the shot is a miss, the player forfeits his or her marble, and the next player may shoot at either marble.

The player to collect the most marbles wins.

Monkey in the Middle

WHERE TO PLAY
Outdoors

NUMBER OF PLAYERS
3 at a time

EQUIPMENT
A rubber playground ball

OBJECT OF THE GAME
For 2 players to throw the ball back and forth without being
intercepted by the third player

One player is designated as the "monkey" and stands between the other
two players, who are lined up about ten feet apart.

The two outside players toss the ball to one another, over and around
the monkey. They keep the ball going back and forth until the monkey
intercepts it, or gets ahold of it after one of the players has dropped it.

Children often add their own commentary by yelling, "Monkey, monkey!" and, "Monkey in the middle!"

The player who last throws the ball before the monkey catches it, or the
player who drops the ball, must change places with the monkey. No one
really wins or loses this game—it will probably keep going until a frustrated monkey finally quits. If after a set amount of time (two minutes or
so) the same monkey is still in the middle, one of the players should
switch positions so the game isn't so one-sided.

(This game is also known as Keep Away when there are more than two
people doing the "keeping away.")

Mother, May I?

WHERE TO PLAY
In a driveway, on a playground, or on a sidewalk, depending on the
number of players

NUMBER OF PLAYERS
4 or more

EQUIPMENT
None

OBJECT OF THE GAME
To follow "Mother's" directions in order to reach her at the finish line

Choose a player to serve as "Mother" and designate start and finish lines, about twenty-five feet apart.

The player selected to be Mother stands at the finish line. The others line up at the start. One at a time, the players suggest how they would like to move toward Mother, and Mother tells the players how they may move.

For example, Johnny asks, "Mother, may I take two giant steps?" Mother may respond, "No, Johnny, but you may take five baby steps."

Johnny must then ask, "Mother, may I?" If Mother replies, "Yes, you may," Johnny is allowed to take five small steps toward the finish line.

Mother also has the option of refusing Johnny permission: "No, Johnny, you may not." In this case, he is not allowed to move.

This continues along the line of players until all are moving toward the finish.

Any player who advances without asking, "Mother, may I?" must return to the starting line and begin again. The first player to reach Mother wins.

This game is controlled at the whim of Mother, but if each player is given a chance to be Mother and direct the game in his or her own fashion, all will end well.

O'Leary

WHERE TO PLAY

Against a wall

NUMBER OF PLAYERS

1 or more

EQUIPMENT

Any bounceable ball

OBJECT OF THE GAME

To throw the ball against the wall and complete a series of motions
while reciting the "O'Leary" rhyme

O'Leary is similar to **Seven Up.** The motions are less complicated, but having to state the rhyme makes up for this. O'Leary is a diverting way to pass the time when you are alone, but it can be played by two simultaneously, to see who finishes first, or by a number of players in series, to see who can get the farthest through the series of motions in one turn.

Each of the motions listed below should be repeated four times, while chanting:

(continued on next page)

O'Leary (*cont.*)

1, 2, 3, O'Leary
4, 5, 6, O'Leary
7, 8, 9, O'Leary
10, O'Leary, postman.

The motions are as follows:

1. Throw the ball under the right leg, bounce it against the wall once, and catch it.
2. Throw the ball under the left leg, bounce it against the wall once, and catch it.
3. Bounce the ball against the wall and catch it under the right leg.
4. Bounce the ball against the wall and catch it under the left leg.
5. Bounce the ball against the wall and catch it on a circle formed by holding your right thumb and forefinger together.
6. Bounce the ball against the wall and catch it on a circle formed by holding your left thumb and forefinger together.
7. Bounce the ball against the wall, twirl around to the right once, and catch it.
8. Bounce the ball against the wall, twirl around to the left once, and catch it.

Pottsie

WHERE TO PLAY
On pavement, on a sidewalk, or in a driveway

NUMBER OF PLAYERS
2 or more

EQUIPMENT
Chalk; any bounceable ball

OBJECT OF THE GAME
To step through a series of boxes while bouncing the ball and naming items to match the categories in the boxes

Pottsie is a cross between **Hopscotch** and the pencil-and-paper game **Categories.** Quick wits as well as quick feet are tested in this game!

Mark off a diagram on the pavement with chalk. There should be six to eight boxes, each about two feet wide and one foot deep. Fill in each box with a different name of a category that is familiar to all players, such as animals, colors, fruits, movie stars, television shows, girls' names, states, and desserts.

The player chosen to go first stands outside the diagram and rolls the ball into the first box (in the bottom left corner), stopping it with hands or feet before it rolls out of the box. If it rolls out of the appropriate box, the player loses a turn.

Before progressing to the next box (the second box in on the left), the player must name something that fulfills the category of that box. For example, if the box is labeled *Animals,* the player must name a type of animal.

After giving a correct answer, the player moves on to the next box. From the second box on, while stepping into a new box, players must simultaneously bounce and catch the ball and give an appropriate answer.

If the player loses control of the ball, hesitates, or gives a wrong answer, he or she loses the turn and play proceeds with the next player.

After mistakes are made, players can either be returned to the first box or begin where they left off, depending on the skills of the players.

The first player to get through all the boxes is the winner.

Prisoner's Base

WHERE TO PLAY
Outdoors, on pavement or grass

NUMBER OF PLAYERS
8 or more

EQUIPMENT
Chalk (optional)

OBJECT OF THE GAME
To capture all the members of the opposing team by tagging them or by entering their prison when no prisoners are in it

If you have chalk available, Prisoner's Base can be played a little more precisely, since the playing area will be clearly designated. If you don't have any, just make sure that everyone understands the boundaries.

Mark off a court, about thirty by fifty feet for eight to twelve players. Opposite corners should be marked off as "prisons."

Form two teams and send them into opposite sides of the court. At a starting signal, each team ventures into the other's territory.

At the beginning of the game, when there are no prisoners, some players should concentrate on getting to the opposite prison, while others remain back to defend their own.

Players can be tagged and imprisoned once in enemy territory. They may be freed by another team member who gets into the prison without being tagged. Both may be tagged, though, on the way back to their own territory.

The game ends when one side has captured all of the opposition or succeeds in entering an empty enemy prison.

Prisoner's Base is an extremely old game, though historians seem unable to agree upon exactly when it was developed. Some claim it was featured in the ancient Olympic Games, while others date it to the reign of Edward III of England (1327–1377).

Running Bases

WHERE TO PLAY
Outdoors, on a sidewalk or playground

NUMBER OF PLAYERS
3 or 4 at a time

EQUIPMENT
A rubber playground ball

OBJECT OF THE GAME
To score runs by running between two bases without being tagged by the fielders

While no serious baseball player wants to be caught in a rundown (also known in baseball circles as a "pickle"), younger players often find the rundown one of the most fun and exciting parts of the game. (A rundown is when the runner is caught between two bases and two players who throw the ball back and forth, not allowing the runner to reach either base without being tagged out. The player with the ball tries to run closer to the runner before throwing the ball to the other baseman, thereby "running down" the runner and the amount of space he has in which to maneuver.) In Running Bases, they will get to participate in rundowns as often as they would like.

Two players serve as fielders, and one is the base runner. The fielders take positions about thirty to fifty feet apart, depending on their abilities. They stand next to areas that are designated as bases: sidewalk squares or areas marked with chalk.

To begin the game, the runner stands on one base with a fielder, and the other fielder has the ball. When that fielder throws the ball to the other, the runner dashes for the opposite base.

As the runner sprints, the fielders try to tag him or her. This often results in a rundown, with the fielders throwing the ball back and forth until they tag the runner or drop the ball.

When a runner is tagged, he or she must trade places with the tagger.

Every time the runner reaches base safely, he or she earns a hit. Four hits equal one run. The player who has scored the most runs in a given period of time wins the game.

Seven Up

WHERE TO PLAY

Against a windowless wall of a building

NUMBER OF PLAYERS

Seven Up is really meant to be played alone, but two players can race
to see who can finish all 7 motions first

EQUIPMENT

A small rubber ball or a tennis ball; chalk

OBJECT OF THE GAME

To complete a series of motions while the ball, thrown against the wall,
is still in the air

Establish the playing area by picking a smooth wall and drawing a chalk
line on the sidewalk, at least five feet from the base of the wall.

Standing behind the line, the player will bounce the ball against the
wall and complete a series of predetermined motions ("onesies" through
"sevensies") while the ball is in the air.

Players should feel free to invent their own motions. These are some
suggestions, which vary from place to place:

- Onesies: Simply bounce the ball against wall and catch it, once.
- Twosies: While the ball is in the air, twirl around and then catch it. Do
  this twice.
- Threesies: Bounce the ball against the wall once, clap once, and catch.
  Bounce the ball against the wall again, clap twice, bounce, clap three
  times, and catch.
- Foursies: Throw the ball against the wall, clap the hands once in front
  of the body and once behind the back, then catch. Do this four times.
- Fivesies: Bounce the ball against the wall. Slap the hands on the thighs,
  cross them over the chest, then clap and catch. Repeat this five times.
- Sixies: Throw the ball, lift the knee and clap the hands under it, then lift
  the other knee, clap the hands under it, and catch the ball. Do this three
  times (three times two claps equals six).
- Sevensies: Throw the ball under leg and catch it, seven times.

Sidewalk Golf

WHERE TO PLAY
On a sidewalk or any paved surface

NUMBER OF PLAYERS
2 or more

EQUIPMENT
A small object for every player, such as a stone or a bottle cap, which
can be tossed along the course; chalk

OBJECT OF THE GAME
To flip or toss a small object along a "golf course" laid out with chalk
on a sidewalk, in the fewest number of "strokes"

Select one player to design the first "hole." With chalk, this player draws
a golf hole on the sidewalk or pavement.

Players should used their imaginations in designing the holes. The hole
can be located on an island in the middle of a pond or be surrounded by
trees, sand traps, and water hazards. The hole can be represented by a
circle about three inches in diameter.

One at a time, players should crouch by the tee and toss their objects
toward the hole. Objects landing partially or wholly in hazards must be
placed outside the hazard, and a penalty stroke is added.

When all the players have completed one hole, another player maps
out the next hole with chalk, and the round continues.

The player with the fewest strokes after a predetermined number of
holes wins the game.

Skully

WHERE TO PLAY
On a sidewalk or on pavement

NUMBER OF PLAYERS
2 to 6 at a time

EQUIPMENT
A "shooter" for each player: a checker, bottle cap, or small, smooth
stone; chalk

OBJECT OF THE GAME
To snap a shooter through the 10 bases of the Skully court in
sequential order

(*continued on next page*)

Skully (*cont.*)

Before beginning the game, draw the Skully court on the sidewalk or pavement with chalk. First, mark out a square, three feet on each side. In the center, draw the pit—a rectangle of eight inches by twelve inches crossed with two diagonal lines. Add ten four-by-four-inch squares and number them as indicated in the diagram.

Choose one player to go first. The shooter is placed on the ground at the center of the pit's *X,* and the first player snaps it or flicks it with any finger toward Square 1. If the shooter comes to rest in or on the lines of Square 1, the player can continue by shooting for Square 2 until he or she misses. After a miss, the next player shoots.

A shot is a miss if the shooter fails to reach the proper base, goes out of bounds, or lands on one of the diagonal lines in the pit. If a shooter goes out, it must be placed at the spot where it left the court before being shot on the next turn. If it lands on one of the diagonal lines in the pit, it must be placed back in the last box successfully reached.

After a miss, the shooter remains in the spot where it landed until the next turn. If a player hits another player's shooter, he or she advances to the next square and gets an extra turn.

When a player reaches a square, he or she may move the shooter anywhere within that square to get the best shot for the next square.

In some circumstances, a player may be returned to the starting point. This can happen if the shooter goes out of bounds twice in a row or if the shooter lands in the open space of the pit (not on a diagonal line). Shooters that rest on the boundary between Square 9 and the pit or Square 10 and the pit are considered to be in the pit, and the player must begin the sequence all over again.

The first player to get his or her shooter from Square 1 to Square 10 wins the game.

Skully can also be played indoors on a diagram drawn on a sheet of paper and taped to a tabletop.

(This game is also called Skelly.)

Steal the Bacon

WHERE TO PLAY
Outdoors

NUMBER OF PLAYERS
11 or more (an odd number is necessary unless a supervisor serves as the referee)

EQUIPMENT
An object to represent the bacon: a piece of wood, a hat, a ball

OBJECT OF THE GAME
To be the first player of 2 whose numbers are called to "steal the bacon"

Divide the players into two equal teams and designate a referee. The referee places the "bacon" in the center of the playing area, and the teams line up on opposite sides of it. Players should stand three or four feet apart, and the two lines should be about twenty feet apart. Each team should count off so that each player has a number.

The referee begins the game by calling out a number. The players from each team who have been assigned that number run to the bacon. The first one to grab the bacon and cross over his or her own team's line without being tagged by the other player earns a point for his or her team.

The first team to score 25 points wins the game.

Stickball

WHERE TO PLAY

Outdoors

NUMBER OF PLAYERS

At least 6

EQUIPMENT

A stick (a cut-down broom or mop handle or a bat); a small rubber
ball or an old tennis ball

OBJECT OF THE GAME

To score runs in a street version of **Baseball**

Stickball is a variation on **Baseball,** adapted for the street.

Delineate a field, which should approximate a baseball diamond, making allowances for the irregular shape of many play areas (see **Baseball**). There should be four bases, with locations marked by chalk or objects, or generally agreed upon. (When possible, a wall behind home plate serves as a good backdrop and saves you from having to chase missed or bad pitches.)

The players should form two teams. The fielding team spreads itself around the diamond. It should consist of a pitcher, someone to cover first base, someone to watch second and third bases, and, if possible, one or more players to take care of the outfield.

The pitcher bounces the ball once to the first member of the batting team. The batter tries to hit the ball with the stick.

Another member of the batting team should serve as the catcher, returning missed balls to the pitcher.

Since there's no umpire, pitching is much less formal than in regular baseball. The strike zone is very wide, and there is no such thing as a walk. Players who try to wait for the perfect pitch will most likely be encouraged to swing by the mockings of the other team. *Whiff* (missed) swings constitute strikes, and three strikes make a strikeout. The first two foul balls hit by a player at bat also count as strikes.

When a batter hits a fair ball (one that remains within the boundaries of the first and third base lines as it travels toward the outfield), he or she sprints to first base, trying to reach it before the fielders return the ball to that base.

If the ball is caught on the fly, if the first-base player tags the base before the runner reaches it, or if a player is tagged by the ball while running the bases, an out is made. There are three outs in each half of an inning, after which the batting and fielding teams trade places.

In **Baseball,** a hit is a home run when it is "out of the park." Stickball rules, however, state that any ball going out of the park and into an area from which it will be difficult to retrieve (into an unfriendly neighbor's backyard, for example) is an automatic out, and the player who hit it is responsible for trying to get it back.

Base runners are advanced when their teammates hit the ball successfully, and a runner who makes it to home plate without being put out scores a run.

When Stickball is played with a small group, *ghost runners* can be used. If all the members of the batting team have reached base and no one is available to bat, the player closest to home is allowed to hit again. A ghost runner is said to substitute for that player as a base runner and may score a run if advanced. For example, if a player leaves third base to bat again and hits a triple, not only do players on first and second base score, but also the ghost runner who was on third.

The team scoring the most runs in a predetermined number of innings wins the game.

Stoopball

WHERE TO PLAY
Against a stoop

NUMBER OF PLAYERS
1 or 2 at a time

EQUIPMENT
A small, hard rubber ball, the size of a tennis ball. (A tennis ball would also be fine.)

OBJECT OF THE GAME
To score runs by bouncing the ball off a stoop

Playing Stoopball alone is a good way to prepare to face off against another player.

The player stands at least four feet from the stoop and pitches the ball at the steps, trying to bounce it back and catch it.

If the ball hits both a step and a riser and the player succeeds in catching it, 1 point is scored. Balls that are caught after bouncing directly off the point of the step are worth 10 points (see illustration).

A point is deducted from the player's score if he or she misses a catch or doesn't bounce the ball properly.

(*continued on next page*)

Stoopball (*cont.*)

Players set point goals for themselves—100 is a good start. Those players with watches can compete against themselves, trying to reduce the length of time it takes to earn 100 points.

Basic Stoopball for two is not very different from Stoopball for one. One player serves as the bouncer, the other as the fielder. When the fielder catches a ball that caroms against a step and a riser, he or she earns 1 point; catching a ball that comes off the point of a step scores 10 points.

Balls that don't bounce right count as outs against the bouncer. After three outs, the bouncer and fielder switch roles.

The first player to score 100 points wins.

VARIATIONS

Another way to score Stoopball is to award points to the bouncer when the fielder makes an error. A ball that bounces against a step and a riser and is missed by the fielder gains the bouncer 5 points. Likewise, a missed ball off the point wins the bouncer 10 points. When three outs are made, the fielder and bouncer change places.

If there is enough room, another version, Five-Ten Stoopball, can be played by one or two players.

For a solo game, the player stands about ten feet in front of the stoop. He or she tosses the ball against the stoop, trying to catch it on the fly, before it hits the sidewalk. A ball caught before it bounces scores 10 points, and a ball caught after one bounce scores 5 points.

If the ball bounces more than once before being caught, however, the player's accumulated score total is wiped out. Score to 100, or 500 for talented players.

Five-Ten Stoopball for two players proceeds in the same way, except that a player who catches the ball on more than one bounce loses the turn, and the other gets the chance to score points.

Curb Ball is similar to Stoopball, except that the players must bounce the ball against a curb instead of steps. The bounce options are more limited, but it is a good game when no stoop is available.

Tunnel Relay

WHERE TO PLAY
Outdoors, on a hard surface where a ball can be easily rolled

NUMBER OF PLAYERS
10 or more

EQUIPMENT
A rubber playground ball for each team

OBJECT OF THE GAME
To advance to the finish line while rolling the ball through a tunnel of legs

Establish a playing area with a starting line and a finish line about thirty to fifty feet apart.

The players are divided into two equal teams. One player from each team stands on the starting line, and the rest of the team members form a single-file line in front of that player. Players should be about a yard apart, with feet astride, and should all face forward toward the finish line.

The player closest to the finish line on each team holds the ball. At the starting signal, this player rolls the ball between his or her own legs and through the legs of the rest of the players in the line. The last player in line should catch the ball and run with it up to the front of the line, where the process is repeated.

If the ball escapes the tunnel of legs, it must be rolled again from the point where it escaped.

When one of the players in line runs the ball over the finish line, his or her team wins the game.

Two Square

WHERE TO PLAY
On a playground or sidewalk, or in a driveway

NUMBER OF PLAYERS
At least 2; more can play in tournament fashion

EQUIPMENT
A rubber playground ball and chalk, if necessary

OBJECT OF THE GAME
To be the first to score 21 points

(*continued on next page*)

Two Square (*cont.*)

If you are going to play on a sidewalk, all that is needed for Two Square are two smooth squares of concrete and a small rubber ball.

On other paved surfaces, two adjacent squares, about four feet on each side, can be drawn with chalk. Players stand outside their squares as if they were standing by a Ping-Pong table to wait for the serve, but they can move inside the square at any time to hit the ball.

Hands are used instead of paddles to hit the ball into the opponent's square. As in table tennis, one bounce is allowed on each side. After volleying for the serve, one player begins the game.

The players continue to hit the ball back and forth until one of the two makes an error, such as failing to return the ball or hitting it out of bounds. If the player with the serve makes the error, the serve goes to the other player. If the player who received the ball makes an error, the player who served it gains a point. Points can only be earned by the server.

The winner of each point always get the next serve. The first player to reach 21 points is the winner, but the game must be won by 2 points.

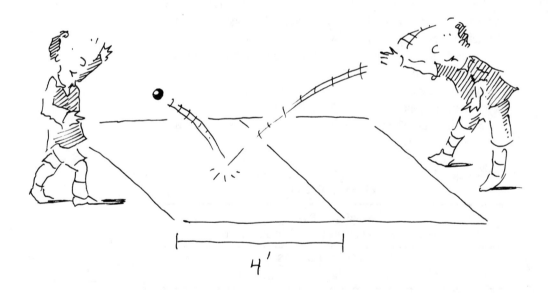

FOUR
Games to Play in Water

Ball Between the Knees Race

WHERE TO PLAY
In any swimming area in which you are able to define a start and finish line

NUMBER OF PLAYERS
At least 2

EQUIPMENT
A ball of any size that can be held between the knees, for each team

OBJECT OF THE GAME
To swim to the finish line holding the ball between the knees

Divide the group into equal teams, and define a start and finish line.

The swimmers on each team must swim to the finish line while holding a small rubber ball between the knees. This can be done while swimming on one's back or front—choose one way before beginning the race.

If a swimmer loses the ball, he or she must chase it, bring it back to the spot where it was lost, and begin the race again from that point.

When there are more than two players, each swimmer, after crossing the finish line, must toss the ball back to the next team member so the race can continue.

Black and White

WHERE TO PLAY
In a pool

NUMBER OF PLAYERS
8 or more

EQUIPMENT
A two-sided floating object like a Frisbee or a small piece of wood

OBJECT OF THE GAME
To play a game of **Tag** in which a whole team is designated "It"

Before beginning the game, a floatable object must be fashioned for designating which team will be "It" throughout the game. For example, you could use a small piece of wood and color or paint it black (or any color) on one side. A Frisbee that has been marked with a highly visible X on one side is also suitable.

One side of the pool should be designated as a safe zone.

The players should be split into two equal teams, each taking a color that corresponds to a side of the object to be tossed: black or white. The two teams should line up in the center of the pool facing each other. Depending upon the swimming abilities of the players, this game can also be played in the deep end of the pool.

To start the game, one player tosses the object into the air (not too high, and not too close to any of the other players). As it falls into the water, the players should pay close attention to which color or side is floating upward and shout it so that all know. For example, if black is floating up, the players will yell, "Black!" and the black team will be designated to chase and tag the white team before they reach the safety zone. Players can move through the water in any manner they choose (walk, run or swim). Likewise, if the unmarked or white side of the tossed object is visible, the white team will chase and tag the black team.

Once all the swimmers have reached home or have been tagged, the teams regroup in the center of the pool, and the object is tossed again to initiate another round.

Since most of the fun of this game is simply finding out which team is "It," playing for score or elimination isn't as important.

VARIATION

You can vary the way this is played by changing the defined safety zone. It could be any side of the pool, or each team could have its own "safe" area.

Chicken Fights

WHERE TO PLAY
In any swimming area

NUMBER OF PLAYERS
An even number of players (at least 4)

EQUIPMENT
None

OBJECT OF THE GAME
To knock an opponent off his or her teammate's shoulders

(continued on next page)

Chicken Fights (*cont.*)

Players select partners based on equal size and strength, so that the teams are as evenly matched as possible.

One partner gets on top of the other partner's shoulders, imitating a chicken. When all of the "chickens" are ready, the players on the shoulders try to push, pull, splash, and wrestle other opponents so that they tumble into the water, without falling off themselves.

The last chicken left in position on top of his or her teammate's shoulders is the winner. Players should alternate between being the chicken and the base.

Players should be reminded not to get rough and to stay in the center of the pool (away from hard edges) to avoid injury.

Fisherman

WHERE TO PLAY
In a pool

NUMBER OF PLAYERS
6 or more

EQUIPMENT
None

OBJECT OF THE GAME
To swim from one side of the pool to the other without being caught by the "fisherman"

One player should be designated the "fisherman," and the rest of the players are "fish." The fish line up on one side of the pool, facing the fisherman, who stands or treads water between them and the other side of the pool.

When the fisherman gives the signal by shouting "Let's go fishing!" the fish try to swim to the opposite side of the pool without being tagged. Any player who is tagged must join the fisherman in the center of the pool and try to catch other fish.

As soon as there are at least two other players in the middle of the pool, they join hands to form a net for the fisherman, who remains free to swim in pursuit of fish. Swimmers should try to get past the ends of the net or swim under it.

The last remaining fish wins the game and may be the fisherman for the next round.

Marco Polo

WHERE TO PLAY
In a swimming pool or any swimming area with definable boundaries

NUMBER OF PLAYERS
At least 3

EQUIPMENT
None

OBJECT OF THE GAME
To avoid being tagged by "Marco"

One player is chosen to be "Marco." With eyes closed, he or she attempts to locate and tag another player, who will then become the new Marco.

Marco's search is made easier by the clues given by the other players. While Marco blindly roams around the swimming area in search of a player to tag, he or she calls out, "Marco," to which all of the players must respond, "Polo."

Marco may call out for these clues whenever and as often as he or she wants. No matter how close Marco is getting, the other players must answer with "Polo" immediately.

When Marco successfully tags a player, that player becomes the new Marco, and the game continues.

Mount Ball

WHERE TO PLAY
At the shallow end of a pool

NUMBER OF PLAYERS
At least 4

EQUIPMENT
1 ball of any type and size for every 4 players

OBJECT OF THE GAME
To pass the ball as many times as possible from one player sitting on a partner's shoulders to another

Divide the players into groups of two, trying to match them in size and strength as much as possible.

(continued on next page)

Mount Ball (*cont.*)

The players should stand in water about waist deep. In each pair, one player mounts the shoulders of the other player. The bottom player can crouch down in the water while the other climbs on. When the top player is seated on the bottom player's shoulders, the bottom player should hold onto his or her partner's legs to steady their mount.

When both pairs are in position, they should face each other, four or five feet apart. The two top players, rather than the top player and corresponding bottom player, are partners, and the object is to pass the ball successfully between them as many times as possible without losing balance and falling into the water. Players should keep careful count.

When the ball is dropped, the top players and the bottom players switch places. The players who started on the bottom get their chance to get on the other players' shoulders and toss the ball.

The partners with the longest string of successful throws are the winners.

To make the game more difficult, players can stand farther apart.

Mount Ball, originally played on land, was an event in the ancient Olympic games.

Poisen Balls

WHERE TO PLAY
In a pool

NUMBER OF PLAYERS
6 or more

EQUIPMENT
As many floating balls as you can round up (old tennis balls and small rubber balls are fine)—at least 8; a rope to use as a net

OBJECT OF THE GAME
To keep the balls from being on your side of the pool when the whistle is blown

Prepare the pool's playing area by stretching a rope across it to serve as a net.

First, pick someone to serve as the referee. Next, divide the players into two equal teams, one on each side of the net, and distribute the balls between the two teams.

At the referee's signal (any signal such as a whistle is fine), the players should throw their balls over the net into the other team's area. Since the idea of the game is to keep your court free of balls, the teams continually go after balls and throw them back over the net. The greater the number of balls in the pool, the more frantic the action of the players.

A ball that goes out of the pool must be chased by the player who threw it. The ball is considered in the possession of that player's team until he or she returns to the water and throws it again.

Any team to get all the balls to the other team's side automatically wins. If neither team is able to do this, however, the referee should stop the game after a predetermined time period (perhaps three or four minutes). At that point, the team with the fewest balls on its side wins the game. Play a best-of-five or -seven series to continue the fun.

Sharks and Minnows

WHERE TO PLAY
In a swimming pool or any definable swimming area

NUMBER OF PLAYERS
5 or more

EQUIPMENT
None

OBJECT OF THE GAME
To swim from one side of the pool to another without being tagged by a "shark"

This is essentially a water version of **Red Rover** with a few differences. Before you begin, establish the boundaries of the play area (usually the sides of a pool or a roped-off swimming area).

One player is designated a "shark" and stands in the middle of the swimming area. The other players, "minnows," line up on one of the end lines. When the shark calls to them to come swimming, the minnows swim as quickly as possible to the other side, trying to avoid being tagged by the shark.

Any minnow tagged becomes a shark and joins the original shark in the middle of the pool. The game continues in the same manner, with the sharks calling to the minnows to come swimming and the minnows trying to avoid being tagged.

The last minnow is the winner and may select which player should start off as the shark in the next round of Sharks and Minnows.

Still Pond

WHERE TO PLAY

In any swimming area

NUMBER OF PLAYERS

5 or more

EQUIPMENT

None

OBJECT OF THE GAME

To be the first to cross the pool without being seen in motion by "It"

One player should be chosen as "It." The remaining players line up on one side of the pool and "It" on the other.

"It" closes his or her eyes and counts out loud to ten. When ten is reached, "It" calls, "Still pond!" and opens his or her eyes. At this signal, all the players must stop swimming and float in place. Any player caught swimming forward must return to the starting point.

This continues until one of the players reaches the other side, is declared the winner, and becomes the next "It."

A new game can be started or this one continued until all players have reached the opposite side of the pool.

Tunnel Swimming Race

WHERE TO PLAY

In a pool or any swimming area

NUMBER OF PLAYERS

6 to 9 (with 3 players on each team); only for players comfortable with underwater swimming

---

EQUIPMENT

None

OBJECT OF THE GAME

To be the first team to swim across the pool by swimming through a tunnel formed by the teammates' legs

---

Once young swimmers have mastered underwater skills, the Tunnel Swimming Race will become a favorite way to test them.

Split the players into equal teams of three swimmers. Each team should form a line, one behind the other in the water, at one side of the pool. The two players closest to the other (far) side of the pool stand with their legs apart.

At the starting signal, the third player in line swims underwater through the "tunnel" formed by the legs of the other two teammates. Upon surfacing, that player joins the tunnel, and the player in the back of the line now swims through the tunnel.

The first team to travel in this way to the other side of the pool wins.

Underwater Football

WHERE TO PLAY
In a pool

NUMBER OF PLAYERS
4 or more

EQUIPMENT
A rubber ball of any size

OBJECT OF THE GAME
To score goals while remaining underwater

Underwater Football resembles the game as played on land (see **Touch Football**), but all plays must take place underwater.

Divide the players into two equal teams and line them up on opposite sides of the pool, in water about waist deep.

For each play, one player is designated as the ball carrier. To begin play, this player gives the signal for all to submerge. The ball carrier and his or her teammates attempt to swim underwater toward the opponent's goal. The defensive team tries to prevent their movement, also underwater, or stop the ball carrier by tagging him or her.

Any player who breaks the surface of the water is out of the play. Teams have four "downs" to attempt to score, after which the defense and offense trade roles. It is also possible to score more than once during the four downs if a team is particularly skillful.

The team with the most points after a given period of time, or the first to reach a predetermined number of points, wins.

Underwater Tag

WHERE TO PLAY

In any safe swimming area

NUMBER OF PLAYERS

5 or more

EQUIPMENT

None

OBJECT OF THE GAME

For the player who is "It" to tag another player, or to avoid being tagged by "It" by swimming underwater and staying away from "It"

One player is selected to be "It." When he or she gives a ready signal, the chase begins.

"It" can tag any player within arm's reach unless that player is completely underwater and therefore safe. "It" can chase players around the pool or wait patiently until players run out of breath and must surface for air.

Any player touched by "It" becomes the new "It."

Water Ball

WHERE TO PLAY

In the shallow end of a pool or any shallow swimming area

NUMBER OF PLAYERS

6 or more

EQUIPMENT

An old tennis ball or any small ball that will float

OBJECT OF THE GAME

To gain points by catching or throwing the ball

Divide the players into two equal groups and line them up on opposite sides of the pool. The players in each line should stand a few feet apart.

One player begins the game by throwing the ball to someone across the pool, while calling out his or her name. If the called player catches the ball, he or she scores a point and may now throw the ball. If the ball is intercepted, the intercepting player earns a point and throws the ball. If no one catches the ball, the thrower is awarded the point and gets to throw the ball again.

Water Ball is most exciting when played very fast. The first player to earn 25 points is the winner.

Water Bridge

WHERE TO PLAY
In any safe swimming area where you can touch bottom

NUMBER OF PLAYERS
At least 5

EQUIPMENT
None

OBJECT OF THE GAME
For one player to travel along a "bridge" formed across the surface of the water by the other players, without falling into the water

Standing in the water, the players form two lines facing each other. Each player grasps the wrists of the person opposite him- or herself in order to form a "bridge."

One player crawls across the bridge, which is held at the surface of the water. Unless the line is very long, the players at the start of the line will have to rush to the end once the crawler has passed over them in order to keep the bridge going.

If there enough players, two bridges can be formed and a race between the crawlers held.

Players can also rock the bridge in order to make the crawler's passage more challenging.

Water Follow-the-Leader

WHERE TO PLAY
In any safe swimming area

NUMBER OF PLAYERS
3 or more

EQUIPMENT
None

OBJECT OF THE GAME
To follow and imitate the actions of the leader

The swimmer chosen to be the leader moves through the water and performs a variety of stunts, followed by a line of swimmers who imitate the leader's movements.

The leader can use different swimming strokes, dive in various ways, do underwater gymnastic tricks—the more imaginative the better!

After a certain period of time, a new leader should be picked.

Water Keep Away

WHERE TO PLAY
In a swimming pool or any definable swimming area

NUMBER OF PLAYERS
At least 3

EQUIPMENT
A soft, floatable object like a ball or inflatable beach toy

OBJECT OF THE GAME
To keep an object away from "It" and avoid becoming "It" in the process

After defining the boundaries of the play area, taking into account the players' swimming abilities and other swimmers in the area, play can begin.

First, one player is chosen to be "It." The other players attempt to avoid being tagged by "It" while in possession of a selected object such as a beach ball or other soft tossable object. Players pass this object back and forth, trying not to have it intercepted by "It."

If a player is tagged by "It" while holding the object, or if "It" intercepts a player's toss, then that player becomes the new "It," and the old "It" joins the other players in a new round of "keeping away" the object.

(With three players, this is more like a water version of **Monkey in the Middle.**)

Water Volleyball

WHERE TO PLAY
In any swimming area where you can define a volleyball court

NUMBER OF PLAYERS
At least 4

EQUIPMENT
Any ball suitable for a game of volleyball; a net or rope to serve as a midcourt divider

OBJECT OF THE GAME
To win points by keeping a ball in play and by hitting it back to the opponents so that they are unable to return the shot successfully

After establishing the playing "court," players are divided into two equal teams and take their places on the opposite sides of the net.

One team begins by serving the ball, and the other team attempts to keep it in play before it hits the water. Each team is only allowed three hits to get it over the net and back to the other team. No player is allowed to hit the ball twice in a row, but there are no limitations on how the ball may be hit (underhand, overhand, fingertips, fists, etc., are all permissible).

Follow the same rules as in regular **Volleyball** for the proper setup of players and serving rotations.

The team that earns a predetermined number of points first is the winner.

Watermelon Scramble

WHERE TO PLAY
In any swimming area where you can define a playing area and 2 goals

NUMBER OF PLAYERS
2 or more

EQUIPMENT
A watermelon

OBJECT OF THE GAME
To score a "goal" with the watermelon

Divide the players into two equal teams, and designate a goal for each team. Float the watermelon in the center of the swimming area between the teams. Each team tries to move the watermelon to the other team's goal by pushing it through the water.

To add to the challenge, lightly grease the watermelon with petroleum jelly, cooking oil, or shortening. This should only be done with the permission of the pool owner or lifeguard, as it could be somewhat messy.

After the game is over, slice up the watermelon and enjoy it—everyone wins!

Whirlpool

WHERE TO PLAY
In a swimming pool (this works best in smaller pools)

NUMBER OF PLAYERS
3 or more, depending on the size of the pool

EQUIPMENT
None

OBJECT OF THE GAME
To create a "whirlpool" by moving quickly around the sides of the pool

This game provides a different kind of swimming experience than can usually be found in a pool.

The players join hands in a circle at the shallow end of the pool and begin moving quickly in one direction. Soon the water will be rushing along in the same direction.

Players then drop hands and take turns floating along in the current. It is also fun to get the current flowing briskly in one direction and then try to walk or swim against the whirlpool and change the flow to the other direction.

VARIATION

Instead of a whirlpool, swimmers can create a Log Chute. The players form two lines along the shallow end of the pool. All move their arms underwater in one direction toward the deeper end of the pool in order to get the current moving.

When the water is flowing rapidly in one direction, players take turns floating along the current like logs down a river. When they float to the end of the pool, they take their place at the end of the line and begin waving their arms underwater again in order to keep the current going for the other players.

White Whale

WHERE TO PLAY
In a pool

NUMBER OF PLAYERS
5 or more

EQUIPMENT
None

OBJECT OF THE GAME
To avoid being tagged by the "white whale"

Select one player to start as the "whale." All the players move freely about the pool, closer to the center than the sides.

The whale begins as a black whale, swimming and floating casually among the other players. But when the whale declares, "Thar she blows!" he or she becomes a white whale and gives chase to the other players.

Players are safe only when touching one of the sides of the pool. The white whale may call, "Black whale" at any time to make players return to the center of the pool for another chase. Any player tagged by the white whale becomes the new whale.

FIVE

Party Games for Any Occasion

Auction

WHERE TO PLAY
Indoors

NUMBER OF PLAYERS
At least 5 players to imitate the atmosphere of a real auction!

EQUIPMENT
Small party favors (one for each player); tissue paper or gift wrap; tape; peanuts (nongreasy kind; 15 for each player)

OBJECT OF THE GAME
To "purchase" a favor at auction using peanuts in place of money

Before the "bidders" arrive, wrap all the party favors in paper and place them on a table. An adult should function as the "auctioneer" and will sit at the table with the objects.

The players should be seated in front of the table. Fifteen peanuts, representing fifteen dollars, are distributed to each one.

The auctioneer opens the "sale" by asking for bids on the first object, suggesting one peanut as the opening bid. The bidders will probably need to be prompted about proper auction etiquette: don't bid too much at once, but don't bid too little or you may have difficulty buying anything.

As favors are purchased, players should not open them until told to do so by the auctioneer. If it is necessary, less successful players may be reassured that everyone will get favors at the end of the game.

When all the favors have been sold, the auctioneer announces that the auction has closed and that no player will be allowed to keep more than one favor. All those who bought more than one must be asked to choose one to keep and to return the others.

The remaining favors should be distributed among the players who failed to make a purchase at auction.

Balloon Ball

WHERE TO PLAY
Indoors

NUMBER OF PLAYERS
2 or more

EQUIPMENT
String; balloons

OBJECT OF THE GAME
To keep the balloon in the air and going over the net, as in **Volleyball**

Balloon Ball is a form of **Volleyball** appropriate for younger players and an indoor location.

Set up a Balloon Ball court by tying or taping a piece of string across the center of an open area suitable for play. The string should be about a foot above the average height of the players.

Form two equal teams and place them on opposite sides of the "net." One team should toss the balloon over the net to the other team to initiate a volley. Once the balloon is in motion, it should only be hit with an open hand, and a player may not touch it twice in a row.

The balloon may be hit as many times as needed to get it over the net. When it finally drops to the ground, a point is scored for the other team.

Games of Balloon Ball can be played to 21 points.

VARIATION
Balloon Ball can be played more formally—that is, more like real **Volleyball.** Move the net a little higher, add a serve, and require teams to get the balloon over the net in three hits.

Bobbing for Apples

WHERE TO PLAY
Indoors, on a floor surface that won't be harmed if it gets wet

NUMBER OF PLAYERS
2 or more

EQUIPMENT
A clean metal or plastic tub about 3 feet in diameter; apples, newspapers; towels

OBJECT OF THE GAME
To remove an apple from the tub by biting it—no hands allowed!

Prepare the floor by covering the area with newspapers. It will probably get wet, and papers will facilitate cleanup. Place the tub on top of the newspapers, fill it with clean water to within a few inches of the top, and float the apples in the water.

Players may get even wetter than the floor, so it is best to make sure everyone is in play clothes. A towel can be pinned around the players' shoulders if they are particularly concerned about staying dry.

One by one, the players kneel before the tub, holding their hands behind their backs. The idea is to remove an apple from the tub using only the mouth and teeth.

Some players will succeed in pushing an apple to the side of the tub in order to stabilize it and bite into it. Adventurous players will bypass fancy maneuvers and submerge the entire head, biting the apple while pressing it against the bottom of the tub. (Make sure an adult is carefully supervising these activities.)

Everyone who succeeds in getting an apple out of the tub is a winner (and gets to enjoy eating a delicious apple!).

Broken Hearts

WHERE TO PLAY
Anywhere

NUMBER OF PLAYERS
At least 8

EQUIPMENT
Red construction paper; scissors

OBJECT OF THE GAME
To find and match the other half of your "broken heart"

Broken Hearts is an excellent icebreaker for Valentine's Day parties.

While preparing for the party, the planner should cut a number of hearts out of red construction paper—one heart for every two players. Each heart should then be divided into two halves with a few bold and jagged cuts.

When all the guests have arrived, each should be given half a heart. At a starting signal, the players compare hearts, trying to find the missing half.

The first two players to put their broken heart back together win the game. Let everyone else find their missing halves, and then play a game requiring partners, which have just been found.

VARIATION
This game can be adapted for any holiday or theme party. For a Halloween party, you could use a variety of images: a ghost, witch, black cat, or a jack-o'-lantern.

Burst the Balloon

WHERE TO PLAY
Outdoors, near a tree or pole from which a water balloon can be suspended

NUMBER OF PLAYERS
2 or more

EQUIPMENT
String; balloons; a strong stick or bat; a scarf or rag to use as a blindfold

OBJECT OF THE GAME
To be the player to burst the balloon

Burst the Balloon is an adaptation of **Piñata**, and is perfect for a summer party on a hot day. It is most fun when participants wear bathing suits.

Fill a balloon with water and hang it from a tree branch or pole, within batting reach of the players.

One at a time, the players are given the stick or bat, blindfolded, spun around three times, and set in search of the balloon.

The first player to burst the balloon wins the game, as well as a cooling shower. The game will be even more fun if you put up more than one balloon, so more players get the opportunity to burst one.

Cobweb Confusion

WHERE TO PLAY
Indoors

NUMBER OF PLAYERS
4 or more

EQUIPMENT
A ball of string or a skein of yarn; paper or cardboard; scissors; a small favor or edible treat for each player

OBJECT OF THE GAME
To unravel the "cobwebs" in order to reach the favor or treat

Preparing for Cobweb Confusion is almost as fun as playing the game. Though it is a natural game for Halloween, it is also an excellent ice-breaker for any party.

Before the guests arrive, the party planner should cut a piece of string or yarn about twenty or thirty feet long for each player. Different colors of yarn make for a bright web and help players to unravel the mess, but a single color is fine.

To one end of each string, attach a name tag. Tags are easily made from three-by-five-inch index cards, or they can be cut from paper or cardboard. To the other end of the string, tie a small favor or treat.

Weave the strings loosely around the room: around table legs, along a stair rail, through a chair back, and, of course, around each other. The result should be a confused snarl of strings.

When all the players have arrived, send them in search of their name tags. When everyone has located the appropriate tag, they may begin untangling the web.

The first player to reach his or her favor is the winner, but everyone wins by the time the web is unraveled because there are favors for all.

Easter-Egg Hunt

WHERE TO PLAY
Outdoors, in a backyard, or inside a house or apartment

NUMBER OF PLAYERS
2 or more

EQUIPMENT
Hard-boiled or plastic eggs; Easter baskets or other containers to hold the eggs

OBJECT OF THE GAME
To find as many hidden eggs as possible

No Easter celebration is complete without an egg hunt! Eggs that have been hard-boiled and decorated the night before are the most traditional and satisfying kind to hide and search out on Easter morning.

However, depending on the number of players and your tolerance for deviled eggs and egg salad, plastic eggs might be more practical. They also allow you to hide them the night before, well in advance of eager hunters.

Hide the eggs around the play area, keeping in mind the ages and abilities of the hunters. If they vary in age, it is a good idea to pair the youngest ones with older players. Send them out, baskets in hand, in search of the Easter bunny's bounty. The player or the partners to find the most eggs win the hunt.

Egg Polo

WHERE TO PLAY
On a rectangular table

NUMBER OF PLAYERS
2 or more

EQUIPMENT
Masking tape; 1 hollow eggshell

OBJECT OF THE GAME
To score a goal by blowing on an eggshell

Two goal lines should be marked at the ends of the table with masking tape. One player should stand or sit behind each marked goal line. If there are more than two players, they can stand at the sides of the table.

The hollowed-out egg is placed in the center of the table. When a signal is given, both players attempt to blow the egg over the other side's goal line. No hands are allowed. If the egg is blown off the table, it is placed back in the center. The first player to blow the egg over the line wins.

To make the game more difficult, goalposts can be made by standing two thick books on the goal line.

In the early twentieth century, blowing the egg was considered too taxing an activity for girls. They competed by using fans to move the egg.

The empty eggshells make this an appropriate Easter game, but it might be easier to use Ping-Pong balls.

Feelies

WHERE TO PLAY
Anywhere

NUMBER OF PLAYERS
2 or more

EQUIPMENT
A box or basket to be covered in order to hide a collection of objects: an assortment of 10 to 15 articles of different sizes and textures, like fruits or vegetables, jewelry, pebbles, a sponge, etc; and a pencil and paper for each player

OBJECT OF THE GAME
To identify by touch and list from memory as many of the objects as possible

This game can be played at a party as guests arrive or during rest periods, when a player is sitting out or has been eliminated from another game.

Miscellaneous objects are placed within a box or basket (by a nonparticipant) so that they can be felt but remain hidden from sight.

Each player inserts his or her hand into the container and is allowed a short period of time (about one minute) to explore the contents solely by touch.

When the time period has elapsed, the player creates a list from memory of the objects identified. The player with the longest and most accurate list is the winner.

Good Resolutions

WHERE TO PLAY
Indoors

NUMBER OF PLAYERS
At least 8

EQUIPMENT
Paper and pencil (or pen) for each player

OBJECT OF THE GAME
To match New Year's resolutions with their writers

Good Resolutions is obviously suited to end-of-December/New Year's Eve holiday parties, but it can be played at any time of year.

Each player needs a small slip of paper and a pencil or pen. Everyone is given a few minutes to think of the most important resolution they should make for the following year.

Resolutions should be written on the slips of paper and passed to the player who has been appointed to read them.

One by one, the reader recites the resolutions while the other players try to guess their authors.

Winners or losers at Good Resolutions aren't truly discovered until the end of the next year, when you find out whether or not the resolutions were kept. Anyone whose resolution is immediately or unanimously recognized might take it as a hint that he or she should try hard to keep it!

Orange Race

WHERE TO PLAY
In any area large enough to hold two lines of team players

NUMBER OF PLAYERS
At least 8

EQUIPMENT
2 large oranges

OBJECT OF THE GAME
To pass the orange from the first to the last player in line, using the neck and chin only

This is a great game to play at the start of a party in order to introduce the guests to each other.

The players are divided into two equal teams, and two lines are formed.

The first player in each line holds the orange between neck and chin, and upon the starting signal must pass it to the next player, who must likewise use only neck and chin to receive it. The orange is passed in this manner from player to player to the end of the line.

Any player unlucky enough to drop the orange must pick it up off the floor (again using the neck and chin alone) and continue to pass it down the line as quickly a possible.

The first team to get the orange to the last player in line wins.

Peter Piper

WHERE TO PLAY
Anywhere

NUMBER OF PLAYERS
2 or more

EQUIPMENT
A large sheet of paper; tape or tacks; writing or drawing materials; a rod, stick, or ruler to use as a pointer

OBJECT OF THE GAME
To point to pictures illustrating the "Peter Piper" tongue twister while reciting it

Before the party, draw a few illustrations corresponding to the Peter Piper story on a large sheet of paper. Sketch a pepper, a basket to represent the peck, and, of course, Peter Piper himself. The pictures don't need to be elaborate, just recognizable. If you have some creative players, the drawing of the illustrations can be incorporated into the game. On the other hand, if you don't want to draw, you can substitute words instead—write *Peter Piper, peck,* and *pickled peppers* in bold letters.

Attach the paper to a wall within pointing range.

Gather all the players in front of the drawing. To prepare the players, go through the rhyme a few times to make sure everyone has it down: "Peter Piper picked a peck of pickled peppers. If Peter Piper picked a peck of pickled peppers, how many pickled peppers did Peter Piper pick?"

When everyone knows the tongue twister, the players stand before the drawing one at a time. While reciting the rhyme, the player should point to the drawings that correspond to the words: "Peter Piper ... peck ... peppers ... Peter Piper ... peck ... peppers ... peppers ... Peter Piper."

Players who successfully get through the rhyme while pointing to the correct illustrations should be rewarded.

Pin the Tail on the Donkey

WHERE TO PLAY
In front of a wall onto which can be hung a large sheet of cardboard or paper

NUMBER OF PLAYERS
4 or more

EQUIPMENT
A large sheet of cardboard or paper; donkey tail cut out of paper or fabric for each player; pushpins, thumbtacks, or tape; a scarf or rag to be used as a blindfold

OBJECT OF THE GAME
To pin the missing tail back onto the donkey

Before the game, draw a picture of a tailless donkey on the large sheet of cardboard or paper. Don't worry, artistic ability is not required! Attach this sheet to a wall or door with tacks or tape.

The players line up in front of the drawing of the poor donkey without a tail. One at a time the players are given the donkey tail, blindfolded, spun around three times, and pointed in the direction of the donkey.

Each player tries to remember where the tail belongs and attempts to pin it as close to that spot as possible. The player who comes closest to pinning the tail onto the proper site is declared the winner.

(continued on next page)

Pin the Tail on the Donkey (*cont.*)

VARIATION

Instead of drawing a picture of a donkey, hang a large map of the world on the wall. Choose a destination and mark it clearly on the map.

Players are given cardboard cutouts of airplanes rather than donkey tails and must attempt to land their planes as close to the destination as possible. For added difficulty, any planes landing in water are considered lost. The pilot landing closest to the target wins.

Piñata

WHERE TO PLAY
Indoors or outdoors

NUMBER OF PLAYERS
4 or more

EQUIPMENT
A store-bought piñata or the materials for making one (2 paper grocery bags, favors or edible treats, crepe paper or drawing materials if you want to decorate it); stick or bat for breaking the piñata; string; scarf or rag to use as a blindfold

OBJECT OF THE GAME
To break open the piñata and enjoy the treats inside

Store-bought piñatas are colorful and charming, but a homemade piñata will be just as much fun. Artistically minded players can create their own piñatas out of papier-mâché, but most will find it easiest to fashion one from paper grocery bags. Making and decorating a piñata can be part of the game if the group is small enough so that all can participate, or players can be split into groups and several piñatas made at once.

To make a simple piñata, place one grocery bag inside another to form a container. Fill the bag with treats: small favors or healthy snacks that won't break easily. Tie the top of the bag with string. Piñatas can be decorated with crepe paper in the traditional manner, covered with drawings, or left plain.

If outdoors, hang the piñata from a tree branch or if indoors, in a doorway or from a hanging plant hook. It should be above the players' heads but within batting range.

Assign the players a batting order and blindfold the first player. The blindfolded player is given the stick, placed under the piñata, and spun around three times. He or she gets one chance to bat at the piñata. When a player is unsuccessful, the next player in line takes a turn.

Continue through the batting order until one player breaks open the piñata, which will shower candies and treats on the ground. Traditionally, the players scramble for the treats that spill onto the floor. This may mean that the player who broke the piñata doesn't get any, so it is a good idea to have extra treats prepared for that player and any others who might be left without a share of the bounty.

Piñata is a game enjoyed by Mexican children at Christmas. Sometimes a clay pot is used as the piñata rather than a papier-mâché animal.

Scavenger Hunt

WHERE TO PLAY
Indoors with a few players; outdoors with a large group

NUMBER OF PLAYERS
2 or more

EQUIPMENT
If played indoors, a group of items easily found (paper clips, coins, magazines, etc); paper and pencils; bags for collecting items

OBJECT OF THE GAME
To find the items on the list

Before the game begins, draw up a list of objects to find. Some of the items can be general (*any rock*), others more specific (*a white rock*). Long lists keep more players occupied and lessen the chances of a tie.

If the game is played indoors, someone should hide the articles on the list: paper clips, coins, etc. Suggestions to search in books or magazines can also be made: *Find an advertisement for a children's cereal,* or, *Find a book with the word* science *in the title,* for example. (Remind players to mark pages with a bookmark and not to rip anything out of books or magazines.) If played outside, the neighborhood can be the source of all items on the scavenger's list.

Define the search area and the time period allotted for the hunt (up to thirty minutes, depending on the complexity of the list of objects to be found). Distribute the lists and bags for collecting, and let the hunt begin!

The player or the team to discover the most objects within the given time period wins.

Treasure Hunt

WHERE TO PLAY
This is more demanding when played outdoors (in a backyard or a park), but it can be adapted easily on a limited scale for indoor play

NUMBER OF PLAYERS
2 or more

EQUIPMENT
A prize; pencil and paper for making clues; tape

OBJECT OF THE GAME
To be the first to discover the hidden treasure

The party planner should make careful preparations for the Treasure Hunt before the guests arrive. Begin by devising and writing down a series of clues that the players must solve in order to find the treasure. For example, for a hunt in a playground to begin at the slide, the first clue might be: *Climb up my back, and down you'll go, very fast.*

Under the slide, the second clue would be taped. *I used to run on the road, now you run over me* would send players to a row of tires. The next clue would be stashed inside one of the tires. Clues can also involve physical tasks: *Walk ahead twenty giant steps, and look to the right.*

After concealing the clues in their appropriate spots, hide the treasure carefully, to keep it from being discovered accidentally by a player in search of clues.

To begin the hunt, read the first clue out loud to all of the players. Players should try to discover the location of the next clue without sharing their hunches with the other hunters. When a player finds a clue, he or she should read it as inconspicuously as possible and sneak off to the next one.

The first player to discover the treasure is the winner!

SIX

Travel Games for Fun on the Road

Alphabet Objects

WHERE TO PLAY

While traveling in a car

NUMBER OF PLAYERS

At least 2

EQUIPMENT

None

OBJECT OF THE GAME

To spot articles beginning with specified letters of the alphabet

While riding in a car, players look out the windows, in search of items beginning with the letters *a* to *z,* in alphabetical sequence starting with *a.* These can be the actual letters on signs or license plates or objects that begin with the letter.

Each player should call out his or her discoveries as they are made, since each item can only be claimed by one player.

To avoid an impasse, it is a good idea to eliminate difficult letters, especially *q, x,* and *z.*

The first player to finish the alphabet is the winner.

Alphabits

WHERE TO PLAY

Anywhere, but perfect for long journeys by car, train, or plane!

NUMBER OF PLAYERS

2 or more

EQUIPMENT

Paper and pencils, if desired

OBJECT OF THE GAME

To form as many words as possible using the letters in one long word

This game can be played cooperatively or competitively.

If played cooperatively, it is much more casual: one player chooses a long word, and the group communally forms smaller words out of the letters, keeping an informal tally as the words are identified.

If played competitively, a pencil and paper are needed for each player.

One player chooses the word, and the other players create their own lists of smaller words.

After a specified time limit of two or three minutes, lists are compared. A point is awarded for each word, and the player with the highest number of points wins.

VARIATION

To make the game more challenging, points can be scored for each letter used in the newly created words rather than 1 point for each word. This provides an incentive to use as many letters as possible in the new words formed from the original word.

Another variation would be to select words from road signs or any sights along the highway as you are traveling.

Automobile 21

WHERE TO PLAY
In a car, while traveling

NUMBER OF PLAYERS
2 or more

EQUIPMENT
None

OBJECT OF THE GAME
To find the numbers *1* through *21* on the license plates of passing cars

The players read the license plates of passing cars, trying to find the numbers *1* through *21*. Players should call out numbers as they find them, and only one player may use a given plate. Players must find the exact number or a combination of numbers on a plate that add up to the number.

To make the game more difficult, assign an order for the players: if there are two players, each one gets to use the numbers from every other plate, for three players, every third plate, and so forth. The game can be lengthened by counting back from 21.

Billboard Alphabet

WHERE TO PLAY
While traveling in a car

NUMBER OF PLAYERS
2 or more

EQUIPMENT
None

OBJECT OF THE GAME
To discover all the letters in the alphabet on billboards seen alongside
the road

Players take turns reading billboards along the side of the road in search of the letters of the alphabet, each player attempting to be the first to find *a* through *z*. The first player looks for *a* in the first sign. Whether or not he or she finds it, the following billboard is read by the next player, also for the letter *a*. When all players have read one sign, the first player begins again.

One letter only may be used from each billboard.

The first player to find the letters *a* through *z* wins the game. Younger children can play this game cooperatively rather than competitively. Players may want to eliminate the difficult-to-find letters such as *q, x,* and *z* before play begins.

In urban areas there may be enough billboards on both sides of the road for Billboard Alphabet to be played simultaneously rather than by turn. Two players or two teams can play this way, as long is they sit on opposite sides of the car.

Bordering Plates

WHERE TO PLAY
While traveling in a car

NUMBER OF PLAYERS
2 or more

EQUIPMENT
An atlas or a map of the United States; pencil and paper for
scorekeeping (optional)

OBJECT OF THE GAME
To travel on an imaginary cross-country trip by spotting license plates
that match the states to be driven through

Any clearly labeled map of the United States is suitable for Bordering
Plates. Players can plan one trip route across the continent to be followed
by all, or each player can choose a separate course.

Select a starting point—for example, Albany, New York—and a destination on the other side of the continent, like San Francisco, California.

In this example, the player should attempt to spot a New York license
plate to begin the journey. Each license plate spotted may be claimed by
only one player.

Once a player has found a plate to match the starting point, he or she
tries to find the license plate of a bordering state that will continue the
movement cross-country. Ontario and Pennsylvania might be passed
through on the way to California, so both would be correct.

This is when the atlas comes in handy—to solve debates about geog-
raphy and the route. Traveling through Pennsylvania might not always be
the fastest way to the West Coast, but that judgment is left up to the players.

Players continue matching bordering license plates to their itinerary.
The first player to reach the destination is the winner. Depending on
traffic, it might not be possible to complete the journey. The player who
gets the closest to the destination is then the winner.

Shorter routes might also be planned to facilitate the possibility of
completing a journey.

Find All Fifty

WHERE TO PLAY
In a car, while traveling

NUMBER OF PLAYERS
2 or more

EQUIPMENT
Pencil and paper for each player if played competitively

OBJECT OF THE GAME
To spot license plates from as many of the 50 states as possible

---

A good way to start this license-plate game is by making a list of the fifty states. See who can name all fifty first or who can come up with the most if they can't get them all.

Make sure everyone has a complete list. For ease in scorekeeping, you can make a chart. List the states down the left side and the items to be searched for across the top. Label the first column simply for plates from the different states. The second column can be labeled for plates with state mottoes on them and the third for plates with state symbols. If a player spots a plate from a new state that also has the state motto or a symbol, that player gets three points. Otherwise, players get one point for each find.

As players spot appropriate plates, they call out their discoveries, since each plate can be claimed only by one player. The scorekeeper should put the initials of the first player to find a state's plate in the appropriate place on the chart.

At the end of the trip, add up the scores of the license plates spotted. One point is scored for every plate, with a bonus point for the District of Columbia. The player with the highest score is the winner.

Searching for the plates from the fifty states cooperatively is an effective way of teaching younger children about U.S. history, too.

Free Association

WHERE TO PLAY
While traveling or at a party

NUMBER OF PLAYERS
2 or more

EQUIPMENT
None

OBJECT OF THE GAME
To call out a word that is associated with or rhymes with the word
called out before it

The first player calls out a word (it is probably best to start with a noun).
The next player must immediately call out a word that is associated with
the first word or that rhymes with it.

Each player around the group must follow in turn with another appropriate word. A sequence might go like this: *Cat—Dog—Bone—Skeleton—
Closet—Clothes—Hose—Garden—Flower—Power—* etc.

A player who hesitates, or uses a word that is not associated with or
does not rhyme with the previous word, or repeats a word used earlier, is
dropped from the game. The last player remaining wins.

Going on a Picnic

WHERE TO PLAY
Anywhere, but this game is especially wonderful to help pass the time
on long car rides!

NUMBER OF PLAYERS
2 or more

EQUIPMENT
None

OBJECT OF THE GAME
To be the last player able to recite a complete list of items, in the
proper order, to be taken on a picnic

One player begins by reciting the phrase, "I'm going on a picnic and I'm
bringing _____." This first player fills in the blank with an item that
begins with the letter *a,* such as *apples.*

(*continued on next page*)

Going on a Picnic (*cont.*)

The second player must recite this sentence in its entirety and add an item that begins with the next letter in the alphabet, *b.* For example, "I'm going on a picnic, and I'm bringing some apples and bananas."

Each of the following turns requires that the complete string of items be repeated and a new item that begins with the next letter in the alphabet be added to that string. The winner is the last person able to repeat the complete string of items to be taken on the picnic without making any mistakes.

VARIATION

Instead of adding an item that begins with the next letter of the alphabet, players add an item from a suggested category, such as *desserts* or *toys.*

License-Plate Poker

WHERE TO PLAY
While traveling in a car

NUMBER OF PLAYERS
2 or more

EQUIPMENT
None, except a good eye and a basic knowledge of poker hands

OBJECT OF THE GAME
To spot poker hands on the license plates of the other cars on the road

While traveling, players scrutinize the license plates of nearby cars for poker hands, as if the numbers and letters on the plates represented individual cards.

When a player spots one with a decent hand, he or she claims it and announces the "hand": three of a kind, two pairs, etc. Suits, of course, don't matter. Certain letters stand for face cards—*A* for Ace, *K* for King, *Q* for Queen, and *J* for Jack.

For a greater element of chance, players can be assigned an order and given plates in order of their appearance. Played this way, License-Plate Poker is more equitable for players unfamiliar with the card game.

When each player has a "hand," they are compared, and the player with the best "hand" wins.

Below are some of the standard poker hands that might be found in order from least to most valuable, with some examples:

- High Card: When no combinations can be formed, the player with the highest "card" in his or her "hand" wins. (*263-ABD* would beat *927-JTI* because *A* is an Ace and beats *J,* a Jack.)
- One Pair: This "hand" has one pair of matched "cards." (*223-AMD* has one pair.)
- Two Pair: Two sets of pairs. (*LF-4334* has two pairs.)
- Three of a Kind: Three matched "cards." (*2227-JM* is Three of a Kind.)
- Straight: Five "cards" in sequence is a true poker straight. For License-Plate Poker, you might relax this requirement to three or four in sequence. (*23456-MM.*)
- Full House: Three of a kind and a pair (*JJJ-2234* has three *J*s and two *2*s, for a full house.)
- Four of a Kind: Four matching "cards" (*MBP-7777.*) Of course, with vanity license plates standing in for cards, it is possible to get five or six of a kind!

License-Plate Spelling

WHERE TO PLAY

In a car, while traveling

NUMBER OF PLAYERS

2 or more

EQUIPMENT

No equipment is necessary, but if you want to play competitively, pencil and paper for each player come in handy.

OBJECT OF THE GAME

To form words incorporating the letters found on license plates

---

This is an entertaining game for passing travel time when played cooperatively or competitively.

If you want to play cooperatively, simply note the letters from the first available license plate. Everyone joins in to try to find a word that incorporates those letters in the order in which they were seen. For example, from *134-CMT* you could get *computer, cement,* and *crumpet.*

To play competitively, the first player to think of a word will score a point.

With pencil and paper you can get more complicated. Write down the letters from six to ten license plates and see who can come up with the most words in a given period of time or who can complete the word for each item on the list in the shortest period.

Miles to Go

WHERE TO PLAY
While traveling in a car

NUMBER OF PLAYERS
2 or more

EQUIPMENT
A working odometer makes it possible to guess distances to tenths of miles. A watch can also be used if you choose to substitute guessing minutes to a destination rather than distances. Pencil and paper for recording guesses and distances and keeping score are helpful but not required.

OBJECT OF THE GAME
To guess most accurately the distance between two points on the travel route

---

Miles to Go can be played in two ways: guessing the distance to a landmark that is in sight; or predicting the distance to a spot that will eventually be reached but that is not yet within sight.

For the most immediate results, players take turns pointing out a landmark that can be seen but is still some distance ahead on the trip route: a hill, a silo, a billboard, a bridge, etc.

Each player estimates the distance to be traveled before reaching the object, to the tenth of a mile. For example, guesses as to the span to be covered before reaching the barn seen ahead might range from .9 mile to 1.2 miles.

A willing and patient driver or another player should monitor the odometer to determine the actual distance. (Players should be reminded to be considerate of the driver's need to concentrate most on the driving and not the game.) The most accurate guesser wins the round.

For a more speculative version of Miles to Go, pencil and paper are useful for recording guesses. Make a list of things that may be sighted along the itinerary: a fast-food restaurant, a high school, a stoplight, and so forth.

Each player makes a guess as to the distance to be traveled before finding the next example of one of these things. One player might estimate three miles to the next fast-food restaurant and twenty-five to the next high school.

Write down the mileage at the point when guesses are made and again as each item is reached. The player who comes closest to the actual distances traveled wins.

A variation on this would be to substitute travel times for distances—six minutes to the next high school, fifteen minutes to the next stoplight, for example.

Name That Tune

WHERE TO PLAY
While traveling in a car

NUMBER OF PLAYERS
2 or more

EQUIPMENT
None

OBJECT OF THE GAME
To guess the name of the tune hummed by the other player or playing on the car radio

Select one player to be the first hummer or whistler. He or she selects a relatively familiar tune and sounds the first note. The other players call out their guesses as to the identity of the song.

With only one note as a clue, it is not too likely that anyone will guess the tune. Therefore, the hummer or whistler continues to add notes to the tune, one at a time, pausing between notes for guesses.

The first player to identify the correct song may hum or whistle the next one.

VARIATION
You could also use the car radio to play this game. By controlling volume, you can turn up the sound to reveal a few notes of a song playing, then turn it off until someone guesses the tune correctly.

100 Points

WHERE TO PLAY
In a car, while traveling

NUMBER OF PLAYERS
2 or more

EQUIPMENT
None

OBJECT OF THE GAME
To gather 100 points from the numbers found on license plates

This game not only requires a sharp eye but also tests one's skill at quick addition and memory.

The first player adds the digits on the license plate of the first car spotted. For example, *326-MDR* will equal 3 plus 2 plus 6, for a sum of 11.

The second player takes the next plate and adds the numbers for his or her first sum.

When all players have added the digits from one license plate, the first player begins again, adding the new sum to his or her original point total.

The first player to reach 100 points is the winner.

For younger children who may find it difficult to remember large sums from one round to the next, point totals from a single round can be compared instead, with the player with the highest sum being the winner.

VARIATION
Another game to play with license-plate numbers is Motor Bingo. Write the numbers *1* through *9* on a sheet of paper. Players take turns spotting license plates. They may choose one number per plate to scratch off their list. The first to find all nine wins.

The Preacher's Cat

(Also known as The Minister's Cat)

WHERE TO PLAY
While traveling or at a party

NUMBER OF PLAYERS
At least 2

EQUIPMENT
None

OBJECT OF THE GAME
To describe and name the preacher's cat with an adjective and a name beginning with every letter in the alphabet

To start the game, the first player forms a sentence by filling in the blanks of the sentence, "The preacher's cat is a(n)——— cat, and his name is ———" with an adjective and a name that begin with the letter *a*. The initial sentence might be, "The preacher's cat is an artistic cat, and his name is Arthur."

The next player must also find an adjective and name beginning with the letter *a* to complete the sentence in order to continue the game. This player might say, "The preacher's cat is an awful cat, and his name is Andrew."

All the players in the game must likewise supply adjectives and names beginning with the letter *a* to complete the round.

When all have had their chance to form a sentence, the first player then fills in the blanks with words beginning with *b*: "The preacher's cat is a beastly cat, and his name is Brandon."

Each player must complete the sentence with *b* words, then *c* words, and so forth, through the remainder of the alphabet.

If the game is played competitively, a player must drop out if he or she repeats a previously used word or is unable to find appropriate new words. The last remaining player wins.

Ten Pairs

WHERE TO PLAY

While traveling in a car

NUMBER OF PLAYERS

2 or more

EQUIPMENT

None

OBJECT OF THE GAME

To score 20 points by finding 2 or more of a digit on license plates

Before beginning the game, each player chooses a different number between *1* and *9*. Simultaneously, the players watch cars in search of license plates that bear two of their chosen numbers. For example, the plate number *323-TEL* would score one point for a player who seeks the number *3*.

The discovery of a consecutive pair on a license plate such as *577-DSS* earns the player 2 points. Rare triple repeats of digits score 3 points. The first player to tally 20 or more points wins the game.

Travel Scavenger Hunt

WHERE TO PLAY

While traveling in a car, bus, or train

NUMBER OF PLAYERS

2 or more

EQUIPMENT

Pencil and paper for each player

OBJECT OF THE GAME

To spot all the items on a list while traveling

Travel Scavenger Hunt requires a bit of preparation before the trip, but it will keep younger travelers happily occupied for some time.

Before setting out on the road, draw up a list of items to be spotted along the travel route. Try to take into account the terrain to be covered—if you are going through both city and country, the options are greatest.

For travels through the city, the list of items to spot might include a pet store, a movie theater, a policeman or policewoman, a dog, a green car, someone carrying an umbrella, and so on. In the country, a silo, a person pushing a baby carriage, a cow, a white church, and a library are all possibilities.

Depending on the length and difficulty of the list, play can continue until the trip ends, with the player who spots the most as the winner. Alternatively, the first to complete the list wins.

VARIATION

If you have ample time for preparations, the different items on the scavenger-hunt list can be assigned point values in keeping with the likelihood of their appearance. For example, a cow might be worth only 1 point in the country, while a swan would equal 10 points. The first player reaching 100 points, or the player scoring the most points by the end of the trip, wins.

Appendix A: Games Listed by Player Age

Early Childhood Games for Ages 2 to 5

Around Ball
Balloon Ball
Bobbing for Apples
Broken Hearts
Colin Maillard
Contrary Children
Drawing in the Dark
Duck Duck Goose
Easter Egg Hunt
Follow the Leader
Ha, Ha, Ha
Hot and Cold
How Do You Do, Shoe?
Jack Be Nimble
Johnny-Jump-Ups
Kitty Wants a Corner
Lemonade
London Bridge
Mulberry Bush
Musical Chairs
Musical Clapping
Orchestra
Pass the Present
Pin the Tail on the Donkey
Prince Tiptoe
Rain
Ring-Around-the-Rosy
Simon Says
Sneeze
Threading Grandmother's Needle
Toesies
Twine the Garland

Middle Childhood Games for Ages 5 to 9

Action Spelling
Aesop's Mission

Alphabet Objects
Alphabits
Animals
Army
Art Consequences
Auction
Automobile 21
Baby in the Air
Badminton
Ball Between the Knees Race
Ball Punch
Bango
Barnyard Peanut Hunt
Bean-Bag Toss
Beetle
Beggar My Neighbor
Billboard Alphabet
Bingo
Black and White
Blindman's Buff
Bordering Plates
Boxes
Bronco Tag
Brooklyn Bridge
Buck, Buck
Burst the Balloon
Buzz
Call Ball
Cat and Mouse
Cat's Cradle
Cheat
Chicken Fights
Chimp Race
Clockwise Dice
Coffeepot
Cootie Catcher
Cops and Robbers
Cowboys and Indians
Crossing the Brook
Danish Rounders
Dizzy Izzy

Dress Me
Drop Dead
Drop the Handkerchief
Egg Polo
Errors
Farmer in the Dell
Feelies
Fifty Points
Find All Fifty
Fisherman
Four Square
Fox and Geese
Free Association
German
Go Fish
Goal Kickers
Going on a Picnic
Going to Boston
Gossip
Greek Ball Game
Guess the Number
Guggenheim
Handball
Handball Tennis
Hangman
Happy Families
Hide-and-Seek
Home-Plate Baseball
Hopscotch
Hot Potato
Huckle Buckle Beanstalk
Human Hurdle
Hunt the Key
Hunter and Rabbits
I Draw a Snake Upon Your Back
I Packed My Bag
I Spy
Ice Cubes
Jacks
Jump Rope
Kick the Can
Kickball
Leapfrog
Letters by Numbers
Log Roll
London
Magazine Storytelling

Marbles
Marco Polo
Maypole
Miles to Go
Monkey in the Middle
Mother, May I?
Mount Ball
Moving Statues
My Ship Sails
Name That Tune
Newcomb
O'Leary
Obstacle Course
Octopus
Odd Bean
Old Maid
100 Points
Orange Race
Peter Piper
Piñata
Poison Balls
Pom Pom Pull Away
Pottsie
Prisoner's Base
Rabbit
Racetrack
Races and Relays
Red Rover
Ring-A-Levio
Rolling Stone
Run for Your Supper
Running Bases
Sardines
Scissors, Paper, Stone
Seeing Green
Seven Up
Sewing Up the Gap
Shadow Buff
Sharks and Minnows
Sidewalk Golf
Skully
Slap Jack
Spelling Bee
Spit
Spud
Statues
Steal the Bacon

Stickball
Still Pond
Stoopball
Tag
Taste
Ten Pairs
Tic-Tac-Toe
Tiger and Leopard
Tip-Tap-Toe
Tongue Twisters
Travel Scavenger Hunt
Treasure Hunt
Tug-of-War
Tunnel Relay
Tunnel Swimming Race
Two Square
Underwater Tag
Up, Jenkins!
War
Water-Balloon Ball
Water Bridge
Water Follow-the-Leader
Water Keep Away
Water Volleyball
Watermelon Scramble
Western Union
What Are We Shouting?
Whirlpool
White Whale
Wink
Word Lightning
Wrestling Games

Late Childhood Games for Ages 9 to 14

Assassin
Baseball
Basketball Games
Battleball
Battleship
Bombardment
Botticelli
Bounce Ball
Capture the Flag

Categories
Charades
Circle Dodge Ball
Circle Golf
Concentration
Crambo
Crazy Eights
Cross-Over Dodge Ball
Crosswords
Dodge Ball
Donkey
Dumb Crambo
Egg Toss
Firing-Squad Dodge Ball
Foul-Play Race
Frisbee Golf
Ghost
Good Resolutions
Hat Grab
Hearts
Initials
King of the Hill
License-Plate Poker
License-Plate Spelling
Magazine Scavenger Hunt
Mathematical Baseball
Memory Game
Muggins
Password
The Preacher's Cat
Questions
Rigamarole
Scavenger Hunt
Sentences
Snip Snap Snorum
Square Tic-Tac-Toe
Stairway
Tetherball
Touch Football
Twenty Questions
Ultimate Frisbee
Underwater Football
Volleyball
Water Ball
Yacht

Appendix B: Games Listed by Number of Players

Games for 1 or More Players

Cat's Cradle
Jacks
O'Leary
Seven Up
Stoopball

Games for 2 or More Players

Alphabet Objects
Alphabits
Automobile 21
Badminton
Basketball Games
Ball Between the Knees Race
Balloon Ball
Battleship
Beanbag Toss
Beetle
Beggar My Neighbor
Billboard Alphabet
Bobbing for Apples
Bordering Plates
Boxes
Buck, Buck
Burst the Balloon
Buzz
Circle Golf
Clockwise Dice
Concentration
Cootie Catcher
Crosswords
Dizzy Izzy
Drawing in the Dark
Drop Dead
Easter-Egg Hunt
Egg Polo
Errors
Feelies
Fifty Points
Find All Fifty
Free Association
Frisbee Golf
Ghost
Go Fish
Going on a Picnic
Guess the Number
Guggenheim

Ha, Ha, Ha
Handball
Hangman
Hopscotch
I Packed My Bag
Initials
License-Plate Poker
License-Plate Spelling
London
Magazine Scavenger Hunt
Magazine Storytelling
Marbles
Memory Game
Miles to Go
Musical Clapping
Name That Tune
Obstacle Course
Odd Bean
100 Points
Pied Piper
Pottsie
The Preacher's Cat
Questions
Races and Relays
Ring-Around-the-Rosy
Scavenger Hunt
Scissors, Paper, Stone
Seeing Green
Sidewalk Golf
Skully
Spelling Bee
Spit
Square Tic-Tac-Toe
Stairway
Ten Pairs
Tetherball
Tic-Tac-Toe
Tip-Tap-Toe
Toesies
Tongue Twisters
Travel Scavenger Hunt
Treasure Hunt
Two Square
War
Word Lightning
Watermelon Scramble
Wrestling Games
Yacht

Games for 3 or More Players

Animals
Art Consequences
Bango
Bingo
Botticelli
Cheat
Chimp Race
Coffeepot
Crazy Eights
Donkey
Going to Boston
Happy Families
Hearts
Hide-and-Seek
Jump Rope
King of the Hill
Letters by Numbers
Marco Polo
Monkey in the Middle
Old Maid
Rain
Rigamarole
Running Bases
Sentences
Slap Jack
Snip Snap Snorum
Taste
Twenty Questions
Water Follow-the-Leader
Water Keep Away
Whirlpool

Games for 4 or More Players

Action Spelling
Aesop's Mission
Army
Bounce Ball
Categories
Chicken Fights
Cobweb Confusion
Dress Me
Egg Toss
Four Square
Fox and Geese
German
Goal Kickers
Hot and Cold
I Spy
Maypole
Mother, May I?
Mount Ball
Moving Statues
Muggins

Mulberry Bush
My Ship Sails
Pass the Present
Pin the Tail on the Donkey
Piñata
Racetrack
Rolling Stone
Statues
Touch Football
Underwater Football
Water Volleyball

Games for 5 or More Players

Auction
Crossing the Brook
Follow-the-Leader
Huckle Buckle Beanstalk
I Draw a Snake Upon Your Back
Kick the Can
Kitty Wants a Corner
Orchestra
Password
Shadow Buff
Sharks and Minnows
Simon Says
Still Pond
Underwater Tag
Water Bridge
White Whale

Games for 6 or More Players

Assassin
Brooklyn Bridge
Charades
Contrary Children
Cops and Robbers
Crambo
Dumb Crambo
Farmer in the Dell
Fisherman
Foul-Play Race
Hat Grab
Home-Plate Baseball
Hot Potato
Kickball
Leapfrog
Musical Chairs
Obstacle People
Poison Balls
Prince Tiptoe
Sardines
Sneeze
Stickball

Tag
Tug of War
Tunnel Swimming Race
Ultimate Frisbee
Water Ball
Water Balloon Ball

Games for 8 or More Players

Baby in the Air
Ball Punch
Black and White
Blindman's Buff
Broken Hearts
Call Ball
Capture the Flag
Cat and Mouse
Colin Maillard
Danish Rounders
Drop the Handkerchief
Good Resolutions
Handball Tennis
How Do You Do, Shoe?
Hunt the Key
Hunter and Rabbits
Ice Cubes
Jack Be Nimble
Lemonade
Log Roll
London Bridge
Newcomb
Octopus
Orange Race
Pom Pom Pull Away
Prisoner's Base

Rabbit
Spud
Threading Grandmother's Needle
Twine the Garland
Up, Jenkins!
Western Union

Games for 10 or More Players

Around Ball
Barnyard Peanut Hunt
Baseball
Battleball
Bombardment
Bronco Tag
Circle Dodge Ball
Cowboys and Indians
Cross-Over Dodge Ball
Dodge Ball
Duck Duck Goose
Firing-Squad Dodge Ball
Gossip
Greek Ball Game
Human Hurdle
Johnny-Jump-Ups
Mathematical Baseball
Red Rover
Ring-A-Levio
Run for Your Supper
Sewing Up the Gap
Steal the Bacon
Tiger and Leopard
Tunnel Relay
What Are We Shouting?
Volleyball
Wink

Index